Ready for Sea

Ready
for Sea

by
H. P. K. ORAM

SEELEY, SERVICE & CO LTD

First published in Great Britain, 1974 by
SEELEY, SERVICE AND CO. LTD.
196 Shaftesbury Avenue
London WC2H 8JL

Copyright © 1974 by H. P. K. Oram

ISBN 0 85422 082 8

Printed in Great Britain by
Hazell Watson and Viney Ltd
Aylesbury, Bucks

To
My Shipmates

Contents

Illustrations

The painting of the Port Jackson *is reproduced by kind permission of Calendars of Distinction, Ltd*

Ready for Sea

CHAPTER I

Outward Bound

In the dim light of an early September morning in 1911 the ocean-going Barque *Port Jackson* sailed from London Docks outward bound for Sydney, New South Wales. Ready for sea, with hatches battened down and loaded to her Plimsoll marks, she warped across the dark still waters of the West India Dock basin into the lock to await high water.

The sun, rising like an orange balloon clear of the dockland roofs, lifted the morning mist. The lock gates opened and a red funnelled tug tautened her hawser. Casting off her last links with the shore, *Port Jackson* towed slowly out into the muddy river to begin her 15,000-mile voyage to Australia.

This routine departure from a busy port attracted little shore-side interest and, apart from a few shouts from a group of pier-head loungers, the ship left without ceremony.

But for me, a 'first voyager', it was a big day and as we moved ahead I stood gulping in the excitement of this significant moment. Looking up at the steeple-high masts, crossed by slender yards, I conjured up a romantic vision of my ship clothed in a cloud of canvas. Imagination running riot I pictured gale-strained rigging and felt sick at the thought of myself, way up aloft, battling with an unruly sail.

Though I had become accustomed to climbing the nursery rigging in the training ship *Worcester* I was now faced with stark reality. First voyagers are traditionally classed as utterly useless articles and as I gazed at the cats-cradle of ropes above my head

I realized, only too clearly, that I was no exception to the general rule.

I was not left long to ponder my fate. As the ship's head pointed down river I was roused by a harsh hail.

'Boy, what do you think you are – a passenger? Don't stand there sucking your thumb, lay hold on a broom and get busy.'

Under the lash of the Mate, an awesome figure with a Cape Horn voice, nobody had leisure for thumb-sucking as we towed steadily down river on the ebb tide, pausing at Gravesend to pick up the Channel Pilot, and then on into the broad estuary.

The *Port Jackson*, and her sister ship *Medway*, were destined to be the last in a line of ocean-going sailing vessels owned by Devitt and Moore, an old established shipping company which, exceptionally among ship-owners at that time, made special provision for training Cadets in their cargo carrying fleet.

The *P.J.* herself was an iron hulled ship of 2,300 registered tons, rigged as a four-masted Barque with square sails on the Fore, Main and Mizzen, and fore and afters on the Jigger mast.

Built at Aberdeen in 1882 she was a beautiful example of the ship-builders craft with her delicate sheer, lofty white spars and sides immaculate in the traditional black and white 'Painted ports' livery she looked, on that day of sailing, superb.

She belonged to a type of ship known as 'Wool Clippers', the heavier successors to the wooden hulled 'Tea Clippers', such as *Cutty Sark*, which in earlier days had won fame for their phenomenally fast passages from China with the first of the season's tea crop. The iron ships designed for carrying Australian wheat and wool were larger and had more hold space than their tea-trade predecessors. They were, nevertheless, capable of a good turn of speed and were staunchly sparred to stand up to heavy weather in high southern latitudes.

The *P.J.* had earned a reputation as a fast sailer and, in the twenty-eight years of her life, had made a number of notable runs. Her 286 feet from stem to stern-post may not seem large by modern standards but, in my eye, she seemed immense and the quintessence of adventurous perfection.

In a sailing ship it is the gear aloft that really counts and *Port Jackson* was well found. The truck of her main-mast towered 167 feet above the sea – only three feet short of the height of Nelson on his column – and though she had a few more lofty rivals she was justly a 'tall ship'.

The technique involved in supporting masts of such height to withstand violent movement and the stress of straining sails had evolved from centuries of practical seamanship. This art reached its peak when steel wire ropes became available for standing rigging.

The masts of the Wool Clippers were customarily built up in three sections – stout steel tubular 'Lower-masts' stepped in the keel and rising to a height of about 70 feet above the deck; above this strong wooden 'Top-masts' and, higher still, wooden 'Top-gallant-masts'. Each of these individual masts was held firm by wire rigging; 'Stays' leading forward; 'Backstays' leading aft; and a number of 'Shrouds' at their sides to prevent lateral movement. A wooden platform was fitted, slightly below the 'Cap' of the lower-mast, to give spread to the top-mast shrouds; similarly 'Crosstrees' near the cap of the top-mast gave spread to the t'gallant shrouds.

I had only joined the ship the day before and I took advantage of a stand-easy in the Dog watches to explore my new home. The whole of the space below the upper deck was used for the storage of cargo and stores. Above deck level a raised fo'c'sle running from the eyes of the ship to the fore-mast, and a raised poop deck abaft the mizzen-mast, provided accommodation for the Seamen and Officers respectively. Between these two extremes the Cadets lived in the 'half-deck', a long deck-house between the main and mizzen masts.

That evening I was told off to stand watch on the poop as messenger. This sounded all right in theory but, in practice, it was puzzling because at that time I knew nobody nor where I was likely to find him. All the same it was a beginning and, apart from a brush with a shadowy figure who sharply ordered me off the sacred weather side of the poop, the watch passed pleasantly enough, striding the deck and feeling important.

The lights of Ramsgate twinkling to starboard raised superior thoughts of gentlemen of England lying abed while stirring things were happening offshore. Four bells called a new helmsman to the wheel and, as we towed out from under the lee of the land, the ship curtsied gently in a slight sou-westerly swell. For a time I found the motion exhilarating but, leaning over the taffrail and hypnotized by welling water under the ship's counter, I became uneasily aware of internal heavings synchronizing with upsurging seas. It was touch and go and I was just waiting for the inevitable when my backside was smartly kicked by the Second Mate who, brushing my protestations of human frailty aside, ordered, 'Walk the poop. If I catch you throwing up you'll get the leathering of your young life.' This brusque therapy was effective enough to last me a life-time!

At dawn the next day the ship, still under tow, made steady progress against a freshening head wind. There was no chance of sailing, so I was told, until we reached the broader waters of the Channel. By noon the Captain evidently felt he had sufficient sea-room and hands were sent aloft to cast off gaskets in preparation for making sail. The first voyagers, in a high state of excitement and not a little trepidation, gazed in awe at their experienced ship-mates working like busy spiders on a dizzy web.

The sails, loosed from their stowed position but still confined by running rigging, hung in bights below the yards and flapped fractiously in the fresh head wind. The hands mustered aft and I heard the Captain order, 'Set fore, main and mizzen stays'ls, Mister, and cast off the tow.' The ship, under helm, sheered out to port, the stays'ls filled and quietened and we made slow headway on the starboard tack. The tug, released from duty, ranged round and embarked the Pilot and, making off to the eastward with a farewell toot, severed our last contact with the shore.

For the next hour I followed the old hands and hauled on hal-liards, tacks and sheets. Far above our heads the sails without apparent human aid sheeted home as if by magic and, taking the wind, stretched out in taut curves. This was big stuff and, with a glorious sense of adventure, I felt the ship tremble and become alive as she heeled to port and gathered speed.

The wind increased that evening; it was cold and dark on deck and taking refuge in a dim corner of the half-deck the voyagers nursed blistered hands and aching muscles and wondered, rather ruefully, what we had let ourselves in for.

I was one of the twelve Cadets in the port watch, eight of whom were hardened veterans who paid scant attention to the problems of newcomers. We clustered together trying to adjust ourselves to the unaccustomed motion of the ship and looked gloomily at our future. The senior Cadets, wise in the way of life at sea and knowing that in four hours we would be roused out for the middle watch, were already flat out on their bunks. I followed their example and drearily watched the swinging oil lamp over the table until, dog tired, I fell asleep.

The next ten days were dismal. The ship, fighting her way against persistent head winds, tacked doggedly across the Channel making distance to the westward on the ebb tide and losing most of it again on the flood. We sighted Start Point on three successive days and everybody cursed as the ship clawed her way out to the open sea. Being, as yet, unused to 'watch and watch' routine*, which breaks up every night's rest, I groped around in perpetual weariness. The pully-hauly on ropes seemed never-ending and my flabby muscles groaned in protest. The voyagers, taunted by their seniors, chivied by the Chief Cadet, scornfully thrust aside by the experienced fo'c'sle hands and roared at by the Mates, had little to laugh at as they tottered from rope to rope on unsteady sea-legs. The whole ship seemed wrathful and, as we saw it, all hands took fiendish delight in venting their angry frustration on our innocent heads.

Though restricted to jobs on deck we were, twice a watch, ordered to climb over the crosstrees to break us in to working aloft. The ship was heeling well over to port when for the first time I climbed on to the bulwark and on up the main rigging. I was, correctly, on the weather side with the wind pressing me against the rigging and this first stage was not too bad as I gingerly found foothold on the rope ratlines stretched between the shrouds of the lower-mast. I followed advice not to look down and climbed slowly towards the main-top. This, I knew, was a tricky bit. The platform 'top' projected out several feet and to climb on to it I had to tackle the 'futtock rigging'. I looked up and saw my rope ladder inclining outwards at an angle of forty degress. Spurred by a shout from deck I gripped the futtock shrouds with sweating

* Four hours 'watch on deck' alternating with four hours 'watch below'.

palms and, feeling like a fledgling fly on a ceiling, I struggled up and over.

With a sigh of relief I found myself standing in triumph, sixty feet above the deck, on a haven of solid wood and, pausing for breath, I looked round. Just below my perch I could see the main-yard, pivoted on the fore side of the lower-mast and braced round at an angle to point to windward. This great steel spar, 84 feet long and weighing many tons, seemed colossal. Depending from it the Main-sail, the largest sail in the ship, curved out stiffly in the strong wind and, at close quarters, I was staggered by its sheer size. Climbing on upwards I passed the Lower and Upper Tops'ls, the Lower and Upper T'gallants until I reached the Crosstrees more or less level with the foot of the highest sail of all, the Main Royal. Here, clutching the mast, I felt safe enough to look down. Far below the pencil slim hull of the ship cut cleanly through the choppy sea. Ahead, the six square sails on the foremast strained at their sheets and, looking aft, I saw their counterparts on the mizzen-mast stretched in full-bellied purpose. It was a supreme moment and such fears as I had were swamped by this bird's-eye view of the beauty of a square-rigged ship under full sail.

Down again on deck I looked up at the lofty crosstrees with a sense of achievement. By the end of the week this exercise, six times a day, made running aloft almost carefree.

Like most of the older hands our Sailmaker was a man of rugged character. Years of lonely stitching with palm and needle had made him something of a solitary and he had a reputation as a recluse with a caustic tongue. In fact this crabbed shellback had a soft centre and, in his mellow old age, he was disposed to be helpful. I stopped to listen one evening as he unravelled the pattern of the 'running rigging' to a couple of green Ordinary Seamen.

Rummaging round in his bag he fished out his yard-stick and a small rectangle of canvas. 'Imagin' that this 'ere is a yard,' he said, 'an' that there is its sail.' Taking the canvas in hand he selected one of the longer sides and deftly stitched in short lengths of twine at intervals along its length. 'That's the "head" of the sail, see, an' these short bits of twine are "robands" – an' it's these what secures the head of the sail to the "jackstay" what you'll find runnin' along the topside of the yard.' With quick fingers he hitched his demonstration robands to the yard-stick and held it up so that they could picture a rectangular sail hanging from its yard. Prodding the canvas in emphasis he pointed out, 'The four sides of the sail are – the "head" secured to the yard; each side is know'd as the "leech"; an' the bottom edge is called the "foot".' He then went on to explain that the two top corners are fitted with 'head earrings' to take the strain when the head of the sail is stretched bar-taut between the two yard arms and that the two bottom corners are called the 'clews'. Hitching a couple of lengths of twine to the two clews of his dummy sail he said, 'These are the "sheets", wot pulls the clews downwards and outwards to the yard arm beneath them. Then, when you've "braced" the yard round to the right angle to catch the wind, there's yore sail set an' drawin'.' 'What abaht furlin' the sail?' 'Back yore mains'l, lad, an' 'eave to,' he said, 'I'm comin' to that.'

With great patience the old man fitted a number of additional lines on his model explaining as he did so the function of each. 'Clewlines' to lift the lower corners upwards and inwards, 'Leechlines' to pull the sides up and in to the yard, several 'Buntlines' lifting the foot up vertically and gathering in the 'Bunt' or centre of the sail, and all leading through blocks down to the deck.

The ship, when under full sail, set eighteen square sails each of which was fitted with at least ten items of running rigging. She also carried four Jibs, four main and mizzen Stays'ls, and a Spanker and Gaff tops'l on the jigger mast. Each of these ten fore-and-afters was rigged with hoisting halliards, sheets and downhauls. All in all there were rather more than 280 individual ropes for setting and furling sails arranged in an orderly pattern and each secured to its own specific belaying pin.

The voyagers were given a few days' grace to learn the ropes. Under dire threat of penalties for ignorance we spent anxious hours examining each other and arguing hotly in the dark about the identity of a rope which might well have been the 'main upper t'gallant outer buntline' the 'main royal weather clewline' or something else equally puzzling.

Within our berth our life was depressed by the three 'third voyagers' in our port watch who, in the arrogance of their own toughness, lost no opportunity to bear down on unsophisticates. The Chief Cadet, whose responsibility it was to take the youngsters in his watch in hand, was a pernickety type whose sardonic sense of humour pricked our follies with unerring sharpness. We respected his authority but were not enamoured .

The 'second voyagers', revelling in their new found emancipation, were pleased to air their wisdom and their mature advice on pitfalls kept us out of a lot of trouble.

Eight days out, on a morning when the fleeting shadows of flying clouds darkened an emerald sea, the yards were squared and in warming sunshine the crew thankfully welcomed easement from the labour of constant tacking. The Captain, walking the weather side of the poop, was reputed to have been seen smiling. The Mates belayed their barking and the fo'c'sle hands stopped grousing. The ship sparkled with a cheerfulness that spread even into the darkest corner of the half-deck. Up till then we had felt hunted, bewildered and useless; suddenly, we were basking in occasional bursts of gruff encouragement. The change seemed too good to be true.

As the ship made steady way to the southward the crew settled down to normal sea routine. We carried twelve Able-seamen, split into the port and starboard watches, and these men together with the twelve cadets in each watch, gave us a 'watch on deck' strength of eighteen working hands. In this respect we were well off in comparison with ordinary commercial freighters of comparable size which in those days were flogged round the world with ten hands in a watch or even less.

In the *P.J.* the cadets were relied upon to carry out the full duties of able-seamen and, as we gained experience, we were expected to become as useful as the most trusted 'old hands'. We lived separately and spent one forenoon each week learning Navigation but, apart from this, our life and work was identical to that of the fo'c'sle hands.

As in all windjammers our complement included three Petty Officers – the Bosun, Sailmaker and Chips the carpenter – who lived in a little cubby hole just abaft the fo'c'sle. These key men were day workers and since they could, in theory, spend the whole night hogging it in their bunks they were traditionally known as the 'Idlers'. In addition we carried a Ship's Cook and a Steward to attend on the Officers in their saloon under the poop.

With a total ship's company of 47 we were considered to be well manned but, even so, in heavy weather we often felt that double that number would have been too few to cope with the hard manual labour involved in working the ship. Everything had to be done by hand for the ship was not fitted with power appliances of any sort and the strain at times bore heavily on all hands.

But, as far as I was concerned in those early days, I knew little of hardships to come and as day by day the sun grew warmer so life became progressively brighter.

Our day's work started at 6 a.m. when the watch on deck turned to for cleaning the ship. As a junior I spent this time heaving round on the hand pump to provide water for washing down. The tedium of this morning chore was lightened by the company of our six pigs in their adjacent pen. At the start of the voyage, before their number was reduced by one each fortnight, these passengers lived in close quarters and in fine weather were inquisitively companionable and highly vocal when hosed down. We knew them well and lamented as the lottery of death removed loved ones from our daily converse. These fellow first voyagers were, however, fair weather sailors and looked a sorry lot sliding *en masse* on their backsides as the ship rolled. Our favourite, Denis, developed cunning in anticipating the coming roll and would scramble into an upper position so that his slide down was cushioned by less agile pigs. Later in the voyage, as the last survivor, he had to bear the brunt on his own but by that time he had become wise and knew it was safer and more comfortable to travel stern first.

During the day the watch on deck were kept hard at it scouring off dockside dirt, chipping rust and repairing gear but, apart from essential work, all hands were free in the Dog Watches, (4–8 p.m.). In fine weather it was the custom to foregather on the fore-hatch to spin yarns, mend clothes, argue and skylark. This social corner of the day was the time for sizing up and shaking down.

We had a mixed crowd in the fo'c'sle ranging from shellbacks calloused by years of hard seagoing to young lubbers as green as a starboard light. Rather to my surprise I found dark personalities, which at the outset had seemed rough and forbidding, blossoming into a bunch of variegated characters.

We had four experienced A.B.s in our port watch – Marnier, an old sailor of dubious French parentage, Wallaby, a certificated deck Officer from down under, working his passage back to his homeland, Hans, a giant 'squarehead' with the strength and temper of a bull, and Dai, a wizened Welshman from the back streets of Cardiff's Tiger Bay. We also had two Cockney Ordinary Seamen who, until they learned to pull their weight, bewailed the misbegotten impulse that had prompted them to go to sea.

Our port watch, bonded by common work, quickly grew into a compact fraternity. Because of our 'box and cox' routine the starboard watch, oddly enough, were comparative strangers and we sniffed them warily until, in the course of time, we became matey. At our evening sessions on the fore-hatch we developed superficial likes and dislikes but it was the work aloft that really counted in sorting out relationships. I learned later that it was up on a yard battling with a vicious sail that one recognized true worth and, in this school, I was educated to a better and more realistic sense of values.

This was only one of many adjustments I had to make in settling down to shipboard life. After the first few days in the Channel in sight of ships and brief glimpses of distant headlands we moved out of the steamship lanes and the sense of separation from the world was strange. Wireless telegraphy, then in its infancy, was a big ship luxury and from the time we cast off the tug we were entirely on our own. The tracks followed by sailing ships, determined by the prevailing ocean winds, passed through unfrequented seas and the chances were that we would not make human contact again until, three months later, we made landfall in South Australia. Isolated from outside distractions our little company became introspective in a world bounded by our own bulwarks. Whatever might be happening ashore –

change, upheaval or even war – was far away and, as there was little purpose in conjecture, we lost interest in matters so far beyond our immediate horizon. Wrapped in our own affairs we concentrated on the progress of the voyage and our talk was mainly concerned with daily happenings and plans for the extravagant binge-up we would have when, released from bondage, we rejoined the world. In a rather curious way we passively accepted our lonely state stretching interminably ahead while, at the same time, we were consumed with daily impatience to make a fast passage.

In contrast to conditions ashore, where the weather is usually a mere incidental to life, the strength and direction of the wind was all-important. We never came on deck without cocking an eye aloft to see if we were beating against a head wind or running free with squared yards. Our moods of depression or elation fluctuated with the vagaries of the weather.

Having no refrigerator we had to subsist on tinned foods which, in those days, were unappetising and ancient beef and pork stowed in brine in 'harness casks'. At first this preserved meat was barely edible but hunger soon made one stomach it with no more than a passing qualm of revulsion. Even when disguised in a hash the stringy, odorous, qualities of salt beef were strongly evident. Bread, a sour variety baked by the cook, alternated with hard ship's biscuit which not only taxed the teeth but kept one alert for the wily weevil. Three meals a day were eased down by bitter coffee and meagre rations of tinned butter and jam. From time to time we shared in the carve up of fresh mutton, pork or chicken but as our stock of livestock was severely limited we only savoured these tough delights on festival occasions. Most of us carried small, jealously guarded, stocks of cocoa and condensed milk which we used sparingly to drive out the chill of night watches in harsh weather. Despite shortcomings in our diet, and we grumbled incessantly at the parsimony of our 'owners', we had enough to keep body and soul together and, in fact, enjoyed rude health.

Water was always a problem in sailing ships and it took time to become accustomed to making do with a daily ration of three pints for all purposes. I usually drank about two-thirds of this allowance and saved the rest for shaving and washing.

On the whole it was fairly hard living and creature comforts were minimal. Our home from home in the half-deck was a bleak steel box of a place sparsely furnished with metal-framed bunks and wooden tables and benches screwed firmly to the deck. Apart from faint warmth from two swinging oil lamps the half-deck was unheated and, in bitter weather, it was so perishingly cold and damp that we were driven to seek self-induced warmth in our bunks.

As a newcomer my youthful pride was pricked by my lowly status at the bottom of a society in which pecking order was determined by strength and seamanlike skill. At the age of seventeen I was, by shoregoing standards, reasonably fit but, in comparison with more seasoned seamen, I was a weakling until, in a short time, the constant manual work in strong sea air opened my lungs and built up muscular toughness. In common with 'first voyagers' throughout the ages my feelings during those early weeks at sea were a mixture of apprehension in what seemed to be an unsympathetic environment and rebellion against harsh authority. They certainly purged me of romantic ideas of life on the ocean wave and brought home the realization that unless I showed willing and quickly hoisted in the tricks of my new trade my life was going to fall short of my expectations.

CHAPTER II

Trades and Doldrums

LOOKING at a faded photograph of our six Officers it is difficult to rekindle the awe they at first inspired. The Captain, then in his sixties and nearing the end of a lifetime in sail, was an aloof but not particularly forbidding personality. Stocky in build and silent in temperament he was, in every sense of the word, the Master. His browned weatherbeaten face, lightened by a white walrus moustache, gave a merited impression of benevolence. A man of vast seagoing experience and a seaman to his fingertips, I seldom saw him rattled though he could flare into irascibility at moments of stress.

In his earlier days in command of clippers he had been known as 'Crack-on Charlie' but, in his mellowing, he became disinclined to live up to his former reputation as a 'driver'. The half-deck were critical of his tendency to shorten sail prematurely instead of holding on to his canvas till the last moment which, in our impatience for speed, we counselled him, from a safe distance, to do.

The Captain was respected fore and aft for his mature judgement and his sympathetic concern for the wellbeing of his working hands. We did not see a great deal of him on deck for he had the gift of trusting his Officers and letting them get on with it without over-riding their authority. He had, however, a keen nose for scenting trouble and at moments of crisis he could invariably be seen climbing deliberately up the companionway from his cabin to the poop to stand, silently grasping the weather rigging, while he sized up the position. His orders, when he decided that it was time to intervene, were decisive and crisp enough to make all within earshot jump to it. He was a strict disciplinarian and, though his temper was generally equable, he was not a man with whom to take liberties.

By contrast, the Mate, a tough 'Blue-nose' Nova Scotiaman, was loud of mouth and swift of wrath. He had served some twenty years in sail and, from his manner, we guessed that much of this time had been spent in flogging ill-found ships and mutinous crews round the world. A tall, hungry-looking, scraggy man he had yellow teeth and a squint which gave the impression that one eye was roving round looking for a handy belaying pin to use as a truncheon – which it probably was. He was so dissimilar to the Captain that we found it difficult to understand why he had been signed on. He certainly knew his job and his rasping drawl and coarse invective kept all hands on the hop.

The Captain, who was not a man given to violence, exercised a restraining influence but it was the general opinion in the fo'c'sle, and in the half-deck, that if the Old Man should, inadvertently, drop off his perch the Mate would soon be hazing us in proper hard-case fashion. Though not bad all through, for he had his moments of sarcastic relaxation, something in his life had turned sour and he seemed to be constantly seeking revenge. He did not remain long with us, after one round trip he was paid off, but whenever he was in sight we were on a split yarn to take heed of the old sailors' cautionary cry 'Stand from under' and kept ourselves ready to nip clear at the first hint of trouble.

The Second Mate was a beefy strong-arm specimen, aged about 30 with a bully-ragging sense of humour, and an infectious cheerfulness when things seemed to be at their worst. He and the Mate were frequently on a collision course but the Second had the wisdom and good nature to give way even when, with justice, he could have afforded to 'stand on'. We liked him for his approachability and, though he had a rough side, he was usually ready for a companionable yarn. He was a fine seaman and when, in emergency, he worked aloft with us he had the strength and power of three men.

The Third Mate was a quiet type, just out of his apprentice-ship and serving in his first job as a certificated Officer. At the beginning of the voyage he kept watch under the Mate's supervision and obviously found it trying to suffer hot correction breathing down his neck. He was, at first, too unsure of himself to feel aggrieved, but later, when the Captain found trust in his competence, he acted on his own and blossomed out. Having been so recently promoted to Officer status the half-deck looked upon him as one of us and he kept us titillated with scraps of 'saloon' gossip.

Being an 'Ocean Training Ship' we carried a Navigational Instructor with whom we were closeted, on average, about one day each week. A dapper pedagogue who coached us for eventual examinations with friendly patience, he was a Captain in his own right and had commanded ships, and it was rather a mystery why he had elected to serve in an undemanding appointment with little active responsibility. We came to the conclusion that either he had, from choice, taken on a cushy job or that there was a dark patch in his former career. He was not communicative on the subject and we never knew the answer but he was popular and we garnered sound wisdom from his wide fund of experience.

The sixth, and last, member of the afterguard was the Doctor. Here we were certain that there was some grim skeleton in his cupboard whose rattling bones had driven him to seek sanctuary at sea. We knew that he couldn't have been struck off the register, for that would have disqualified him for a position as our medical practitioner, but he reeked of malpractice. As a Doctor he was useless and most of our company would have opted for the Bosun's rough and ready first aid rather than put their ailment in the hands of such a seedy physician. He was a flabby, porcine, little man whose threadbare beard and whiskers insufficiently masked his pale sweating face. He spent the entire voyage in his cabin which stank like a badger's set. Much later in the voyage I discovered his dark secret when he rolled up his sleeve to dress a whitlow on my finger and I saw his arm dotted with the marks of morphine needles.

Two weeks out I had had, in the opinion of my seniors, ample time to find my way round and was put to the test. The ship, with all sails set, slipped serenely along on a light breeze. The Mate, prowling like a panther, pounced on three of us chipping the scuppers and took us in tow round the deck, snapping out questions about the rigging. Having survived this trial without apparent disaster we were startled to be told 'Clew up the mizzen royal.' With muttered argument we eased off the sheets and lay back on the running rigging. Looking aloft at the sail looped obediently below the yard we were congratulating ourselves on our prowess when the Mate ordered 'Up and stow', in tones so compelling that we were over the futtocks and up to the royal yard before we had time to think what we would do next. Edging out to windward on the swaying footrope, hanging on its 'stirrups' below the yard, we felt tremulously inadequate for the job in hand. From the deck the sail had seemed to lay quietly in its gear. Up here the canvas ballooned out and flapped fretfully in a wind that seemed, unaccountably, to have freshened to angry proportions. Reaching over we dug our fingers into the swelling sail and, heaving together, lifted a flap of canvas and tucked it between our stomachs and the yard. As we stretched out for another handful the sail pulled free and billowed out with a violence that made us clutch the jackstay in alarm. Back to square one we tried again and, at long last, worked the sail into an untidy roll on top of the yard and, having secured it with a snaked gasket, we moved over to the lee yard arm to repeat the process. Flushed with success we went down on deck by the quickest route, the lee rigging, to be greeted with biting sarcasm and ordered aloft again to come down in a seamanlike manner on the weather side. No sooner were we back on deck when I was sent up to cast off the gaskets we had so carefully secured. Three times in all we furled that blasted sail and our exercise seemed set to go on indefinitely. Fortunately eight bells released us to collect our dinner ration of salt beef from the Cook.

Our efforts had not passed unnoticed and in the half-deck we were bully-ragged for our amateur performance. The sting of this leg-hauling, however, was eased by the Chief Cadet who told us that henceforth we would work aloft with the watch, which made us feel pleasantly professional.

Until this time I had been too preoccupied in finding my bearings to pay much attention to the ship's progress and I welcomed a break from manual labour when, in a spell of fine weather, the voyagers were told off for occasional sessions in 'school'.

Our Instructor, starting us off on ocean meteorology, explained how the Captain, taking advantage of the patterns of prevailing winds, would make his passage round the Cape of Good Hope to Australia.

Oceanic weather, he told us, was primarily affected by alternate belts of low and high barometic pressure encircling the globe. In the vicinity of the Equator the power of the sun overheats the lower levels of air and, as this hot air rises, the barometer readings at sea level tend to be lower in this tropical region than in adjoining regions to the north and south. Since nature abhors a vacuum, cooler air flows steadily into the tropical low pressure belt thus creating the phenomena of the Trade Winds which, due to friction caused by the revolving earth, blow constantly from the North-east in the northern hemisphere and from a South-easterly direction in the southern hemisphere.

To the north and south of the Trades light variable winds are commonly experienced and, beyond these, in latitudes 50° N and 50° S, roughly equivalent to the latitudes of the British Isles and Cape Horn, there are broad belts of comparatively low pressure traversed by frequent east-going cyclonic disturbances giving rise to prevailing westerly winds.

On leaving the English Channel the Captain's first objective was to work out to the westward to ensure that, in an area where predominantly westerly winds could be expected, the ship would have ample sea-room to clear the north-western corner of Spain by at least 200 miles. Having reached a position well out in the Atlantic it was then safe to shape course to the southward until, just short of the Tropic of Cancer, the outward-bounder could expect to pick up the North-East Trades which could be relied upon to carry the ship to within 300 miles of the Equator. Here the Trades would fade away in the aptly named Doldrums where we would have to make what little way we could in a region renowned for its glassy calms. It might take days, or at worst weeks, of boxing the compass in light airs to drift through to the welcome South-East Trades which could usually be expected shortly after crossing the Line. Since a wind from the south-east was dead against us making a course towards the Cape of Good Hope we would, perforce, have to sail across the Trades on the port tack and run parallel to the coast of Brazil down into the area of variable winds to the south of the Tropic of Capricorn. From then on it was a matter of working down to seas beyond latitude 40° S to the belt of the Westerlies where, in the notorious 'Roaring Forties', the ship would 'Run her Easting down' to the Great Australian Bight. This was the tough leg of the voyage which, as everyone was at pains to tell us, would sort out the men from the boys.

These forebodings of trouble did not disturb us overmuch as we dawdled in fine weather through the 'Horse latitudes' – so called because, in bygone days, ships were sometimes forced to jettison horses owing to shortage of fodder and water arising from undue protraction of a voyage through this area of light variable winds.

On a day of light airs with the ship ghosting to the south-west at a bare 2 knots all hands were turned-to after breakfast to change our suit of sails. Up till this time we had been wearing heavy weather sails but, at this stage of the voyage, it was customary to bend on an older set so that the strength of our strong storm canvas would not be impaired by chafing in the desultory Doldrums. Half watches were told off to work as competitive teams on the fore, main and mizzen masts. Up aloft we furled each sail in turn, cast off its running gear, passed a gantline round its bunt, cut away the robands and lowered the sail down on deck to be snaked up and stowed away in the sail locker. Reversing the process we hoisted, bent on and set the older sail and moved on without pause to start on the next one.

For my part I enjoyed the two sweaty days it took us to finish the work which broke me in to laying out on the yards and gave me a gratifying sense of participation in a seaman's job.

We spent a week in the Trades in idyllic weather. Logging an average 7 knots we covered the best part of 1,000 miles without being called upon to trim the sails in the steady nor-easterly wind. In typical trade wind weather occasional clouds cruised lazily to leeward across a clear sky, their cotton-wool whiteness matching sun-brilliant wave crests flashing against a background of deep blue sea. A school of porpoises played round the forefoot and flights of flying fish, disturbed by hungry predators, made hasty airborne escape. On the horizon a family of whales broke surface to blow plumes of spray.

The now cleansed ship, heeling gently to starboard, reflected the cheerful weather and all hands revelled in this expected, but nonetheless welcome, fair wind boost to the southward.

We stripped down to virtual nakedness and though, through carelessness, I suffered a novice's sunburn my skin and bare feet soon hardened to leathern immunity. Earlier aches and pains were forgotten and I decided that if this was seagoing it fully lived up to my expectations.

Though these halcyon days were pleasurable in themselves it is the Trade wind nights that live in my memory. Our watches on deck, peacefully undisturbed by calls to man the braces or shorten sail, were drowsily idle. We had a waning moon at the time and I recall blissful hours lying on my back on the top of our deckhouse looking up at the sheer beauty of the tapering sails glowing in gentle golden light. The trucks of the masts sweeping in slow arcs across a background of brilliant stars had a lulling effect. The sails, arching out in satisfying curves, tugged at their gear, livening leading blocks into murmurous chatter and setting up faint creakings as the rigging reacted to their pull. Apart from these soft noises and the constant rustle of water as the ship slipped through the phosphorescent sea those nights were beatifically reposeful – except when cruising Mates turfed us out of our nests of coiled rope to save us from the hazard of becoming moon-struck!

Four weeks out we held the 'Dead horse' ceremony. This traditional fo'c'sle festival marked a significant day in the sailor's log.

The crews of ships when paid off at the end of a voyage were easy prey to shore-side sharks who smartly relieved gullible mariners of their hard-earned cash. Deep sea John, though well-rigged with sterling qualities when afloat, was not the most provident of men ashore and, dazzled by the bright lights of dockland, he was soon stripped to a gantline and reduced to pawning his pitiful belongings. Despite earlier vows that he would never again sweat his guts out at sea, harsh hunger weakened his resolution and, broke to the wide, he joined the queue when the buzz got round that a ship in port was going foreign.

As an inducement to sign on, it was the custom to hand out a month's wages in advance – a philanthropic gesture to enable ill-equipped sailors to redeem their oilskins and seaboots and stock up with a few small comforts, or a skinful, to fortify themselves against hardships to come. In John's logic the first month of a voyage was dead time during which he worked for nothing. By his reasoning the 'owners' were 'flogging a dead horse'. The beginning of the fifth week at sea was, therefore, an occasion for celebration.

At two bells in the first dog watch the fo'c'sle hands gathered by the fore-mast and formed into a straggling procession with Hans at the head astride a canvas and oakum hobby-horse of his own making. The 'ploddy Dotchman', as he described himself when taunted with being a squarehead, had to be in the centre of things and, neighing like a randy cart horse, he led the party aft. The hands shuffled along at funereal pace singing the old traditional sea song in a minor key:

> They say, old man, your horse will die,
> An' we says so – an' we 'opes so.
> They say, old man, your horse will die,
> Oh! – poor – old – horse.

Halting at the break of the poop and confronting the Captain, flanked by his officers, the ill-used sailors, in mock aggrievement, chanted:

> Old horse, old horse, what brought you here
> After working hard for many a year,
> From Bantry Bay to Ballywhack,
> Where you fell down an' broke yore back.

> Now, after years of crool abuse,
> They'll salt you down for sailors use,
> They'll tan yore hide an' burn yore bones,
> We'll send you down to Davey Jones.

The Captain, playing his part, looked over the mutinous assembly with a bleak eye and demanded 'What do you want?', to which Hans in a lather yelled 'Ve vants to bury der horse'. Taking advantage of the occasion the Old Man handed out a homily on the virtues of hard work and passed down a bottle of rum to the expectant crowd.

Hauled by its bridle the now reluctant horse was hurried forrard where, with a noose round its neck, it was triced up to the fore yard-arm and cut away to drop overboard with such scant ceremony that, before the body had drifted astern, the mourners were in the fo'c'sle for the wake.

This was an anti-climax for the cadets who, barred from entering the crew's quarters, slouched into the half-deck where the seniors eased their disgruntlement by ordering the voyagers to scrub the deck.

The North-east trades slackened and finally left us slumped in a dead calm. Far from being a time of passive idleness waiting for a wind, the passage through the Doldrums is a period of purgatory. Days of frustration with the tropical sun blazing, the ship rolling lazily in an oily swell and lifeless sails slatting against the masts. Throughout this enervating time restless Officers on watch scanned the horizon looking for signs of wind. At intervals, sensing a zephyr, they called the hands to trim the sails in an endeavour to coax the ship a few miles onwards. Several times a watch, in scorching heat, we lay back on the braces swinging the heavy yards round, grumbling at the effort of a task that, even before it was finished, left us despondent at the sight of drooping sails. No sooner had we squared up and coiled down the gear than we were at it again, cursing the Mate for his wind fantasies which, we suspected, he conjured up with malice aforethought. Tempers flared as old pessimists gloomily recalled memories of ships taking months to drift through to the South-east trades.

From time to time a bank of distant clouds lifted above the horizon and, mounting towards the zenith, blotted out the sun and we sensed menace in their darkening passage across the sky. Still becalmed we watched the encroachment of slate grey forerunners heralding opaque black rain clouds, and we knew we were in for a cloudburst. Though some of these tropical phenomena brought no more than a drenching deluge, there were some that had strong winds in their bellies. The Captain, with wary experience, looked for the worst and, whenever he saw a dark marshalling of clouds he sharply ordered us aloft to furl t'gallants and royals to guard against the threat of more than a capful of wind.

As the leading edge of a squall advanced in our direction, its black heart veiled by a fringe of falling rain, we braced ourselves, and the yards, to meet the blast. Doldrum squalls strike swiftly – at one moment we would be sweating in airless unease and, within minutes, half drowned in a gale-lashed torrent. As the ship, lying over under the strain, scudded through the murk we splashed through turmoil to stand by the tops'l halliards with heavy rain striking our bare skins with cold ferocity. A few hands were told off to block up the scuppers to prevent the precious fresh water running to waste. Grabbing buckets to top up our water tanks we wallowed in the luxury of a freshening bath.

For the best part of a quarter of an hour the squall raged un-abated until, suddenly, as quickly as it had begun, the wind died away. The rain stopped as if turned off by a tap; the sky cleared and the ship lay becalmed once more with decks steaming under the hot sun and drying sails hanging limp and slack from the yards.

We were lucky that voyage and, in less than a week, we were roused by the distant sight of a coruscating shimmer on the face of the glassy sea. This was more than a cat's-paw and, feeling the first breath of a steady breeze we knew that we were through purgatory and into the South-east trades. Braced up sharp on the port tack the ship cantered away to the sou-sou-west to begin her long slant of untroubled sailing down into the South Atlantic.

We crossed the Line the next day with the customary initiation ceremony in which the voyagers were lathered, shaved and well nigh drowned in a canvas bath by Neptune's loyal, and far from gentle, Bears.

While still in the Trades I was allowed to try my hand at steer-ing. With the ship close-hauled on a steady breeze I was told to sail as close to the wind as possible and cautioned to use as little helm as I could. In such fine weather it was not too difficult to get the feel of the ship and I soon picked up the knack of keeping the weather leeches of the royals just shivering with no more than a few spokes turn of the wheel. It was a boost to morale to be trusted with this responsibility and, after a few tricks at the wheel, I was cocksure that I was a hell of a helmsman.

As we made our way to the southward the Trade wind, as is usual, backed a bit and we were able to make good a course to the east of south. Just beyond Capricorn we lost the Trades but, after a couple of days of light airs, we luckily picked up a fair wind that took us well down into the lonely waters of the South Atlantic.

The weather grew perceptibly cooler and at this first whiff of trials to come the old-timers fished out and refurbished their heavy weather gear. With painstaking care each man scrubbed off the goo-ey surface of his long-stowed and sticky oilskins and re-coated with a patent panacea of his own choice. Sea-boots, grown hard and unyielding with disuse, were made supple with grease. Change was also foreshadowed by two days' work shifting over to our strong, storm-canvas suit of sails.

We were well to the south when our Instructor drew our attention to the fact that we were now, technically, in the 'Roaring Forties'. It was a fine stimulating day which did not at all fit in with forecasts of weather to be expected in those rough latitudes. There was, however, an abnormally long swell rolling up from the sou-west which gave clear indication that we were already in the belt of 'Westerlies' where great seas driven by frequent gales coursed round the world.

I had noticed, when writing up the log, that the sea temperature had dropped suddenly and I was told that this showed that we had entered a fertile region of the southern seas abounding in marine life. There was little evidence of this until, the following morning, I sighted my first albatross. The sun was shining and a fresh nor-westerly wind turned over the tops of the long swell in creamy crests. Suddenly, out of nowhere, there he was – a great white solitary bird skimming close to the water about half a mile to windward. As I watched he banked, making a flashing white cross against the deep blue sea, and turning into the wind soared up and swooped across our stern. Fascinated by this magnificent creature, rather bigger than a swan and with narrow wings with a spread of at least ten feet, I saw him circle round and take up close station abreast the main yard, riding the wind effortlessly without apparent wing movement.

For a time he hung there motionless until, attracted by a bucket of slops dumped overboard, he turned and glided with astonishing speed to settle with upturned wings on the water a quarter of a mile astern. We were sailing at around ten knots but in less than a quarter of an hour, having finished his meal, what there was of it, he was back in station with a roving eye for the next course.

That evening I noticed old Marnier hammering out a piece of tin into a 4"-sided triangle and asked him what he was up to. The ancient mariner cocked an eye aloft and grunted, 'Ze vind 'e drop – tomorrow we 'ave calm an' I go catch plenty albatross.' He was dead right and next morning the ship lay becalmed, rolling in the undulating swell and barely moving ahead.

Our friend the albatross, who had been joined by a smaller companion, was about 100 yards astern floating with high freeboard and paddling round with a weather eye lifting for anything tasty in his vicinity. Marnier mustered his gear and dumped a bucket of water over the side. His quarry, alerted, started to get under way and, with thrusting webbed feet, worked up such speed as he could. Normally, in a wind, he would have paddled to the crest of a sea, pointed his beak to windward and, with spread wings, have lifted off without effort. But, in such a flat calm it was a matter of flapping sea-touching wings, assisted by frenzied feet slapping the water to lift his one and a half stone body into flight.

Marnier, watching this manoeuvre, uncoiled his line and muttered, 'Bon – 'es 'ungry or 'e wouldn't start walking on ze water.' Lowering his cork-floated triangle, its sides wrapped in putrid pork, over the side he paid out his line so that the bait lay invitingly at rest on the sea's surface. Our friend, tired of flapping in the still air, lost no time in gliding down, alighting alongside and making a jab at this free meal. Quick as a flash old Marnier jerked his line taut and, in doing so, jammed one side of his triangle behind the hooked beak of the astonished bird and, keeping a constant strain on the line, he hauled in hand over hand. The albatross, with spread webbed feet and wings flapping full astern, fought this outrage with all his strength but, with muzzled beak, he was unable to resist his captor's pull.

I felt compassion for this magnificent bird in his indignity and was relieved when, in a careless second, Marnier slackened the strain and the great white captive, shaking free, paddled off in obvious aggrievement. Marnier, in disgust, spat out a lewd French oath and told me that we had lost a prize – a fully grown male Wandering Albatross.

In his years of seagoing the old sailor had picked up a fund of knowledge on the habits of these tremendous travellers, tirelessly scanning the wide wastes of the southern seas for sustenance. He told me that they breed on desolate wind-swept islands on the edge of Antarctica such as Kerguelen and the Crozets in the Indian Ocean's deep south. After a few months ashore, feeding their newly hatched Goneys, they set off once again on their solitary voyaging remaining at sea, so it was said, two years or more out of sight of land.

While we waited for a second chance I asked the ancient mariner why he was not scared by the legend that the killing of an albatross brought bad luck. 'Zut!' he said scornfully, 'We bin catchin' them birds for centuries, 'tis said though,' he added, crossing himself, 'that they is the souls of sea-captins who 'ad sich a fat arse time when they was alive that they've bin sentenced by ole Nick to cruise lonely after they've bin drownded.' This, in Marnier's opinion, was ample reason for catching the bastards whenever possible.

Before long he made a catch, this time the smaller bird, which was successfully pulled up the ship's side and released, unharmed, on deck where after a few ungainly and unavailing runs to get airborne he disgorged the evil smelling contents of his stomach. Thinking it strange that a bird so used to violent movement should be seasick I asked if this was usual. 'It ain't seasick 'e is – 'es just pumpin' out 'is bilges to lighten ship.' With that, to my distress, he dispatched this wandering soul and carved up its beautiful body with meticulous care.

For weeks after I was intrigued to watch the old Frenchman using his spare time to fashion profitable products from the dismembered carcase. The webbed feet he made into tobacco pouches, the breast he cured and made up into a white muff, the fine head with its 6″ hooked beak was mounted on a wood backing and the long hollow wing bones were cleaned and made into pipe stems and cigarette holders. The oily skin, so he said, was better than any dubbin for sea-boots.

'Reckon that lot'll make a tidy bit when we gets to Sydney,' said the unfeeling craftsman with miserly satisfaction.

CHAPTER III

Roaring Forties

THE first hard gale of the voyage hit us as we were rounding the Cape of Good Hope. In latitude 45° South, the ship was well in the 'Roaring forties' and the violence of this blow, and its effect on our lives, was a revelation.

In the higher southern latitudes strong 'Westerlies' prevail, on average about three days in five and set up a mammoth swell which, untrammelled by land, sweeps round the world. Even on days when the wind shifts to other quarters this great swell persists and, when thrashed by a westerly gale, the sea builds up into one of nature's most spectacular demonstrations which, once seen, is never forgotten. Day after day long lines of mighty combers march eastwards in inexorable procession. The height of these formidable waves, measuring forty feet or more from trough to grey-beard crest, seems dwarfed by the hundreds of yards between successive seas but, when seen from the deck of a labouring ship, their towering mass is awe-inspiring.

The 'Westerlies' are generally more boisterous, and the seas greater, in latitudes beyond 50° South and windjammer Masters making the 7,000-mile passage from the Cape to Australia were faced with the choice of pressing down into the 'Fifties' on a 'Great circle' track or keeping within the 'Forties'. The former shortened the distance to be run at the risk of damage to the ship or encounters with ice; the latter took longer but was marginally safer. Our Captain, no longer driven by the urge to break records, opted to run our 'Easting down' on the 45th parallel, a decision which was endorsed by the older hands as being preferable to skating about on the fringe of Antarctica.

Just before that first hard blow – it happened to be memorably fierce and prolonged – we were beating to windward under all plain sail on a moderate easterly breeze. It was a fair day and the ship, close-hauled, lifted to a long but smooth swell under her counter. On watch on the poop I heard the Captain and Second Mate, attracted by grey clouds creeping up from astern, discussing the portents and I was told to take a barometer reading every half-hour. By the end of the watch the glass had fallen perceptibly and, forewarned, I was not altogether surprised when, shortly after going for a mug of tea in the half-deck, I heard 'All hands' called to shorten sail. The weather was still fine but the whole sky was now overcast and the wind had fallen light. It did not take us long to hand the royals and t'gallants and I was just thinking that it was about time to carry on with my watch below when our port watch was ordered aloft again to furl the Crojick * while the watch on deck manned the braces to square the yards.

While we were still up on the yard the sky darkened into rain and, cursing because we had not had time to put on our oilskins, we hurried down on deck. I finished my cold tea and went out on deck just in time to notice the wind suddenly chop round to the west and breeze up in bad-tempered gusts. At midnight, when we mustered for the middle watch, it was pitch-dark and blowing very fresh with slanting hail stinging the flesh with icy pricks. The ship scudded along before the wind and the sea looked ugly as wave after wave swept past with bared teeth. The Captain, standing with broad-legged stance by the weather rigging, held on to his canvas but, to be on the safe side, he kept our watch handy and we huddled together taking what shelter we could under the break of the poop and the gap between the half-hour bells seemed interminable.

About three bells the whine of the wind in the rigging went up a tone and we heard the Captain sing out, 'Call all hands, Mister, and take in the upper tops'ls'. For our part this order was not

* The Crossjack or Crojick is the lowest and largest sail on the mizzen mast—comparable to the mainsail and foresail.

entirely unwelcome for we guessed that with worsening weather the sooner we got on with it the better and knew that activity aloft would warm our chilled marrows. As we staggered off in the darkness to stand by the halliards we smirked at the thought that it was now the turn of the starbowlines * to lose part of their watch below.

The upper tops'l yards – and the upper t'gallant yards for that matter – were held by sliding bands encircling the mast allowing the yard to be hoisted by its halliards when setting sail or lowered when shortening down.

By the time the port watch climbed aloft to tackle the main upper tops'l it was blowing hard and as I went over the futtocks on to the main-top I felt the full blast of its fierce breath and shivered with cold and excitement. With lungs distended by streaming air I braced myself for an ordeal. I looked down but, in the driving rain, there was nothing to see beyond the loom of immediate wave crests surging past.

Out on the lee yard-arm I gripped the jackstay with cramped fingers. The foot-rope, wet and slippery, jumped wildly as the flapping sail jerked the yard, and sagged and tautened as my work-mates struggled on either side. Great balloons of stiff canvas reared above the yard, threatening my tenuous hold. The spiteful wind lifted the back of my short oilskin jacket and flipped my souwester over my face and I began to lose my temper at its ill humour. This was a proper state to be worked up into and, disregarding the old adage 'One hand for yourself and one for the owners', I made a two-fisted grab at the billowing sail.

Flanked by the giant Hans and the sinewy Wallaby I helped to heave up a fold of canvas but no sooner had we got it tamed between our bellies and the yard than it broke free with a cunning that caught me napping. My sea-boots slipped and with an anguished squawk I slithered down to fetch up sitting on the footrope. Holding on to the stirrup to regain my foothold I felt a hoisting hand on my collar and heard Wallaby, chuckling like a Kookaburra, shout, 'C'mon sport, it ain't no good hollering till you're in a safe place to holler. Save your breath and hang on by your eyebrows.' Too right he was! Restored to my place at his

* A term used often for the Starboard watch.

side I went back into battle with the sail, forgetting all else except the imperative need to master the malevolent beast.

For a full half-hour we clutched and hove up in unison, gaining and losing, but finally imprisoning, our enemy within a snaked gasket. Wet with sweat and rain we struggled down to return to our draughty stand-by station under the break of the poop, short of breath but warmed through for the remainder of our watch on deck.

Four hours later we were turned out for the forenoon watch and found the ship running under fore-sail, three lower tops'ls and fore topmast stays'l. A cheerless day but at least it was light and we could see what we were up against. The wind, stronger than ever, strained the taut sails to the pitch when it seemed that the canvas must split. The rain had eased up and under a leaden sky we looked out on a panorama of heaving grey seas. Mighty rollers with blown spray flying ahead of their tumbling peaks and their valleys streaked with the aftermath of broken crests. A bottle-green wall of water reared up astern lending a slight touch of colour to a scene of drab uniformity.

In the wake of the preceding wave the ship, though driving fast before the gale, seemed to lose way in comparison with the onrush of the overtaking greybeard. I could sense the poop lifting under my feet, hesitatingly at first under the influence of the moderate incline in the trough, but ever more acutely as the great sea rolled up. The steepening front grew closer and it looked as if the towering mass must break over and 'poop' the heavily laden ship. Miraculously the buoyant stern rose to the occasion and the thwarted wave snarled under the counter and swept forrard to lift the bow until the bowsprit pointed high in the murky sky. Despite the sea's anger the ship, pitching like a crazy rocking horse, stormed along with decks comparatively dry.

Steering a ship in heavy weather is a fine art, requiring a trained but indescribable sense that becomes an instinct. A good hand at the wheel meant a dry deck and a helmsman who could sense the feel of the ship through the spokes of his wheel was popular fore and aft. In a gale, particularly with a following sea, it needed strength to keep the ship on course. Stressed by surging water the rudder made the hand wheel kick like a mule and the helmsman had to sweat to stop it from taking charge, so much so that, in really foul weather, it was necessary to give him an extra hand as 'lee wheel' to share the labour of heaving on the spokes. A great deal depended on the amount of canvas carried – with too little the ship had insufficient steerage way, with too much there was grave danger to the gear aloft. In either case the man at the wheel had to be quick off the mark and use every ounce of his instinct for, if he failed, the ship broached to and with wind and sea abeam rolled gunwales under and shipped green water over the bulwarks.

I was not yet competent to be a full-blooded helmsman but I stood my trick as leewheel and shared, vicariously, the tingling excitement in handling the ship in heavy weather. The overtaking threat of a storming southern ocean sea could be terrifying – some ships rigged a screen to check an inexperienced man at the wheel from looking over his shoulder and losing his head. I felt this apprehension myself at first and remember muttering the Breton fisherman's prayer, 'Have mercy Lord, your sea is so big – my barque so small'.

One gained confidence in the ship's staunch buoyancy and qualms subsided, but everyone recognised that the danger of being pooped was very real and this possibility always flitted about at the back of the mind. Pooping, by all accounts, was the acme of disaster and old hands told tales of badly handled ships being ravaged from stern to bow by an irresistible wave sweeping the Captain and his Mate, the Helmsman and his wheel far along the deck and leaving the ship out of control and helpless. The voyagers hoisted in these dire yarns with a pinch of deep sea salt – but kept their fingers crossed!

The gale had more or less blown itself out on the third day and in the First watch the wind had moderated sufficiently to set the lower t'gallants. At 4 bells I went to the poop to take over a trick as lee wheel. The wind was still fresh enough to cap the long, heaving swell with breaking crests. The sky had cleared and the ship galloped along, pitching and yawing under a canopy of brilliant stars and a half moon. My helmsman, a trusted third voyager, tutored me good-humouredly as we wrestled with the lively wheel. In the brightness of the night it was fascinating to look aloft at the straining sails and sense the whims of the labouring ship under our hands. With the compass jumping about in its gimbals it was difficult to read the card in the dim light of the binnacle lamp and we were steering on a star just clear of the fore t'gallant. It was not too easy to hold the ship on a steady course but I soon found myself instinctively anticipating the need for helm to check the yaw, and I was indulging in mild confidence when my mate was sent forrard on a job and I was told to take over the wheel. Flattered by this trust I moved over to the weather side and, grasping the spokes with determination, sang 'Blow the man down' to myself in the exhilaration of the moment.

For a time all went well, and I was just thinking that under my expert helmsmanship the decks were dry, when fate took a hand. A squall blew up and without warning the wind backed four points, a black cloud masked my guiding star and, in a sudden gust, the binnacle lamp blew out. This combination was too much and, sensing the ship sheering off course, I frantically struggled to put the helm down to check the swing. But I was too late – with the great swell now on the beam the ship rolled heavily and a green sea flooded the deck amidships. The Third Mate, thrusting me roughly aside, took over and yanking the helm down regained control. In scorching words I was roundly cursed for being a useless 'sodger' and told to get to hell out of it. My cup of misery overflowed – but worse was to come. The green sea that had flooded the deck to bulwark level took time to drain away through the washports and, under the lift of the bow, tons of spent water surged aft and, flooding through a door left carelessly open, well nigh washed the Mate out of his bunk. With rasping sarcasm the wet and angry blue-nose blew such remnants of pride that I still carried out of their bolt ropes and I spent the rest of my watch, and half my watch below, with bucket and swab dolefully mopping up the aftermath of my unwitting lapse from grace.

This foretaste of the Roaring Forties was typical of many wet and dreary days to follow as we ran eastwards. It was not all bad; there were days of relatively fair weather and, even when careering before a westerly, our hardship was compensated by the comforting knowledge that we were covering 200 miles or more towards the end of the voyage. But always, fair or foul, the great swell rolled on, the ship groaned and creaked in constant violent movement, the southern spring was lamentably cold and, despite careful helmsmen, heavy seas crashed on board all too frequently. Life deteriorated into an endurance trial against discomfort and weariness. Food, at best of times unattractive, was even more so when the cook's galley fire was dowsed by a sea and our hot meal dowsed with it.

Within the half-deck it was cold and damp. The inner walls of our steel house streamed with condensation, the deck was often wetted by water spurting through cracks and positively drowned when the door was stupidly opened at the wrong moment. Battened down against the elements there was no ventilation to freshen the dank air and, lacking heating, we shivered in chilly humidity. We ran out of dry clothes at an early stage and, thereafter, turned into our bunks 'all standing' in our damp gear to ensure that we would at least be warm when turned out four hours later. At meal times one had to juggle to eat while keeping control of plate and pannikin with both hands and a sheath knife stuck in the table.

After my experience on the tops'l yard I quickly learned to make my oilskins reasonably watertight with 'soul and body' lashings round neck, waist, wrists and ankles but, even so, salt water encroached and rain had the seeping power of Satan – one could never keep that out.

Watches on deck had few idle spells. In addition to the labour of shortening down, and setting sail again when the weather served, there were innumerable jobs to be done on deck and aloft making good the ravages of wind and sea.

Work on deck was harassed from time to time by seas cascading inboard. Tailing on a lee brace one felt the ship make an untoward lurch to leeward. Someone would yell 'Hang on!' as a wall of green water the size of a house reared up and thundered over the bulwark on top of us. Groping instinctively for something solid, but more often than not finding nothing to hand, the unlucky ones would be swept away along the deck in the maelstrom.

It was a curious feeling to be up-ended and helpless in the

surging rush of water, lacking all sense of orientation but knowing that one was travelling at speed. Within seconds, though it seemed longer, one fetched up against something hard and firm and clung on till the flood drained away through the washports leaving one stranded and gasping with the Mate bawling, 'Stop porpoising about – blast ye. Get back on the brace.'

It was quite an art to move about the deck in heavy weather. With the aid of life-lines one developed the habit of sensing the safe moment to dash from one secure handhold to the next, but it took time to pick up this knack by trial and error. It was the rule of the half-deck that two voyagers shared the chore of making cocoa in the night watches. We were barred from using a primus stove in our living quarters and had to perform our culinary miracle in a small wash place just abaft the fore-mast. Choosing the right moment to open the door we lurched forrard along the deck, loaded with the necessary gear. Once inside the wash place, unloading stove, cocoa, condensed milk, jug and water from their stowage in our oilskin coats it was relatively easy going – apart from the problem of holding our paraphernalia on a metal shelf while trying to get the stove alight with damp matches. This, at long last, achieved we brewed up and with steaming jug in hand hastened to deliver our product before it lost its heat. Looking anxiously out into the black night to sense the temper of the tempest we seized an apparently propitious moment to get under way – one with the jug and the other as forerunner to herald our arrival by thumping on the scuttle through which we were to hand our offering. If all went well and we had a fair passage this meant no more than a hurried dash along the heaving deck but, if our timing was at fault, we fetched up in the scuppers in a welter of cocoa-stained water.

It took us rather more than three weeks to cross the South Indian Ocean and during this time I became inured to discomfort and phlegmatically accepted the hardship as inevitable. Time did not drag, each day had its element of excitement and working together under difficult conditions drew us closer as a team. I sensed, too, a subtle change in the general attitude towards the voyagers. In the early days we had been left in no doubt that we were worthless. Now, after hard weather initiation, we were accepted as tested members of the tribe and it was satisfying to feel that we had graduated from uselessness to the status of working hands.

In the half-deck our seniors dropped their irritating superiority and fraternized with amiable condescension. One, in particular, went out of his way to be pleasant. 'Molly' Morgan, so called because somebody on the previous voyage had said that he had the face of a 'Mollymauk',* had a ravenous appetite for fun and, like his namesake, for food. I had the bunk beneath his and, as this was conducive to spontaneous yarning, we developed a lasting friendship and I owed much to his invigorating goodwill.

Though we were boosted by a fair number of westerlies there were days of contrary winds and, looking at the plot of our daily progress on the chart, we became resigned to the fact that our voyage was going to be rather longer than average. Pessimists forecast that it would be many weeks before we dropped the hook in Sydney harbour. Things looked better when we saw our track slanting north-eastwards towards Tasmania and, when we crossed the meridian of Cape Leeuwin, everyone made extravagant calculations to prove that we would be home and dry by Christmas.

Half way across the Great Australian Bight we picked up a fresh northerly wind carrying an enticing scent of land far away on our beam. Working aloft on a brisk morning of streaming wind and warming sun I sighted a smudge of smoke right ahead on the horizon. It was more than two months since we had seen another ship and, feeling uplifted at this tangible evidence that our period of utter isolation was nearly over, I hailed the poop with my momentous news.

With all kites set and drawing strongly, the ship seemed eager with anticipation as she stormed along at twelve knots. Everyone found an excuse to make a trip to the fo'c'sle head for a personal look at the distant steamer. During the forenoon the upperworks of the ship ahead became visible and it was clear that we were catching up. The wind held and throughout the day we raced on, gradually overhauling the plodding stranger who was now seen to be a single funnelled tramp.

By six bells in the afternoon watch she was barely a mile away

* A handsome sub-species of the Albatross family.

on the port bow and the Captain hauled up a point to pass close along her lee side. With signal flags fluttering at the peak we asked her name and destination and, on hearing that she too was bound for Sydney, we hoisted the signal 'I will report you on arrival,' to which the unhappy steamer made no reply beyond belching black smoke in a vain endeavour to ward off her ignominy.

This high comedy reached its climax when we swept past, scornfully hanging a hawser over the taffrail and signalling – 'XZ – Shall I take you in tow?' This was a supreme moment and everyone tucked away the incident for later use when, no doubt, the tale would be embellished by a running commentary on our yard by yard overhauling of a crack ocean liner!

This contact had given the Captain a check on his longitude and, sure of his position, he cracked on with confidence towards the Bass Straits. The following night the light on Wilson's Promontory loomed up on the port bow and I spent most of my watch gazing in fascination at this significant welcome.

Next morning, with less than 500 miles to go, the anchors were unlashed from their sea stowage on the fo'c'sle and catted in readiness for use on arrival. As we stamped round the capstan we reckoned that the girls of Sydney had got us in tow and that they'd have us in harbour on Christmas Eve. But hopes are gossamer things and ours were blown into limbo by the persistent north wind. It took us a full week's tacking up the Tasman Sea and it was New Year's Eve before we made our final landfall.

This check had rather dampened the Christmas spirit but a present of a handful of black cheroots from the afterguard and a slice of Denis, who was not as tender as his confiding nature had led us to expect, helped to ease our frustration.

Ten miles off Sydney the tug *Heroine* loomed up like a wraith out of the misty morning and, after an exchange of pleasantries, passed the tow. We had been 102 days on our own and the twang of Australian voices had the quality of greetings from another planet.

We needed no urging to roll up the sails for the last time in a tight harbour stow. Two hours later we towed past Sydney Heads and, with a rare rattling of cable, anchored in Rose Bay on the southern shore of the finest harbour in the world.

Nothing comes up to the tranquillity of arrival after a long voyage. All my senses combined in conjuring up a feeling of magical euphoria. The ship, never still at sea, was strangely motionless; my eyes, so long accustomed to long focus on distant horizons, were drawn irresistibly to a close view of a red-roofed village against a background of green trees; my nose quivered in response to exotic shore-side scents and even the acrid smoke of a passing ferry smelt delicious.

I was lucky enough to be told off as one of a boat's crew to take the Captain ashore and, after landing him at the pier, we wandered up to the village store. It seemed odd to walk on solid earth and this, my first glimpse of a new land, was entirely captivating. In stained dungarees, with sheath knives slung on our belts, we must have looked a piratical lot but this did not dismay the store-keeper's daughter who, with a typically Aussie greeting, handed out fruit which, as we couldn't muster a bob between us, was a welcome bonus. I sat on a bench sucking an orange and, in utter contentment, absorbed the peace of the placid village.

CHAPTER IV

Cape Horn

SYDNEY was one of those comparatively rare harbours where visiting ships are part and parcel of city life. Unlike most ports, where the docks are thrust aside in an environment of mean streets, the ocean liners arriving in New South Wales berthed on Circular Quay close to the town's centre. This was also the terminal point for ferries feeding surburban bays on the periphery of a superb land-locked harbour and commuters were thus brought into daily contact with ships in port.

Being the main entrepôt serving a fast expanding country there was an intense, two-way, traffic in cargoes through the port and the harbour was always full of ships of all kinds. Sydney was a vigorous, bracing, city with a gift for boisterous, open-handed friendliness.

Two days after arrival we were moved to an unloading berth in Wooloomooloo Bay, an indentation on the southern shore quite close to George Street and the bright lights of city enticement. The ship was taken over by stevedores and in an atmosphere of chaos we had a feeling that we had done our bit and hankered for the flesh-pots. In my innocence I reasoned that I had earned a little relaxation from watch and watch routine and heavy toil. It was certainly pleasant to enjoy 'all night in' in my bunk but I hadn't reckoned with 'all day work'. Turn to at 6.30 a.m. and pack up at 5.0 p.m. was our daily ration which left us with little energy for an evening run ashore. Even so, it was shortage of cash that was the real factor in clipping our eager wings. As Cadets we were not entitled to pay but it was the custom for parents to lodge money with the Captain to be disbursed at his discretion. It happened that the Old Man was circumspect to the point of miserliness and there was a wide gulf between his idea of an adequate hand-out and what we knew was the minimum necessary for our essential, and urgent, needs. The Captain considered that he was rather overdoing it when he disgorged five bob for a week's dissipation. Any fool could have told him that such a paltry sum would evaporate in about five minutes in the Marble bar. This lack of understanding of the rights of youth left most of us dead broke by sunset on Saturday nights. We put on a wheedling act each week and, occasionally, one of us would spin such a plaintive plea that the Old Man's heart would be wrung to the extent that he reluctantly handed over £1, much of which, inevitably, was spent in subsidising less persuasive sufferers pledging their dead certain success in next week's hand-out gamble. Things being what they were we normally hoarded our meagre resources for a splash on Saturday afternoons and Sundays when we were left, more or less, to our own devices.

Fortunately the ferries were cheap and most of our week-ends were spent surf-bathing in summer sunshine at Bondi beach as a prelude to a gentle pub-crawl in the evenings. There was not much scope for social adventure but, for me, it was all brand new and alluring.

With the best part of our cargo discharged we towed to Newcastle, 70 miles up the coast, to complete unloading and spent five days in company with some 25 windjammers most of which were waiting to load coal cargoes for the west coast of South America. Back in Sydney we dry-docked to clean the bottom and returned to Wooloomooloo to load our homeward cargo of wheat.

I was intrigued by the Sydney stevedores – a gang of tough larrikins with lusty independence and a stinking scorn for authority. When they felt like it they put their backs into lumping and stowing the heavy sacks of wheat – when they didn't they were quick to scrounge off into a dark corner of the hold to sleep off last night's beer. Their incessant good-humoured back-chat was an education in pornography and our vocabulary of four-letter words was vastly enriched. They had their own simple code of verbal abuse. A mate could be showered with any obscenity without offence but, curiously in all the circumstances, the appellation 'bastard' invariably led to a bloody fight.

In the middle of our loading our gang unanimously agreed it was high time for a holiday and, working up a grievance, they went on strike. This was a fairly normal procedure, particularly during Randwick Race-week, but from our point of view their absence meant that we had to stand-in and carry on the loading. Those three-foot sacks of wheat had looked manageable in the hands of experts but, on our amateur backs, they weighed a ton. For eight hours a day we backed up to a built-up platform to shoulder a bag and, with wilting knees, staggered across the hold to throw the load over the head into its allotted place. By the end of Race-week we were getting the knack but I have had a fellow-feeling for stevedores ever since.

With loading completed and hatches battened down, we towed out to anchor in Neutral Bay and prepared for sea. On 4 March, 1912, the wind came fair and we stamped round the capstan cheerfully singing the traditional 'Rolling home' shanty. Our old friend the tug *Heroine* started us off on our long journey and on an afternoon of sparkling sunshine we towed out through Sydney Heads. Looking back at the thronged harbour for the last time most of us had mixed feelings at this severance from easy living.

Five miles off shore we cast off the tug and set course to the south-east to pass to the south of New Zealand. Nine weeks in harbour had left us with little relish for sea routine and the prospect of a month's slog across the cold South Pacific before we could turn the corner into warmer seas was not particularly inviting.

The Tasman Sea was boisterous and within a couple of days we were hard up against a 'Southerly Buster'. We had heard that these blustering local storms had a habit of striking 'blunt end first – without warning'. This one certainly did and before we had time to shorten sail the sudden violence of the wind laid the ship over on her beam ends. The weather rigging, taut as fiddle strings, stood up to the tearing strain but it seemed that something must give way and that the sticks would be whipped out of the crazily heeling ship. The Second Mate, throwing his full weight on the wheel spokes, managed to heave the helm up. The ship paid off the wind and, running free, righted herself as we hurried aloft to take in sail. That was not the end of our trouble. Under the stress of the squall the ship had laid over so far that the top layers of the wheat cargo, carelessly stowed in Sydney, shifted over to port. As we could not carry on the voyage with an uncomfortable list the Captain ordered all available hands down the hold to re-stow the cargo as best we could.

It took us two days of hard labour to finish the job. Those sacks of wheat, which we had felt to be back-breaking when loading during the strike, now seemed twice as heavy as we sweated in the confined space to lift and shift their bulk. Battened down in the semi-darkness of the heaving hold we cursed the bastard steve-dores who had let us in for this trouble. Apart from short spells for meals there was no respite and we were a sore and sorry lot when, at long last, we finally climbed out into the fresh air to re-set sail.

The last remnants of cheerfulness at being homeward bound evaporated when, on the seventh day at sea, we were headed by a vicious easterly blow. There had been some warning of this and the upper kites had been furled before the wind built up to gale strength. By midnight when we mustered for the middle watch it was only too apparent that we were in the grip of a snorter, and on being ordered to furl the main lower tops'l we knew it was worsening. As we groped along in the darkness to manhandle the gear the starboard watch, straggling down from reefing the fores'l, jeered at us as they hurried below to their bunks.

At this time, so we heard later, the watchkeeper on the poop hearing what he at first took to be the plaintive cry of a sea-bird, had second thoughts and, to be on the safe side, threw a life-buoy over the side. Four hours later, when the starbowlines gathered for the morning watch, Bazalgette, their Chief Cadet, failed to answer the roll call. We searched the ship but he was never seen again. This, our first fatality, was emotionally up-setting. All of us, at one time or another, had had our own scares to ram home the possibility of an accident but the actuality was difficult to accept.

41

I had been yarning to Bazalgette the previous evening and it seemed beyond the bounds of credibility that he had gone from our company.

The Captain held an enquiry next morning but little tangible evidence was forthcoming. Those who had been reefing the fores'l reported that Bazalgette had been seen on the lee yard arm and that he was probably the last man down. Nobody had actually seen him come off the yard and it was assumed that he had either slipped off the footrope and dropped into the sea or that he had come down the lee rigging and that the fierce wind had torn away his handhold and blasted him overboard. Though his ultimate cry had been heard there would have been no hope of rescue on such a dark tempestuous night.

Later that morning we were called aft for a memorial service. This was the first occasion on which the Captain had suffered the loss of a cadet and he was visibly distressed. As we listened to the sombre words of committal I looked out at the streaked turbulence of the angry sea and, imagining Bazalgette's loneliness, took comfort in the thought that his dark ending must have been mercifully swift.

One hundred miles or so to the south of New Zealand we steadied up on the 50th parallel of latitude for our long run to the east and for the next three weeks experienced typical westerlies alternating with brief days of contrary winds. The great swell, rolling on day after day, seemed if anything to be more stupendous than on the outward voyage but this impression was probably illusory as the Roaring Forties do not vary much from ocean to ocean. We were, however, farther to the southward and the autumnal weather had more than a hint of winter cold particularly when southerly winds gave us a taste of the icy breath of Antarctica. We had an average quota of high winds; the decks were often ravaged by flooding seas, the ship bucketed about incessantly and, more often than not, the sun's occasional warmth was blotted out by grey clouds.

A fortnight after leaving harbour we crossed the International Date Line. Throughout our voyage from west to east round the world the ship's clocks had been put forward day by day and now, on reaching 180° East longitude, we had to adjust by adding an extra day to our calendar. This, of course, was normal practice when making easting across the Pacific. Windjammer crews, unaware of the ship's actual position, used to accuse Masters of craftiness in always choosing a full working day for this adjustment and the phrase 'Never on Sundays' became accepted deepsea lore. I don't remember whether or not this applied on our particular voyage but I do recollect that when the Captain announced that we would have a second Friday the crowd in the fo'c'sle suspected dirty work.

I had good reason to remember that extra day. I was busy with Molly Morgan on a splicing job and, as the fore-deck was awash most of the time with seas breaking on board, we took our work on to the top of the half-deck where it was comparatively dry. Settling down in the lee of the hen-coop we braced ourselves against the violent movement of the ship which, wallowing in the heavy swell, was rolling a full 30° each way. The sun was shining and we were agreeing that this was not at all a bad way to spend our afternoon when our attention was roused by maternal cluckings within the coop. Molly, who always kept an ear cocked for a quick chance, thought that a fresh egg would go down well with our tea and told me off to investigate. Taking a look round to check that the Second Mate was not in a position to witness our abstraction I cased the joint and got on with the job. I had just thrust my hand under the protesting mum when, without warning, as if in retribution for felony, a bloody great sea reared up and with an almighty rush swept clean over the scene of the crime. The next few seconds were hectic and confused and I had not got over my surprise when I found myself lying on my back holding on like grim death to the keel of the starboard lifeboat which had been lifted out of its chocks by the now receding sea. Molly had been equally lucky and had fetched up wrapped round a stanchion. But the fowls, and our egg, had gone overboard leaving no trace of their habitation except the wire rope that had formerly lashed them to the deck.

By this time we had become accustomed to accepting general hardship as our way of life but as time went on work on deck was made painful for most of us by nagging sea-cuts – cracks on the palms of the hands which, under the aggravation of constant hauling on salt soaked ropes, stubbornly refused to heal.

A month out from Australia, two thirds of our way across the Pacific, we began to work to the southward to round Cape Horn. This took us into the Fifties and a tearing westerly gale during which we logged eleven knots under three tops'ls and fores'l and made good 250 miles in 24 hours – the best day's run of the voyage. Though it was a grim day of lowering clouds and blinding squalls the dark threat of the weather was lightened by the ship's exultant speed.

Cape Horn has a legendary, and well deserved, reputation for harsh treatment of ships and sailors. One hundred years after the great Magellan probed through the passage to the Southern Sea that bears his name, the Dutch brothers, Schouten, pressing on into hitherto unexplored waters discovered that there was an open sea route to the Pacific. From that day in 1616 when they sighted the uttermost point on the American continent and named it after their home town in Holland, the wild waste of water to the southward of Cape Horn has taken heavy toll. All the elements conspire in frustrating the Pacific-bound sailing ship endeavouring to round Cape Stiff, as sailors call this bleak headland. Fierce westerly winds prevail, great seas roll eastwards and an adverse current checks progress. In the face of such opposition it was common experience for ships to beat to windward for weeks on end striving to make sufficient westing to weather the storm-battered coast of southern Chile.

At the best of times the west-bound ships had a bitter struggle to claw their way round – at worst they were stressed to the limits of endurance, and many, dismasted, had to limp back to the Falklands under jury rig. Through the centuries a tragic number of battered vessels succumbed and foundered without trace.

With such a long history of battle and disaster it is not surprising that the term 'Cape Horner' epitomises the ultimate in hard seagoing.

In comparison with the trials of west-bounders the passage from west to east presented relatively few hazards. Helped by prevailing winds, and carried on their way by a favourable east-going current, Atlantic-bound ships customarily rounded the

Horn with no more difficulties than they had experienced while running their easting down across the Pacific. In bad weather and poor visibility the Masters of east-bound ships, always anxious about their longitude, were naturally on edge at the prospect of making a landfall on such a treacherous lee shore but, unless the weather had been exceptionally cloudy, they had confidence in their latitude and kept well to the southward and clear of danger.

This applied in our case and with a strong wind under our tail we ran into the South Atlantic without sighting the dreaded Cape Stiff.

It had taken us five and a half weeks to sail 6,130 miles across the Pacific at an average speed of $6\frac{1}{2}$ knots. A log of daily distances run shows that we covered 200 miles or more on no less than thirteen days of this 38-day passage from Sydney to the Horn which, though by no means a record, was not bad going.

Having rounded this significant corner we really felt that we were on the homeward stretch and wisecrackers cautioned the look-out to keep his eyes skinned for the smoke of a tug on the northern horizon. In reality we were still a week short of the half way mark and still had to sail the best part of 8,000 miles before we could hope to pick up soundings to the west of Land's End.

Six weeks in the roaring forties had given us a bellyfull of heavy going and it was a relief to sail in relatively moderate seas under the lee of the Falklands. We happened to strike lucky winds and covered 2,000 miles to the northward in a week and a half. It grew warmer day by day, the ship dried out and almost before we had realized our good fortune we were coming up to Capricorn and the south-east Trades with our salt-caked sea-boots stowed away and the rigours of the Southern Ocean all but forgotten.

By this time we were in the middle of a drive to get everything shipshape in readiness for inspection by hawk-eyed owners on arrival in London. For the past ten days we had been on our knees like a bunch of ardent Mohammedans scouring the decks with gritty holystone 'bibles', and urged into back-aching genuflections by our blue-nosed Mufti. We were then swayed aloft in bosun's chairs with a pot of black paint preservative and a rag to coat the standing rigging – and hell to pay if a drop fell on the spotless deck. We then spent most of the fine weather time in the south-east Trades slung over the side on stages with chipping hammers and scrapers to flake off sea-wracked paint and rust. This was an agreeable way to pass the time, sitting in the hot sunshine and cooled by the blue sea beneath our feet. It was peaceful, too, providing one kept up sufficient clatter to check the Mate from sticking his ugly face over the bulwark.

With the south-east Trades abaft the beam most north-bound Masters aimed to cross the Line in mid-Atlantic, round about 30° W, and it was not unusual to sight other windjammers in this area. Sure enough, on our 65th day at sea we sighted and spoke *Loch Torridon*, a famous rival. We had sailed from Australia on the same day, we picked up the north-east Trades together and, after a day in company we lost touch. She had better luck than we had and beat us home by three days.

We averaged six knots during ten days in the constant Trades. Sailing full and bye on the starboard tack we made good distance to the north towards the belt of westerlies but, in doing so, were driven far out to the westward. Fetching up in the Horse latitudes, with the ship's head boxing the compass in light airs, we spent five days shifting sail and painting the ship's side.

On the 83rd day at sea, in a position midway between Gibraltar and New York, the wind came out of the west and we were able, at long last, to steer directly homewards at nine knots.

By this time we were in the lanes of steamer traffic and, on 24 May, the Cunard liner *Carpathia* hastened past. She promised to report our position by wireless but was in too much of a hurry to tell us where we were. Having had the sea to ourselves for so long the almost daily sighting of ships made us feel overcrowded and the Old Man, scornful of the quality of look-out kept by steamers in general, and mindful that our oil-burning side-lights were far from brilliant, kept the watchkeepers on the poop on a split yarn to let off a signal flare to ward off heedless steamers blinding along at full speed.

At this time the Captain began to grow tetchy at the prospect of making landfall. The chronometers on which we had to rely for calculation of longitude might well have gained or lost time during the three months we had been out of sight of land. Inaccuracy of a few seconds from correct Greenwich time meant an error of a mile in position as calculated by observation of the sun or stars. Since last checked the chronometers had been subjected to violent movement and changes of temperature and their accurate time-keeping might well have been affected by this rough treatment. The old precept 'When in doubt – lead, log and look-out', was very much in mind as we felt our way eastwards and the watch on deck was kept busy making casts with the deep-sea lead as we approached the Channel. We did not have to rely on the lead alone because arrival in 'soundings' was indicated by a change in the colour of the sea from dark blue to green. We also knew that land was not far ahead when we saw solan geese, seagulls and a French trawler, all confirming that we had entered the shallow water fishing grounds on the Atlantic Shelf.

We spent a day heaving round on the capstan, lifting and catting the anchors and, that evening, our gathering on the fore-hatch buzzed with argument about the expected date of arrival in London. Discussion livened up when we heard a rumour that the Captain had forecast that we might make landfall some time after midnight. As the light failed after sunset the look-out on the fo'c'sle roused all hands by reporting a light on the port bow. The chronometers had been only a minute or so in error and we had come up to the Bishop Light four hours earlier than expected.

This famous light, the last and first link with home for generations of sailors, flashed with exceptional brightness on that clear night. Looking at this evidence that I had indeed gone round the world I found it difficult to recall my disconsolate feelings when I had last watched the loom of the Bishop dip beneath a dark horizon.

We galloped up Channel next day with a fresh nor-west wind on the quarter and, by midnight, our old friend Start Point was abeam. Shortly after dawn the next morning the tug *Progress*, which had been cruising the western Channel looking for us, steamed up to within hailing distance and, after bellowed greetings, offered her tow rope. 'How much?' shouted the Old Man. 'A hundred pounds to you, Captin'.' With the end of the voyage in sight this seemed reasonable enough to us but the Captain thought otherwise and, to our disgust, replied – 'What do you take me for – a philanthropist? I've got a fair wind and can make the Downs without your help.' 'Please yourself Captin' – but the breeze is fallin' light an' it's settin' in for a calm I shouldn't wonder.'

The tug-master, hoping for a change of mind, hung around for a bit and his crew shouted the news that the *Titanic* had struck an iceberg on her maiden voyage and had been lost. It seemed inconceivable that this great liner, publicised as unsinkable, could have foundered but, as we read later, she had been steaming at speed and the ice had ripped the bottom out of her and, despite her many watertight compartments, she had sunk with heavy loss of life. By a coincidence, as we heard this news, we sighted the *Olympic*, one of her sister ships, tearing down Channel at twenty knots.

The tug-master's weather sense had been just about right and, twelve hours later, we were becalmed to the southward of the Isle of Wight and losing ground on the ebb tide. This time the Captain was not so optimistic and, after a bit of haggling, he clinched a bargain at £50 for a tow to Gravesend.

Up aloft next morning, unbending sails, I felt on top of the world. Windows on the distant Kentish coastline shimmered in the sunshine and even the dirty yellow waters of the Thames estuary were touched with a sparkle that matched the fantasy of homecoming. This air of entrancement persisted and when we came to a buoy off Gravesend to await the tide the novelty of tan-sailed barges tacking up stream; the sounds of a church bell and a barking dog; the sight of strangers climbing on board; all seemed too unreal to be true. Visitors brought papers and filled us in with the headlines of three months back news. We read our mail and tried to pick up the threads joining us to what had become an alien world.

In an atmosphere of effervescent idleness I relaxed with Molly Morgan, smoking cadged Turkish cigarettes the aroma of which, after weeks of pungent plug tobacco, stimulated exotic plans for our shoregoing.

On 7 June, 1912, the 95th day after leaving Sydney, we towed up river on the flood tide and, berthing once again in the West India dock, completed a circumnavigation of some 31,000 miles in the 265 days since our day of sailing in the previous year.

CHAPTER V

Second time round

My second voyage, half as anticipated and half unforeseen, landed me in a situation that changed the entire course of my life.

We sailed on another September morning and the tow down river and the beat down Channel was much the same as before but, this time, I was back in an accustomed environment, thoroughly bitten with deep-sea life and full of ambition to make a career in sail.

Some of the Officers had changed and we now had to adjust ourselves to the whims of a new Mate who, after a week or so of threatening thunder, eased off and became generally accepted as a fair-minded bastard. All hands agreed that he was a vast improvement on old Blue-nose. The Second Mate, too, had been replaced by a more cultured, but just as competent, 25-year-old who took life more quietly than his predecessor who, in moments of stress, had been inclined to bawl and thump anyone within reaching distance.

Up forrard, Bosun Macgregor, Sails and Chips, who were all more or less fixtures in the ship, had faithfully returned. In the fo'c'sle there were new faces but the *P.J.* had a good reputation and a number of the old-timers, including the wizened Dai and the ploddy Dotchman, had signed on again. Even the scrofulous old Marnier had managed to survive his customary shoreside dissipations and was back with yet more wanton tales of excesses.

We now mustered eight seniors in the half-deck all of whom had been on the previous voyage. All my batch of eight had come back for more and, at the tail end, we had eight voyagers. Our port watch was very much as before with the same Chief Cadet and Molly Morgan, now on his third voyage, as his stand-in. With an instinct for discipline we seasoned veterans looked over our four newcomers with fastidious eyes, audibly deploring the drop in quality since the days when we came to sea.

While still in the Channel I was told off to break in our colts. A year at sea had made a big difference to me; I had filled out physically and with experience tucked under my belt I had started to grow up. In my new-found maturity my charges, though in reality only a year younger, seemed to be callow school-boys and just about as helpless as I, no doubt, had looked in my early days. I tried, with difficulty, to remember this as I took my unprepossessing bunch in hand but, despite my assurance that they were in clover in comparison with what we had had to put up with on the previous voyage, they remained unconvinced and woebegone. As a matter of fact they were a good lot and, after the first ten dismal days, they blossomed out – as I had done.

One, in particular, intrigued me. A sprig of Irish nobility with patrician features, dark hair and eyes of blue innocence that veiled a soul full of sin. He was, I gathered, an orphan under the guardianship of an elder brother who, alarmed by a series of night escapades from Eton to Leicester Square, had wisely decided to ship his errant brother off to sea. This did not disturb the stripling overmuch for he was all out for adventure wherever it might be found, and a windjammer seemed as good a place as any to satisfy his ambitions.

His early days were disillusioned by seasickness and irksome authority but, as he had an irrepressible buoyancy, he soon bobbed up from adversity. Full of good nature, infectious gaiety, Irishisms and tall tales told with an air of wide-eyed virtue, we aptly christened him Blarney. If he scented fun he was in it up to the neck with feckless disregard of the consequences. As far as I knew he was absolutely fearless with one, rather curious, exception – he was scared stiff of heights. In his existing situation this was awkward to say the least and it took me days of coaxing backed by threats to get him over the futtocks and on to the royal yard. In time he forced himself to accept the challenge but, though he came to joke about work aloft, I don't think he ever quite mastered his initial fear.

The ship soon settled down to sea routine and, as the majority of us had been together before, our life on board seemed to be a prolongation of the previous trip. Those long windjammer voyages did not differ much in substance and we moved from the North-east Trades through the Doldrums to the South-east Trades and on to the Roaring Forties with a steadiness that varied little from a regular pattern. Individual ships experienced some vagaries in the weather but, by and large, one voyage was very similar to another and, apart from exceptional disaster, the wool clippers could be relied upon to go down under or back within a week either side of a 95-day time-table.

The sameness in our daily lives would have been tedious had it not been for the wide variety of seamanlike jobs to be done to keep the ship well maintained and ready to meet all foreseeable eventualities. All, except the few who by temperament or sheer bloody-mindedness had not got their hearts in it, took pride in their seamanship and this developed an *esprit de corps* in which to be found wanting was equivalent to personal disgrace. This affected all of us to greater or less degree and, for my part, I was fired with determination to become a seaman in the full sense of the word, and I welcomed the more mature jobs that I was given. Old seamen say that the longer you are at sea the more there is to learn and, as this is undeniably true, I had ample scope and plenty of opportunity to practise my expertise.

We were lucky with the North-east Trades and, in idyllic weather, made good time down to the southward. Fishing for bonito was popular on that voyage. The technique was to climb out on the bowsprit with cod-line and hook masked by white and red bunting and to keep the lure bouncing on the surface in the hope that it would be mistaken for a flying-fish. Either I hadn't got the knack or the bonito weren't interested and I was about to pack it in when Blarney decided to have a go and I sat at his back, astride the bowsprit, while he tried his hand. He had not been there ten minutes, bobbing his line up and down, when with beginner's luck he saw a flashing silver body shoot out of the depths and take his hook in mid-air. With a wild cry he gathered

1. 'The ship sheered out to port, the stays'ls filled and quietened and we made slow headway on the starboard tack.' (Page 4)

2. An artist's impression of the *Port Jackson*.

3. Furling the fors'l. 'One hand for yourself and one for the owners.' (Page 29)

4. 'A wall of green water reared up and thundered over the bulwark.' (Page 33)

in his line but, in his excitement, took a turn round his wrist which promptly jammed. I grabbed his belt and we both lay back. Had not the hook, providentially, torn clear that three-foot fish would have had both of us in the ditch. 'Mother of God – that's a bloody shame to lose a spalpeen like that,' said Blarney sucking his bleeding wrist.

This abortive venture whetted his sporting instinct and when, in a calm a few days later, a baited shark hook was dropped over the taffrail into the still water he buzzed round like a blue-arsed fly determined to be in at the kill. Sharks, with reason, are looked upon by sailors as the incarnation of Old Nick himself and there was always someone with a thirst to teach the old devil a lesson. A dorsal fin had been seen cruising round and the splash of the hook quickly attracted a twelve-footer. The shark, though hungry, was cautious and in the gin-clear water we watched him, with his small black and white pilot fish in station just above his snout, swim languidly up and, like an expectant cat, rub the length of his sinuous body against the fid of putrid pork. Satisfied with his reconnaissance, or misled by his eager pilot, he moved off about a hundred yards and came back at the rush, turned on his back, and took bait, hook and chain trace at a gulp. Well and truly curbed he thrashed out viciously as we man-handled the line forrard and, helped by willing hands, hove up and pulled the struggling monster over the bulwark on to the deck. He was a big one all right and as he wriggled about, scattering the party with whipping tail and snapping jaws, he looked far too aggressive to tackle at close quarters. Blarney, yelling 'Erin go bragh,' nipped in and thrust a capstan bar into the cavernous mouth, stiffening the catch sufficiently to allow someone to apply the finishing stroke by hacking off the beast's tail with a butcher's cleaver. We tried to catch the pilot fish in a bucket but he was circling in panic and soon disappeared in search of a new host to protect his vulnerable little life. The tail fin of the shark was nailed to the end of the jibboom as a talisman to bring fair winds.

Boatswain Macgregor was a relic of the great days of a rapidly passing age. A venerable sexagenarian with salt water in his veins and thoroughly deserving the sailor's accolade – 'Every hair a rope yarn and each finger a marlin spike.'

Like all good Bosuns he had more seamanlike foresight and common sense than most of us would gather in a lifetime. A taciturn Scot, he was not given to idle reminiscence and we knew little of his history but, from occasional monosyllabic disclosures, we gathered that in youth he had served in famous Tea Clippers and that his long life had been studded with perils – dismastings, strandings, founderings and extreme privations. Despite all this he was relatively unscarred and, though time had stiffened his joints, he could still work aloft with the agility of a man half his age. He knew no other life than that of the sea, his bosun's locker was his home and, as a dedicated 'ship's husband', he was content to live out his days in that capacity.*

The Bose was always in the forefront in a crisis, tackling the job in hand with unflagging skill and disregard for personal safety. There was a wild day down south when the weather lift of the fore-yard carried away. The great yard canted and jerked; the tops'l sheet parted; the released clew broke free and, within seconds, the whole sail disintegrated leaving nothing but torn strips of canvas streaming from the yard. The roping on the leech of the sail, trailing a length of its broken chain sheet, whipped viciously in the high wind.

The Bosun, who was on the fore-deck at the time, instinctively sized up the trouble and, recognizing that the unsupported fore-yard was in danger of buckling, decided to rig a preventer lift to take the strain. Without waiting for orders he was up the rigging, with a coil of rope and a snatch block slung round his neck, before we were hurried aloft to cut away what remained of the tops'l. As I climbed the topmast rigging I saw the old man edging out crabwise on the bucking fore-yard without, apparently, giving a thought to the risk of being clobbered by the whipping remnant of the tops'l sheet. The sight of this elderly man voluntarily tackling a job which, in his mind, was too dangerous to be passed on to others lives in my memory as typical of the unselfish courage shown by the best of a great generation of seamen.

* Boatswain Macgregor stayed on in *Port Jackson* until, four and a half years later, he died when the ship was sunk by a German submarine on 28 April, 1917.

Sailing ship crews were not all of this calibre – there was always a residue of scrimshankers and scruffy troublemakers – but the majority were rugged individualists who could be relied upon to pull their weight. In a reasonably ordered ship the fo'c'sle crowd faced up to the reality of being cooped up together for months on end and shook down into a pecking order in which the upper levels were reserved for seasoned seamen. On the whole they got on well enough together but, when personalities clashed, they were inclined to settle disputes with fists rather than sweet reason. Most fo'c'sles had a bully who aimed to dominate with a heavy hand but there were usually enough staid hands to keep him in check.

The tone of the fo'c'sle was greatly influenced by the attitude of the Bosun. In our case Macgregor, a respected disciplinarian, did much to de-fuse disaffection and smooth out personal conflicts. He kept his ear to the deck and moved in with forceful authority if, in his opinion, any loud mouthed sea-lawyer started to swing his weight about.

The Bose did not go much on Hans, whose native arrogance was tending to burst out at the seams. The ploddy Dotchman was irritating rather than vicious and, like most bullies, he was vulnerable to ridicule. For some reason or other he had got it in for the diminutive Dai and the two skirmished in a festering feud which came to a farcical climax one bleak day on the lee fore brace.

The trouble between them had started earlier in the voyage when Hans became jealous because Dai was chosen as shantyman of our watch. On long heavy hauls requiring sustained strength and endurance it was necessary to coordinate our efforts. In such cases the halliard or brace was rove through a leading block and strung along the deck so that the hauling hands could lay back to the rhythm of a shanty. These working songs, some of great antiquity, consisted in a shantyman's refrain followed by a heaving chorus. We used a number of shanties in the course of a voyage but usually liked those that had become traditional through long usage – such as *Whiskey Johnny, Ranzo* and *Blow boys, blow*, This last, a favourite, ran :

Refrain.　A Yankee ship came down the river,
Chorus.　　*Blow* boys – *blow*,
R.　　　　　Her masts an' yards they shone like silver,
C.　　　　　*Blow* my bully boys *blow*.
R.　　　　　An' how d'ye know she's a Yankee Clipper,
C.　　　　　*Blow* boys – *blow*,
R.　　　　　By the blood an' guts wot flows from her scupper,
C.　　　　　*Blow* my bully boys *blow*.

To ease the strain between hauls it was normal practice to operate a 'stopper'. This, a short length of rope shackled at one end, had its tail twisted round and round the main rope on which the hands were hauling. With each heave the 'stopperman' slackened his stopper to allow the bigger rope to slide through. As the heave ended he quickly gripped the coils so that they held fast on the strands of the main rope and stopped it running back. This allowed the hands to ease their muscles and shift their grip. A good stopper-man did not lose a single inch of hard-won effort, even though he might at times be smothered by a sea tumbling over the rail.

The art of the shanty-man, who invariably worked the stopper, lay in timing his refrain to get us all pulling together and in improvising his words to keep us entertained. Though the working hands usually preferred the re-telling of their well-known shanty stories in traditional words they were always amused by variations on a customary theme – particularly if it voiced some current grouse against harsh treatment by the Mates.

No one who heard those working songs in the original would claim they were immaculate. Shanties were designed for rough, tough, men and I much prefer memories of the coarse, bawdy, salty words that lightened the toil of countless sailors to the washed-out fresh-water versions that survive ashore.

Dai had been chosen by popular consent for his competence in working the stopper and for the imaginative skill he used in colouring his repertoire. He was a little blackbird of a man whose Celtic spirit reflected the mood of those around him. Like many of his countrymen he alternated between cocksure assurance and an attitude of injured inferiority in the face of opposition. He had a thin nasal voice and, like many Welshmen, he delighted in song. The subtle variety of his improvisations kept us amused and, as he was nippy with the stopper, we had no complaints.

On a day when the wind had been backing and freshening we were called, twice in a watch, to man the lee fore brace. This tendency of the wind to grow ahead set tempers on edge and we grumbled as we came shambling along the deck for the second time to brace up the fore-yard.

Our shantyman jumped up on the rail and with his stopper in hand started us off on *Whiskey Johnny*. At the third verse he turned to look to windward just as a rasping sea whipped over the fo'c'sle head. His mouth, agape in song, caught it and, in a flash, his larynx was awash in salt water. In a paroxysm of coughing he relaxed his grip, the fore brace took charge and rendered back and, with a chorus of jeers ringing in his ears, our soddened songster dried up.

Bully Hans, who fancied himself as a shantyman, roughly pushed the gasping Dai aside and, grabbing the stopper, sang out, 'Gott a'mighty – ve vants a chantymans vot can sing.' Dai bach, looking as sick as he felt, miserably tailed on the end of the brace. The work done we coiled up the gear and went about our several jobs – all but Dai who, smarting from injustice, felt disinclined for company and hid himself in the Bosun's locker where, in solitude, he planned revenge. Sensing that if the wind was in the mood for backing it would back again he guessed that, before long, there would be another call to sweat up the fore braces. Plunging his hand in a tin of tallow he wandered out casually on deck and cleaned his greasy fingers on the stopper of the lee fore brace. His intuition served him well and within half an hour we were stringing out the fore brace once more. This time Hans had no rival and, shouting, 'Vere's my ploddy Velshman now?', jumped up on the rail and, with teuton arrogance, bawled out his shanty. For a pull or two all went well but, as the grease spread, Dai's stratagem paid off. The brace was under strain and as we relaxed between hauls the slipping stopper lost its hold. The great fore-yard took charge, the sail got caught aback, and the Mate came storming forrard spitting out lethal abuse. Dai had been waiting this moment and quick as a bird took a hitch with a handy rope's end and, hopping up on the rail coiled his improvised stopper round the brace. With a cry of, 'Gott a'mighty – inteet we want a stopperman wot can stop – look you,' he burst into an old favourite, – 'Have you heard of Reuben Ranzo?' This shanty relates the hard fortunes of a poor tailor who shipped aboard a whaler but was too lubber-like to learn to be a sailor. Improvising on the normal words Dai piped:

> Have you heard of bully Ha-anso,
> Hanso boys, Hanso.
> Now Hanso was no sailor,
> Hanso boys, Hanso.

As Dai sang the story of Hanso's failure to work a stopper the tale lost nothing in the telling and the ploddy Dotchman, taken aback, was left in no doubt that we were all on the side of David in his victory over Goliath.

The Bose, who had been an approving witness of the whole incident, bawled out the deflated Hans and, with a rare smile, told him off to clean out the 'heads'.*

Apart from a few individual dust-ups personal relationships were exceptionally cordial that voyage. The Officers were friendly and humane in their discipline and the rest of us had little of substance to complain about. This did not, in any way, inhibit the perennial grousing natural to deep-sea sailors but there was no snarl in the backlash against the firm authority of our Master and his Mates.

Coming up to the Bass Straits, with the end of the voyage in sight, past differences and grumbles were jettisoned in an atmosphere of cheerful anticipation.

Sydney was mid-summer bright and the days of our calendar flipped past with the speed of a card-sharper's deal. As the attractions of Australia as a land of promise became more widely known they acted as a powerful magnet in drawing an increasing number of Europeans seeking a new life and Sydney's population was regularly swollen by immigrants decanted by the ship load into the teeming city. A high proportion of these newcomers were

* The ship's company's lavatories.

'townees' with little inclination to rough it 'up country' and, as there were few jobs going in Sydney at the time, hundreds were stranded without money or prospect of work. At the end of the three day's grace allowed after arrival these unfortunates were dumped ashore to shift for themselves and I remember the plight of pathetic family groups camping as best they could in the Domain – a park near our berth at Wooloomooloo. In time these disillusioned venturers were absorbed but many must have been scarred by a greeting that treated them as refugees rather than as welcomed citizens of a new world.

I was at this time half way through my three year apprentice-ship and had learned enough to take a full seaman's part in pre-paring the ship for the homeward voyage. We struck down some of the upper yards to repair the gear; rigged and fitted a new t'gallant mast; replaced worn ratlines and refitted our two heavy ship's life-boats – all of which called for intriguing sailorizing.

We fraternized with the White Star training ship *Mersey* and wasted a lot of idle breath trying to convince their cadets that we had a tougher time than they had. In truth we were all better nurtured than the Brassbounders'* commonly found in the half decks on board the average hard-case windjammers who, as they vehemently pointed out to us when we met, lived the life of dogs.

By the end of January the last of our outward freight had been swung over the side and we spent several days at a buoy waiting for our loading berth to be vacated. During this lull a party of us were put on to cleaning out the hold in readiness for our home-ward cargo of wheat and wool. It was sweaty hot down below and, feeling the need for a breath of fresh air, I climbed up the vertical ladder to lower a bucket of water to my thirsty mates. At the top I reached out to grasp the hatch coaming to heave myself up and over on to the deck. It was not, in any way, a difficult feat but my greasy fingers slipped and, losing my handhold, I fell backwards. I did not take long to drop the forty feet or so to the floor of the hold but, in those frantic moments, I had time for three racing thoughts – what a bloody silly thing to happen; it's a long way down; and there's going to be a hell of a bump. There was! I had

* One of the politer terms used as a title for square-rigged apprentices.

instinctively raised my right arm to protect my head and, by a miracle, landed slap in the middle of a hatch cover – the only bit of wood in the hold – with my arm forced round the back of my neck. Though fully conscious I was dazed by the shock and vaguely remember being hoisted up and taken ashore to a waiting ambulance. My shoulder was sickeningly uncomfortable but the hospital made quick work of me and after a whiff of anaesthetic I woke up in a bed in a large general ward, free from pain and with a pretty nurse telling me that my dislocated shoulder had been reduced. She also told me that I was now as right as rain and extremely lucky and I fully endorsed her sentiments.

Five days later I was discharged and returned on board, feeling physically fit but with my right arm in a sling and paralysed from the shoulder down. The hospital Doctor had told me that my arm would regain feeling before long and, in sanguine hope, I spent several weeks loafing round ashore in pleasant freedom. Our ship's Doctor, looking me over as best he could through his morphine haze, reported to the Captain that I would be fit for work in a week or so but, when the ship sailed on 11 March 1913, my arm was still rigged up in its sling without feeling and incapable of independent movement.

The temperature dropped as we made our way, once again, to the south of New Zealand aggravating a sense of vague depression at the inevitability of many weeks of isolation before we fetched up in home waters. The cargoes carried by sailing ships on their long voyages tended to change hands after the day of sailing and, in the absence of means of communication, it was customary for ships to make for a west-country harbour to be directed on to their port of destination and, on this voyage, we were under instructions to proceed to 'Queenstown for orders'.

Being officially on the sick-list I had little to occupy my time and, in reality, there was not much I could have done with one arm out of action. The smug satisfaction of being able to hog it in my bunk when my mates were roused out for a dirty watch on deck soon palled. Time dragged and, feeling disembodied from the corporate life of the ship, I became increasingly bored with my idle situation. Making my way aft I asked the Captain if I could stand a regular watch on the poop which, I urged, was well within my capacity. Thereafter I had something to do – it was not much but at least it alleviated the frustration of the long voyage home. I found that I could easily cope with the comparatively light duties involved – attending on the Officer of the Watch and running messages; writing up the rough log; striking the bell and calling the hands – and this, in small measure, gave me a sense of participation.

One of my routine jobs as watchkeeper was to organise the 'Heaving the log' ritual. We were not fitted with a sophisticated 'speedometer' and made use of a 'hand log'. This time-honoured device consisted of a hand-held spindle, a log line, and the log itself – a triangular piece of wood the drag of which, when dropped over the stern, would pull the logline off its spindle at a rate equivalent to the ship's speed. The logline was marked at four fathom intervals with small lengths of knotted twine. Each hour I called two operators from the watch on deck – one to hold the spindle above his head, the other to heave the log overboard and let the line run through his hands. As master of ceremonies I held a 15 second sand-glass and when the heaver, feeling the first knot passing his fingers, shouted 'Turn' I reversed my glass. As the last grain of sand dropped through I ordered 'Stop' and the heaver, checking the line running out, reported the number of the knot nearest his hand. Heaving the log in wintry weather was a tiresome chore, particularly when the ship was eating up the miles and, say, twelve wet knots had to be laboriously hauled back on board with fingers aching with icy cold. This primitive, but really quite effective, method of measuring speed by numbers of knots gave its name to the modern scale by which a ship's speed is recorded.

The passage across the South Pacific was comparatively uneventful until a day when we were slanting to the south-east to round the Horn. On a cold, sunless, forenoon I was watchkeeping on the poop. The ship, on a light soldiers' wind, was making a bare three knots. The visibility was closing down and it soon thickened into dense mist. The temperature dropped and the Captain restlessly walked the weather side of the poop with droplets of mist glistening on his white moustache. He stamped his foot in irritation and I heard him mutter 'Thick as a haystack –

I don't like it.' Swivelling round he sighted me blowing warmth into my fingers and ordered, 'Here boy – get up on the fo'c'sle and start up the fog-horn – there's ice about.' I trotted forrard with this brass instrument, resembling a tyre pump with a handle at the top which, if pressed down with force, caused the horn to let out a plaintive bleat.

Enveloped in isolating mist, it was grey and lonely in the eyes of the ship. Pumping my eerie cry over the waters I strained my eyes trying to pierce the gloom ahead. The risk of running foul of another ship in such unfrequented seas was negligible and I knew that after each bleat on my horn the Captain would be listening to catch an echo from an ice-berg. It grew colder and, in imagination, I saw fantastic shapes looming up in our path – great masses of ice which if encountered could tear the guts out of us. I shivered and sent another mournful note reaching out in quavering anxiety to seek dread ice and come speeding back to warn us of peril. In a calm sea the ship sailed blindly through the murk as I pumped away with my ears rigged out. After a time I sensed what might have been an echo. With thumping heart I thrust my handle down twice in succession and, unmistakeably, heard twin counterparts come faintly back. I caught my breath and, with cold air biting my lungs, shrilled, 'Ice ahead.' The Captain had heard it too and with quick instinct ordered the helm down to bring the ship up in the wind to check her speed. Way above my head I heard the invisible sails slatting against the fore-mast and, as the bows swung round, I saw it – my first ice-berg – as menacing and spine chilling as a ghost. I had time only to see white water fretting its bulk and it was gone – cold death fading like an ugly dream and leaving an icy breath of fear in its wake. Shouts came to me through the fog as the hands started to shorten sail, the Old Man having decided that it was better to drift under bare poles than run the awful risk of collision. The berg was seen no more but the chill impact of its presence lingered on until the memory was off-set by a wave of amusement at a farcical sequel.

Up aloft, out of sight from the deck in the thick mist, Blarney was doing more than his share in furling the mizzen royal when he realised that Marnier, his working mate, was drunk. This was an entertaining, and puzzling, phenomenon and he was wondering how the old Frenchman could have scrounged a skin-ful when he remembered that his partner had been lumping provisions in the lazarette and, putting two and two together, he guessed that the light-fingered old bastard had lifted a bottle of liquor from the Captain's store.

With their job more or less finished Marnier, bemused by hot spirit and cold air, laid his head on the rolled up canvas and lapsed into drowsiness. Blarney, with samaritan goodwill, shook his lethargic mate and, getting no response, passed several turns of a gasket round the recumbent figure and secured the end – out of reach. The sleepy reprobate, far away in a lecherous dream, mumbled 'Cherie,' and hugged the bunt of the sail with amorous arms.

A few minutes later the Old Man on the poop, and Blarney coming down from aloft, heard a banshee wail wafting down through the enshrouding mist. 'What the hell's that?' exclaimed the Captain. Blarney, who could never resist opening his big mouth at the wrong moment, piped up, 'I'm thinking it must be after being an albatross himself.' The Captain, still on edge and in no mood to respond to an Irish wise-crack, thundered, 'Who the hell ever heard of an albatross sitting singing on a yard, if you think it's a bird get aloft and catch it!' Freeing the furious Frenchman Blarney, in all innocence, grinned, 'Ye wouldn't be after having a nip of the Captain's hard stuff to warm me heart – it's sure cold and wet I am.' The angry Marnier brushed past and, with bleary hate in his blood-shot eyes, snarled, 'Keep yore bloody mouth shut or I'll . . .'. Blarney never heard what was coming to him for the ancient mariner, feeling suddenly cold and old, hastened unsteadily down the rigging and took cover in the fo'c'sle.

We rounded the Horn a few days later and, on this occasion in fair weather, sighted the famed headland standing up like a great bastion ten miles away to the northward. This was a rare experience for most of us and, after a month of blank horizons, even the forbidding cragginess of desolate land looked inviting. Once into the Atlantic the days of the voyage seemed to accelerate and in a few weeks we were through the Doldrums and into the North-east Trades.

In the fine weather, with time on my hands, I grew to know the ship's company more individually. Knowing the discomforts and deprivations of sailing ship seagoing I found it difficult to understand why the hard driven fo'c'sle hands chose to go on serving in sail when they could have led softer lives in steamships. Whatever their reasons many elected to come back for more and, despite perennial vows that, 'When I gets paid off after this bleedin' trip I'm going to swaller the anchor an' take up farming,' – a big proportion of the old-timers signed on again and again. Probably most of them did so because they were broke and, with only their seamanship to fall back on, they chose hardship on a miserable wage rather than the prospect of hunger ashore. But, behind this, the average barnacled deep-sea salt looked upon steamships as dirty mechanical upstarts and would have scorned to serve in so-called ships run by 'greasers'. It was really this pride in their calling and, perhaps, the perpetual challenge in pitting their skill against foul weather and angry seas that made them sign on voyage after voyage until incapacitated by rheumatism or death. Like most of those who choose to battle with nature's elements in the raw they developed deep-seated courage and humility in the face of forces so much greater than their own insignificance.

The sea is a great leveller and those men who, year after year, voyaged the seven seas in windjammers were ennobled by their environment and singularly free from the petty characteristics which are all too common in those who lead sheltered lives. The best of them made wonderful shipmates and even the worst could be relied upon to volunteer an unselfish hand at times of stress and danger. There is a lot of truth in the saying that nobody is the worse for contact with the sea and sailors. I learned that then and have had no reason to doubt the sentiment since.

As the voyage neared its end I became increasingly weighed down by gloomy thoughts of the future. Despite voluntary massage by the Steward, who at one time had coached a football team, my arm was still useless. The muscles had wasted away and I was depressed by the daily sight of mere nerveless skin and bone hanging lifelessly in my sling. I could, however, feel returning sensation and could move my thumb and, clinging desperately to this promise of improvement, I hoped for the best.

On mid-summer day we came to an anchor at Queenstown after a passage of 103 days and received orders to await the arrival of a tug to tow the ship to Havre for unloading. I missed this ultimate leg of the voyage because I was discharged to find my own way to London for medical treatment. I packed up my gear with mixed feelings – happy to be going ashore but not relishing this break with *Port Jackson* and her company with whom I had been so intimately related for two impressionable years.

Leaving in the Harbour Master's launch I looked back with my mind full of kaleidoscopic memories. The ship, with yards trimly squared and lofty masts shining in the summer sunshine, showed little signs of wear and tear apart from rust-stained plates near the water-line. Seeing her lying there, so quietly ship-shape in a calm green roadstead, it seemed inconceivable that those slender spars could have borne the stress of vengeful gales or that the graceful hull with its delicate sheer had so recently battled with, and surmounted, the monstrous seas of the Southern Ocean.

My mood of retrospection rapidly evaporated in the warmth of an Irish welcome. It was exciting to be on land again, the prospect was bright and, though the possibility of lengthy disability hung like a cloud over my future it was not black enough to take the edge off my keen enjoyment of present creature comforts – the unaccustomed luxury of a long wallowing bath, the sensuous relaxation of an undisturbed night between sheets in the cross channel packet and lashings of country fresh food for the asking. I can still sense the ecstacy of working twice through the boat-train's breakfast menu – from porridge and cream to three varieties of marmalade – without straining my loading capacity.

CHAPTER VI

Battleship

I SPENT the rest of the summer in London attending hospital for daily therapy. The Doctors told me that the dislocation of my shoulder had crushed a bunch of nerves but they had not been severed and to my great relief, my arm gradually responded to electrical shocks and vigorous massage. It was, however, a maddeningly slow process and, though in sight of recovery, I was still tied to the hospital when the *Port Jackson* sailed without me on what should have been my third, and final voyage.

Frustrated by this setback I pestered Sir Philip Devitt to let me work a steamer passage out to Australia to rejoin my ship in Sydney. But he had other ideas and startled me by saying that he was submitting my name to the Admiralty as a candidate for a period of service in the Royal Navy.

I had been one of four cadets who, on leaving the *Worcester*, had been enrolled as Midshipmen, Royal Naval Reserve, and under a new scheme that had just been announced I was eligible for a year's training in the Fleet.

With my ambitions firmly centred on sitting for my 'Square rig certificate examination' as soon as practicable it seemed to me to be a waste of time to spend a year in a warship when I could have been finishing my three year period of qualifying sea-time in the *Port Jackson*. My arguments were unavailing and, in October, 1913, I received an impressive-looking document from The Lords Commissioners of the Admiralty directing me to proceed to Portsmouth forthwith for service in the Home Fleet. Though still rankled that my personal plans had been capsized, I set about rigging myself out with new uniform gear, including a Dirk which seemed to me to be a peculiarly anachronistic weapon for twentieth century warfare.

The Navy was much in the public eye at the time and the papers were full of heated controversy on the meaning of sea-power. I knew little or nothing about the fighting side of the sea service in which I was about to embark. I was, therefore, intrigued when two passengers on the train to Portsmouth started an argument on naval affairs.

One, a man of commerce, was hot under the collar at the cost of expanding the Navy which, he declaimed, was already the largest in the world and more than adequate for our defence. He objected to his money being squandered on ever more toys for bellicose Admirals. The other took him to task for overlooking the fact that a large proportion of our existing ships were verging on obsolescence. The battle was in good trim to continue but, at this stage, we arrived and the contestants, in self contained rectitude, went their separate ways.

Their subject, however, had been very relevant to my situation for I was about to join one of the new battleships that had been the main bone of their contention.

Boarding a taxi, and looking at my instructions for the hundredth time, I told the driver to take me to *H.M.S. Orion* at the South Railway Jetty.

Accustomed to vessels of modest size I found the dark grey mass of the giant battleship intimidating and strangely unreal. Crossing the brow I was acutely conscious that I was stepping over the threshold into a new and unfamiliar world. The prospect, though exciting, was unnerving. I was formally saluted by the Officer of the Watch in a frock-coat and a Midshipman in a bumfreezer with white patches on the collar. I introduced myself and was taken in tow by the Midshipman through a warren of passages bright with lights and gleaming paintwork to the Gunroom which, so he told me, would be my home from home shared with nine Sub-Lieutenants and thirteen Midshipmen.

The Mess, into which I was ushered, gave an impression of space and luxurious comfort in comparison with the 'half-deck' in which I had lived for the past two years. A long table, covered with a green and black patterned cloth, stretched fore and aft beneath a row of open scuttles through which a fresh breeze fretted yellow-shaded pendant lights. A coal stove at the forrard end was ringed by a semi-circle of well worn leather armchairs. At the after end a battered piano lent a faint air of culture to its otherwise severely functional surroundings.

The only occupants were a Maltese steward laying the table and three recumbent Sub-Lieutenants to one of whom I was presented. He was, I gathered, the senior resident and, in his capacity as Sub of the gunroom, the ruler and arbiter of Midshipmens' fortunes. He gave me a friendly greeting and leading the way to the head of the table called for tea, over which he probed my professional history. Hearing that I had been at sea for two years he relieved my apprehensions by saying that after a month to get acclimatised he would accord me the status of senior Midshipman. This was welcome news because I had heard disturbing yarns about the Navy's treatment of junior 'snotties'.

The Mess filled up and I was turned over to the care of the four junior Midshipmen who were told off to help me shake down. Though they did their best to make me feel at home I was baffled by their eager comments on things and events utterly foreign to my experience, and their conversation was so larded with naval jargon that they might well have been talking a different language.

I turned in that night in a state of confusion and fell asleep in my unfamiliar hammock, surrounded by new mess-mates co-cooned within touching distance in a crowded compartment below the gunroom. I dreamt that I was once again a new boy at school, until roused by shouts of 'Rise and shine' into a strange world regulated by, to me, incomprehensible pipes and bugles.

Dressed in unaccustomed uniform I made my way to the gunroom and, after breakfast, not knowing what to do, I remained at anchor until a breathless Snottie told me to report to the Commander in his cabin.

The Commander of a battleship, under the Captain's overall authority, bore responsibility for the good order and discipline of the entire ship's company and was, as the senior Executive Officer, the prime organiser and dictator of day to day activities.

5. Heaving the Log. (Page 61)

6. HMS *Orion*, October 1913. (Page 70)

7. Rear-Admiral Sir Robert Arbuthnot (*left*) sparring with Lieutenant Bradford, who won the VC at Zeebrugge; HMS *Orion*, Scapa Flow, 1914. (Page 113)

Everything came within his ambit and, as 'Second in command', he had power to enforce his law by the application of summary justice to 'defaulters'. The Commander, or 'Bloke' as he was commonly called, was an awesome figure in a ship's hierarchy and, as it was quickly pointed out to me, it was highly dangerous to drift athwart his hawse.*

Entering the cabin I found myself face to face with a yellow malarial countenance framed by a trim black beard which quivered with suppressed impatience. No time was wasted on formalities and I was promptly catechised with disconcerting directness. I was beginning to feel under stress when the Commander, alerted by a distant bugle, ceased fire and brought the inquisition to an end with, 'As you have been round the Horn I suppose you think you know it all, but you have a hell of a lot to learn so get busy and, as a start, go and see the snotties' nurse.'

By modern standards our particular Bloke would be classed as an eccentric but he was not untypical of big-ship Executive Officers of that time, whose autocratic peculiarities of behaviour were accepted as a matter of course. A man of quicksilver temperament, alert with restless energy and brusque in speech, it was his habit to affect an irascible manner which he found useful in enforcing his authority, but the gale of his anger was short-lived and quickly subsided.

Despite their manifold duties no self-respecting Commander ever forgot his personal responsibility for the upbringing of the 'young gentlemen' – the euphemistic title for common or garden 'snots'. Commander Lewin was no exception and he would drop all else to catch a Midshipman's misdemeanour and had no compunction in sending the culprit hot-foot with a message to the Sub of the gunroom with an imperative order that salutary correction be promptly, and thoroughly, administered.

I made my way to the Snotties' nurse, a senior Lieutenant-Commander who carried responsibility for organizing and supervising Midshipmen's insruction. He was a 'salt horse' † and, to my eye, the beau ideal of a naval officer, suave, quietly mannered,

---

* To run foul of.
† The sobriquet attached to those who elected to remain plain 'seamen' in preference to specialization in Gunnery &c.

impeccably dressed and worldly wise. He was sympathetic to my state of bewilderment and gave me sound counsel. 'Get to know the ship first,' he said, 'ferret round on your own, be inquisitive about the whys and wherefores of everything that happens until you can see the pattern in the organization.'

Following my nurse's advice I set out on a questioning campaign and, in the course of my amateur research, collected information on *Orion*'s vital statistics.

She was the name ship of a class of four battleships of 25,000 tons displacement with a main armament of ten 13.5″ guns in five twin-gunned turrets; a secondary armament of sixteen 4″ guns and two 21″ submerged torpedo tubes.

She had an overall length of 545 feet, a beam of 88 feet and, in common with all battleships, was fitted with heavy armour protection. The four ships of the *Orion* class, which cost £2,000,000 apiece, were the first capital ships to be fitted with 13.5″ guns which, as all the turrets were mounted on the centre line, could fire a $5\frac{1}{2}$ ton broadside. The eighteen coal-fired boilers provided power for four steam turbine units giving a designed full speed of 21 knots and a full stowage of 3,300 tons of coal enabled them to cover about 4,000 miles at 19 knots. *Orion* had a complement of 900 officers and men and, when I joined her at the end of 1913, she was well on into her first two-year commission with a Devonport ship's company.

The 2nd Battle Squadron, to which we belonged, was commanded by Vice-Admiral Sir George Warrender wearing his flag in *King George V*, and *Orion* was the designated flagship of the Rear Admiral of the Squadron.

Shortly after my own inconspicuous arrival we were exposed to the pomp attending a change of flag, an event which, judging by the scale of the preparations, presaged an awe inspiring occasion. As we braced ourselves to receive the Admiral the Bloke stung the ship's company into more than normal activity. We knew that we were to embark Rear-Admiral Sir Robert Arbuthnot and that he was reputed to be a hard nut. Rumours flew and those who claimed previous acquaintance spread the buzz that we were 'for it'. On the mess-deck former shipmates avowed that he was 'an 'oly terror of an old time flogger' with an obsessive passion for 'strict service' and harsh discipline. In the gunroom we retailed all these lurid reports with apprehensive relish.

One intriguing yarn, possibly apocryphal but nevertheless swallowed entire, related to a wet and windy morning at Portland when Sir Robert, then Commander of a battleship, returning from a rare night ashore was delayed by weather and arrived at the gangway just as the hands were falling in at 6.0 a.m. Hurrying to his cabin he changed into uniform but, in his haste, omitted to exchange his shoregoing bowler for his brass hat. On deck the seamen awaiting orders to get busy with the ship's morning ablutions were confronted with an unconventional sight and, so the yarn went, the Commander's discipline was such that not a soul in the ranks of expressionless sailors dared display the unholy delight swelling his bosom. Back in his cabin the Commander, realizing his lapse, promptly put all officers who had witnessed the happening under arrest pending punishment for their deplorable lack of initiative.

A casual visitor gave us warning that the Rear Admiral was a stickler for strict observance of the uniform regulations. This set up a wave of despondency in the gunroom as the subordinate officers balanced the shortcomings in their wardrobes against lack of wherewithal for replenishment. The wearing of 'Ties, black silk, officers for the use of', was imperative and as such articles of adornment were comparatively inexpensive I was sent to Gieves on the Hard to buy 24 regulation ties on tick in the hope that their silken sheen would blind the evil eye to other less respectable aspects of our persons.

The Admiral, so I was told, would be accompanied by his Flag Captain, Secretary and Flag Lieutenant, all of whom by time honoured custom were personally selected officers. We were, therefore, faced with the prospect of a new Captain and, bearing in mind the reputably fierce nature of the Admiral, we could do no other than look askance at the idea of being commanded by a Post Captain of his choice.

On the great day the ship's company in No. 1 dress was fallen in on the upper deck a full hour before the event, a good old practice to safeguard against last minute crises. The Marine guard and band on the quarter-deck stood woodenly at ease. At the gangway the Officer of the Watch fidgetted his Midshipmen, Quartermaster and Boatswains Mates. Frock-coated senior officers pulled on white kid gloves as they paced the port side with clanking swords. Alone, on the hallowed starboard side, the Commander discharged flights of messengers in all directions.

At long last the Chief Yeoman of Signals, whose eye had been glued to his telescope for the past half hour, sang out, – 'Admiral, flyin' his flag, coming up from astern, Sir.' A bugler sounded the 'Still' and the whole assemblage froze into immobility as the barge, its brass funnel belching sparks of urgency, swept alongside to the accompaniment of shrill piping – re-enacting the ritual of the past when a senior officer was hoisted from his boat in a boatswain's chair.

Stationed with the Fore-topmen's division of seamen I was overlooking the gangway and saw a slight athletic figure bound up the accommodation ladder to pause on the threshold to receive our official homage. As one man the Guard came to the 'Present', each Marine raising a little cloud of pipeclay as he slapped the sling of his rifle, while the band burst into a jingling phrase from *Iolanthe* which, for some odd Victorian reason, had been chosen as an appropriate musical salute for officers of Flag rank.

Grim-faced and unsmiling the Rear-Admiral toured the deck to inspect the ranks of bare-headed sailors pausing, from time to time, to fix some unfortunate with a steely eye, ramming home his distaste by curt comments such as, 'Hair cut', 'Boots', 'Dirty silk', and, to a pimply specimen, 'Sick Bay'. This duty done Sir Robert repaired to his cuddy and, though lost to view, his sharp authority lingered on to give rise to gloomy speculation when the hands were piped to dinner.

The new Captain, having followed the Admiral at a respectful distance, was later seen pacing the quarter-deck in frowning conversation with the Commander. An imposing figure, well above average height, he had a pink, heavy-jowled countenance, a deep rumbling voice and ponderous manner. Captain F. C. Dreyer was a gunnery specialist with an outstanding reputation as a prolific inventor of intricate gun-control mechanisms and was acknowledged to be one of the brightest stars in the armament constellation.

Following the change of flag we sailed for Portland. For most of our ship's company this short passage was devoid of interest. For me it was a big event. My sea-going experience in power-driven ships had been limited to brief trips in cross-channel packets and my understanding of even these small steamships was theoretical rather than practical.

With one of the senior Midshipmen I climbed to the bridge to keep the afternoon watch. On the lofty compass-platform I felt far removed from the sea. It was a fair day and the massive bulk of the ship was serenely untroubled by the lively waves. She seemed solid and immovable and from my high viewpoint I found it difficult to realize that we were making a steady fifteen knots.

We had no other ships in company and, the Captain being in his sea-cabin, the Officer of the Watch, a senior Lieutenant, leant against the binnacle smoking a placid pipe. As he looked at his watch and yawned with ennui I admired his nonchalance and said as much to my confrere who, pitying my innocence, opened my eyes to the fact that, in comparison with the Midshipman of the Watch, the O.O.W. was something of a cipher. Being, naturally, surprised at this revelation I enquired the nature of our onerous duties. We were, I gathered, personally responsible for seeing that each item in the ship's complex routine was punctually set in motion and writing up the rough log.

At seven bells the Navigating Commander appeared and, after a couple of snap bearings, rounded up for Portland. This alteration of course brought the wind astern and, as the compass-platform was more or less level with the top of the foremost funnel, we spent an uncomfortable half hour choking in sulphurous fumes. The Captain, between paroxysms of coughing and clearly not in the best of humours, boomed biting blasts at all within earshot.

The ship wakened to life as bugles called the cable party to muster on the fo'c'sle to clear away the anchors. In due course we passed majestically through the breakwater entrance and, with the signalmen in a fever of urgent communication with *King George V*, we came sedately to an anchor in our allotted berth.

I cannot say that I enjoyed my initial weeks which were full of perplexity in an environment that was so complicated that at times I despaired that I would ever get the hang of the Navy's way of life. All my training had been in the pully-hauly school of seamanship in a ship handled by the muscle-power of her scant crew. Here, as I delved into the ship's anatomy, I was lost in a mechanical maze.

It was a world of drills, inspections and a host of, seemingly, useless formalities. I had been used to practical and economical seamanship and in this new setting I felt frustrated and rebellious in the face of apparent fatuity. The Navy's way of life struck me as being riddled with petty restrictions and taboos and I missed the easy going, flesh and blood, relationships that had warmed our dog-watch sessions on the fore-hatch.

Gradually, as I burrowed about, I began to glimpse reason in the ceaseless activity. In the same way that, as a first voyager, the gear in *Port Jackson* had appeared to be a tangled cat's-cradle until I perceived its purposeful pattern, so growing understanding of the layout of my new ship led me to appreciate reason in the complex organization that ruled our lives. When, at last, I realized that the size of the ship's company in a man of war is determined by her function in battle I began to recognize that, in times of peace, a superfluity of men have to be kept fit and alert by drills and exercises, some inherited from the Navy of byegone days.

As the picture cleared I appreciated the flexibility in an organization which, at the call of a pipe or a blast on a bugle, could bring six to 600 men on deck at the double to deal with anything from menial task to major emergency and that good seamanship, though of a different order, is just as essential to efficiency in a highly mechanized ship as it was in the days of sail.

I discovered a honeycomb of compartments housing men, munitions, machinery and stores, met many friendly souls and spent hours with 'sweepers' as they burnished brightwork and jealously guarded their preserves from contaminating intruders. I heard entertaining mess deck gossip from this tribe of troglodytes who seemed well content to live hermit-wise within their shells, seldom emerging unless 'Clear lower deck' brought them blinking into the light of day.

At the end of the first month, full of acquired knowledge I reported to my nurse who, to my relief, was sufficiently impressed to put me on to the normal duties of a junior snotty.

I took my turn as Midshipman of the Watch on the quarter-deck, a duty which taught me the details of the ship's daily routines. I also served as 'doggie' to the First Lieutenant. 'Jimmy the One' was the senior Lieutenant Commander and, as the Commander's right hand man, he carried delegated responsibility for the cleanliness and good order of all living spaces. Delivering his many messages brought me in touch with the ship's company and their way of life.

The main body of our company lived in 'broadside messes' and took their meals off portable tables projecting from the ship's side. At one end of the table a hanging contraption of metal shelves housed cutlery, at the other a wooden bread-barge squatted on the deck. The sailor of those days had bottom space on a bench, a scrubbed plank table to eat off, a canvas bag and 'ditty box' in which to keep his kit and personal belongings and his hammock into which, when permitted to sling it at night, he could climb for brief comfort. The layout of the mess deck was a legacy from the days of the 'wooden walls' when the seaman lived, ate and slung his hammock over the gun he served in action.

Life between decks was grossly congested, hard on the arse and without privacy. A man off watch seeking relaxation had the choice of sitting at his mess table amid the noisy clamour of his messmates or, if sleepy, 'taking a caulk'* on some unoccupied stretch of deck space. At night the mess deck became a crowded dormitory with row upon row of touching hammocks swinging rhythmically with the roll of the ship. Nightly rounds of inspection in the dim illumination of 'police lights' were eerie, necrogenic experiences as one groped and bumped under the crowded concourse of sailors dead to the world.

Chief and Petty Officers were slightly better off in 'enclosed messes', but they too lived in acute congestion though their re-

* The spaces between deck planks are 'caulked' with oakum and pitch. In hot weather the pitch softens and adheres to clothing. Hence to lie asleep on the deck is to 'take a caulk'.

laxation in the mess was shielded from the vulgar gaze by brown rep curtains.

Food has always ranked high in the seaman's list of priorities and, through the ages, poor quality provender has been a major cause for grumbling disaffection. The ship's 'Pusser'* was responsible for the commissariat drawing his supplies from victualling depôts. All hands were entitled to a ration of meat, bread, sugar, etc., priced at 1/1d. a day. Each mess appointed a 'cook' to draw the ration for his messmates and, within the limits of his resources, he prepared the food and took it to the galley for cooking. Fifteen minutes before meals a bugle released 'cooks' from their duties to collect their mess tins ready for dishing out when their hungry messmates were piped to dinner. This method allowed for popular choice of menu, but much depended on the skill of the 'cook' who was, at best, an amateur doing what he could with, sometimes, unpromising foodstuffs.

As far as the ship's company was concerned life on board was a teetotal affair and dire punishments were whacked out to malefactors smuggling liquor on board. The daily tot of rum was, therefore, a much prized privilege and the pipe 'Up spirits' and the subsequent issue to 'cooks' from a grog tub emblazoned 'The King God bless him' was a ceremonial occasion. Until the mid-eighteenth century it was the practice to serve out neat spirit until Admiral Vernon directed that rum should be watered before issue. It was the Admiral's habit to wear a grogram cloak and the sailor, never at a loss for sardonic comment, christened the puny mixture 'grog' in memory of its innovator. Under pressure from Victorian reformers those sailors opting for teetotalism were allowed to draw a pittance in lieu of their ration of spirits but the vast majority relished their tot which took the edge off the irritations of crowded existence. Although strictly against orders the more frugally minded hoarded up unconsumed portions of their tots for celebrations such as birthdays and Christmas when a rum loving-cup was passed round messmates for 'sippers'.

In 1913 an Able-Seaman drew £3 on to his upturned cap at the end of each month, a figure which, even after allowing for dif-

* Paymaster.

76

ference in the value of money, was a poor return for his service. It is not surprising that marriage was out of the question for younger men and even those who advanced to Petty Officer rating found it hard going to maintain a family ashore on £60 a year. Bundlemen* were left with very few pence to satisfy their personal needs. An occasional pint of beer and duty free ship's baccy were about the sum total of their self-indulgences.

Officers were brought up on the principle that they had 'married the Service' and, on the rates of pay then obtaining, it was rare to find anyone under the rank of Commander who could afford the luxury of a wife. Snotties were paid the princely sum of 1/9d. a day, supplemented by a compulsory £50 a year allowance from their parents. After paying for clothes and food there was precious little left over for secular amusements. The finances of the young gentlemen were usually at low ebb and in this state they found it particularly irksome to be forced to hand over threepence a day to the Naval Instructor, usually the Chaplain, in return for tuition in nautical astronomy, an irritation as rankling as a stone in the shoe.

As I grew to know and like my messmates life became increasingly enjoyable. We were a boisterous party and, being of roughly University age, we had much in common with the undergraduate's customary idealism and urge to create a bright new world. In this we were rather inhibited by the Navy's monolithic traditionalism but this in no way curbed ebullient ideas on what we would do to shake things up if we were given half a chance.

The Gunroom, as an institution, had deep historical roots and, though it had greatly changed from the odorous squalor of Smollet's day, it still played an essential part in moulding 'young gentlemen' into an acceptable professional pattern. Within its walls a strict caste system was tacitly observed. In pride of place the Sub-Lieutenants, commissioned officers, were the privileged and oligarchic masters of the Mess. Next in rank the Senior Midshipmen, veterans of a year's service at sea, and confident in their vast experience, exercised a lordly superiority over their juniors. Lastly the Junior Snotties, those 'warts on the face of humanity'

* Married men were called Bundlemen because they were reputed to bundle up spare food to take ashore to their families.

who from time immemorial had been distinguished by their use-lessness, languished at the bottom of the table.

By the custom of the Service the gunroom enjoyed autonomy to the extent that senior officers would not enter without invitation and, within his kingdom, the Sub of the Mess administered self-government. His rule was absolute, he set the tone of the Mess and it was his hand that normally applied the dirk scabbard to the bottoms of those who, in his judgement, merited a taut half dozen. The agreeableness, or otherwise, of a snotty's life depended to a great extent on the characters of the Sub-Lieutenants and, in particular, on the temperament of the Sub of the Mess. We were fortunate in having a just and likeable Sub of the Mess whose prowess as a member of the Navy Rugger XV endowed us with vicarious glory.

Within the Fleet there were good and bad gunrooms. Some contemporary authors told tear-jerking tales of horrific hell-holes in which tender 'middies' were flogged unmercifully but, in the vast majority of gunrooms the snotties, though undoubtedly strictly disciplined in obedience, were happy enough.

The adolescents of those days, at least that section choosing the sea as a career, had few inhibitions about corporal punishment. A straightforward beating for a known offence was the accepted order of things and, by and large, the discomfiture was momentary and inflicted no lasting injury. It was undignified, certainly, but the average snotty was tough and would have chosen quick sharp correction over a gunroom chair rather than face the alternatives of having his leave stopped, being mast-headed or standing extra watches.

In comparison, the Wardroom, the home of nineteen Commissioned Officers, seemed to us a formidable sanctum presided over by the Bloke and redolent of starchy authority. We seldom crossed its portal except when on duty and even then with apprehensive embarrassment.

CHAPTER VII

Home Fleet

In January when the Home Fleet sailed for the spring cruise to Gibraltar *Orion* was in the middle of a refit in Devonport dockyard and our Admiral shifted his flag to *Thunderer*. A ship in dockyard hands is a poor thing analogous to a patient in hospital. Nothing works properly, normal habits have to be abandoned and trim appearance deteriorates. For the majority of our company with the bright lights of Plymouth under their lee this was fair enough and they welcomed respite from spit and polish. But the Bloke, being a firm believer in the tenet about idle hands, set about finding occupation for all who were not already engaged in such pleasurable ploys as chipping the cable and cleaning boilers.

The Naval Barracks was well equipped to provide opportunities for healthy fun and bright and early each morning reluctant 'training classes' were dispatched at the double to be inoculated against the disease of indolence. The young gentlemen were, of course, particularly prone to be infected by sloth. The Admiral in person, on the eve of his departure, had said that as we were to be deprived of the health-giving scrambles over the mountains of Spain which he planned for our opposite numbers in *Thunderer* we must be compensated by daily body building activities. Throughout those cold winter weeks we assembled in the dark at 6.0 a.m., drank an obligatory mug of glutinous ship's cocoa and, with rumbling stomachs, ran a brisk mile and a half round the dockyard basin and up the hill to the swimming bath. After three compulsory lengths, we hurried back on board to shift into uniform ready for a signal exercise at 7.30 a.m.

The Navy in those days was, to a great extent, run by Gunnery officers who argued that as men in action had to carry out their duties even when distracted by horrific events they must be conditioned to a state of automatic performance. Much time, therefore, was devoted to drills of diverse kinds on the assumption that training in absolute obedience was the only way to ensure high morale in the heat of action. Some cavilled at this theory on grounds that intelligent men and not automata were required for the operation of sophisticated equipment but the dictum 'Their's not to reason why' held sway. We spent many foot slogging hours on the barrack square being taught obedience through the medium of small arms drill. This was my first introduction to Gunnery Instructors on the rampage in their own element.

Masters in the knack of reducing squads to a state of fumbling incompetence, the G.I.s brought us by sweaty repetition to what we imagined to be shining smartness but, judging by the scathing invective showered upon us, our self-satisfaction was not entirely endorsed by our instructors. Though those long hours of 'square bashing' might not have developed our thinking powers to any great extent they certainly taught us to obey and raised our standards of smartness in bearing and, if our egos were pricked in the process, in the eyes of our instructors that was all to the good.

Most instructors leavened the dull dough of the drill book by adding bubbles of personal commentary. One, I remember, used to embellish the staid wording of 'funeral drill' by interjecting his own patter. 'When the corp' come out of the mort-u-ary or dead 'ouse you "Rest on your arms reversed" an' assume a mournful an' melan-colly haspect. Mournful because your shipmate 'as gone to a better 'ome – what none of you lot will go to – an' melan-colly because 'e 'asn't paid 'is mess bill.' The efficacy of this method of tuition is evident. To this day I retain this crumb of funerary etiquette.

Outside working hours we had few duties while the ship was alongside the dockyard wall and, providing that an application for leave was not vetoed by the snotties' nurse, we were free to push off for a run ashore. We were, however, under standing orders to be back on board by 8.0 p.m. unless we could invent some credible reason for late dissipation. This restriction did not irk us much because we were usually too broke for social adventure and the cost of shoreside meals was beyond our resources. Plymouth in the dog watches was a gay place and it was our custom to congregate for pink gins in a favoured bar. Freedom to take an occasional nip of the hard stuff was a privilege denied to us on board. Subordinate officers, though allowed to run up a wine bill of 30 shillings a month, were not allowed the luxury of spirits.

As the ship's refit neared completion 'dockyard mateys' in slow progression returned refurbished bits and pieces on incongruous hand carts. Life on board was quickened by the Bloke back from leave. Drafts of men, including many youngsters, came down from the Barracks with their bags and hammocks to replace numbers of ratings who had been discharged at the beginning of the refit.

At the beginning of March the boilers were fired and trailing clouds of black coal smoke drifted over the roofs of Devonport as an acrid farewell to sweethearts and wives. We moved down to Plymouth Sound to shake down and wash away layers of dockyard grime which fouled the ship.

Ships' boats loomed large in the training of Midshipmen. *Orion* carried fifteen boats in all ranging from two 50-foot steam picquet boats down to a brace of diminutive skiffs. Only the two steamboats were power-driven, all the remainder – launch, pinnace, cutters, whalers and gigs – were double or single banked pulling boats fitted with masts and sails for use when the weather served. Befitting my immature state I was given charge of one of the smaller boats, a five-oared whaler, and in this modest craft I sailed in to the Hamoaze several times a day with the postman, stewards and sundry passengers.

On a wet and windy morning we sailed for Bantry Bay on the south-western corner of Ireland and, steaming out from under the lee of the land, met the full force of a big sea sweeping in from the Atlantic. Some ships in a seaway ride as daintily as swimming gulls others are stiff and uncompromising. Battleships with their big guns and weighty carapace of armour tend to push through rather than over the waves and to be ponderous in movement. Life between decks is always uncomfortable in heavy weather because flying spray makes much of the ventilation inoperable. The thick atmosphere, particularly on the mess deck, had to be breathed to be believed. Dirty weather after a prolonged spell in harbour is unsettling and there were many owners of heaving stomachs who heaved a sigh of relief when we came to anchor off the village of Berehaven.

The purpose of our visit to this isolated harbour was to calibrate our 13.5″ guns by firing each in turn along a marked stretch of the bay to check their ranging accuracy. This, for me, was a momentous occasion. Hitherto the great guns, passive and inert, had been no more than a massive back drop to scenes of shipboard life. Now I was to hear the vehemence of their bark. At that time I was acting as 'doggie' to the Gunnery Lieutenant and when 'General Quarters' summoned the ship's company to their action stations I followed him up to the foretop from which high viewpoint he controlled the guns. As he ordered the turrets to be trained on to a bearing pointing down the firing range I fingered wads of cotton wool in my pocket but, as nobody seemed in the least perturbed, I was too shamefaced to plug my ears.

Having reported his readiness to the Captain in the conning tower, Guns announced that the trial would begin by firing the right gun of 'A' turret. Then, beckoning me to follow, he disappeared down the mast and made his way to the fo'c'sle where, handing me a stop watch and a signal pad, he lay down on the deck and calmly focused his binoculars. I have never forgotten the awe of that moment. Immediately above our heads the two great gun muzzles oscillated like mammoth antennae sensing their prey. Muffled sounds percolated through the armoured walls of 'A' turret, all else being unnaturally quiet. I began to wonder why any rational person would choose to rest in a position fraught with such obvious risk of bodily harm. Later I learned that an expert eye if positioned near a gun muzzle can follow the trajectory of a projectile and doubtless that is what the Gunnery Officer aimed to do. My personal tension mounted when I heard rumblings as shell and cordite clattered up from the bowels of the ship to be rammed home into the right gun of 'A'. A pause, then the faint sound of a fire gong, then cataclysmic upheaval. I was not thinking very coherently at the moment but my senses recorded a blinding flash, a searing blast, an acrid smell of burnt cordite and painful descent to the deck after being whipped up in the air. I did not record much else. My pencil had snapped, the stop-watch was obviously suffering and, having forgotten the cotton-wool, I was deaf to any pearls of gunnery wisdom that had passed my way. Guns was understandably peeved but he overlooked my lapse and, by the end of the day, I was almost blasé.

After calibration trials we lay peacefully at anchor smartening up in preparation for our impending return to the Fleet.

The First Lieutenant, a fanatical believer in the creed that fitness is all, induced the Bloke to order the hands to canter round the upper deck for a quarter of an hour each morning enlivened by the Marine band and hoarse shouts from Jimmy to speed the feet of sluggards. Naturally the Snotties were singled out as being in especial need of exercise and our days opened with half-hour sessions of physical jerks to brighten our bleary eyes. We were sent off on strictly planned excursions into the hinterland to toughen us up. Despite the stress of covering ten miles or so, much of it at the double to keep up with our time table, we enjoyed those balmy spring afternoons on the hills of Cork and Kerry. If for nothing else the exercise was well worth the effort in working up a ravenous appetite for a gargantuan tea of eggs, soda bread, jam and lashings of cream at a friendly farm house nestling on the lower slopes of Hungry Hill.

After ten days on our own we sailed for Portland on a day of sparkling sunshine. It was good to be at sea again and to feel at one with the throbbing ordered life of the ship. Now thoroughly acclimatized, my initial sense of uselessness forgotten, I keenly anticipated the exciting prospect of being in company with the Home Fleet.

We entered Portland harbour as the sun broke through the morning mist to flood the ships in the crowded anchorage with mellow light. It was the first time that I had seen the assembled might of the Home Fleet and my eyes ranged round registering the majesty of the scene. Entering harbour is a ceremonial occasion with seamen in serried ranks on the upper-deck, Marine

Guard and trumpeting Band on the quarter-deck and the rest of the company incarcerated below behind closed scuttles to prevent protruding heads from marring the symmetry and, as we moved up between the lines to our appointed anchorage, we knew we were watched by critical eyes. Smart seamanship was generally held to be one of the main criteria in judging a ship's war efficiency and it was traditional for ship's companies to be exercised in competitive drills. Some of these, which were common and necessary in the days of sail, had lingered on into the twentieth century and generations of Admirals had amused themselves by simulating the past and thinking up seamanlike activities to keep the maximum number of men circling in complicated drills.

A forenoon at 'General drill' normally commenced with such stereotypes as 'Furl awnings' and 'Out nets' but after that individual Flag Officers exercised their sense of humour, or malice, by introducing more exotic happenings. One, I remember, was particularly gifted and 'Chief cooks proceed to Hospital ship with fried egg', 'Marine bands pull round the ship playing the Siamese anthem' and 'Chaplains repair on board Flagship with harmoniums' were three gems in his repertoire. Evolutions were highly competitive and ships' companies looked upon them as sporting events to be won by hook or crook. Many involved the use of ships' boats and the Snotties were invariably in the thick of the fray. I recall agonizing moments when my crew were reduced to fumbling impotence by blasts of megaphoned vituperation. Those sweaty forenoons of General Drill though harassing did not lack excitement and it certainly gave us all a kick to see the 'Evolution completed' signal hoisted a split second ahead of the rest of the Squadron.

The day after our arrival our Rear Admiral struck his Flag in *Thunderer* and rejoined his flagship, fighting fit from his cruise in Spanish waters. Following the prevailing custom I was invited, in my turn, to breakfast with the Admiral in his cuddy. The Flag Lieutenant had briefed me to present myself at two minutes to eight and at that time, in a clean collar and regulation tie, I savoured a fragrant scent of bacon and bangers while awaiting my host. At the first stroke of eight bells he came smartly into view.

Sir Robert was one of those men whose actions are so abrupt that they appear to be moving at the double and his sudden arrival caught me aback. Without checking speed towards his chair at the head of the table he shook my hand and snapped 'Good day, have you taken exercise this morning?' Taking station astern I stammered that I had just returned from regatta practice in the Gunroom gig's crew. 'Very good,' he said waving me to a seat at his side, 'then you will be hungry – eat up.' I was and I did. 'Take more,' he ordered as I speared a single sausage, 'a large breakfast is good for the bowels and good for morale.' For some time we sat in blessed silence broken only by staccato commands for more coffee.

I braced myself for conversation. 'I am told you served in a sailing ship. So did I when I was your age. Tell me about it.'

For a quarter of an hour with unexpected geniality he drew me into esoteric discussion on clew garnets, reefing and clawing off a lee shore. I warmed to my subject and to my host.

'Did you hand the sails personally or did the fo'c'sle hands do the work aloft?' he asked and, on being assured that in *Port Jackson* the cadets formed the major part of the crew, he slapped me on the back and added 'And hard work, what about that? Did you get down on your knees and pray with holystones – eh?' When I told him I was no stranger to such devotions the Admiral, with a glint in his eye, snorted 'Excellent – that's what the Midshipmen in this Fleet should be doing every morning instead of sitting on their arses in the Gunroom.'

Thrusting his chair back and leading me to an open scuttle he pointed at the great concourse of ships. 'There,' he said, 'is the most powerful fleet in the world, built by Admiral Fisher. I don't agree with all his ideas but the fact that we are now serving in modern ships equipped with up-to-date armaments is due, in large part, to his genius, and,' he added prodding me in the chest, 'don't you forget it.' Then, without warning, he turned on his heel and dismissing me with 'Thank you, good day,' moved briskly through the door stimulated, no doubt, by high morale and an active colon. Feeling full of myself I repaired to the Gunroom to spread the buzz that obligatory holy stoning of the deck was about to be appended to our curriculum.

This brief encounter added a new dimension to my experience. Admirals were, by custom, august and aloof, their art was exclusive and they operated a closed shop. This exclusiveness was carried to such extremes that even Rear-Admirals were not always made privy to the thoughts, plans and objectives of their Commanders-in-Chief. When the history of that time came to be written it was revealed that even at the top of the pinnacle the Navy's war plans were locked in the mind of the First Sea Lord who held his cards close to his chest and kept his own counsel.

Brought up in a tradition of omnipotent command Admirals felt no need for aid in performing their function and brushed aside suggestions that the effectiveness of their office might be enhanced by the employment of Staff Officers. Such an attitude had perhaps sufficed in days when sea warfare was relatively uncomplicated but the introduction of sophisticated ships and weapons created new and complex administrative problems.

In the Gunroom, that crucible of bright ideas, we naturally knew what we would do if we were Admirals. We read in the papers that the First Lord, Winston Churchill, was shaking up the Admiralty and creating a Naval staff and we supported his praiseworthy efforts to bring junior officers into participation in the affairs of high command. A few staff officers, we heard, were being appointed but from our viewpoint most Admirals were clinging to the old order and administering their squadrons with no other assistance than that given by their personal secretaries.

As more and more ships assembled at Portland I became increasingly impressed by the sheer size and power of the Home Fleet. *Dreadnought*, at that time eight years old, was moored in an adjacent berth and wondering why the advent of this notable ship had caused such a stir I broached the subject with my nurse.

She was, he told me, the brainchild of the redoubtable Jacky Fisher who had been the first to appreciate that the introduction of 12″ guns which could fire at unprecedented ranges would radically affect battle tactics. When he became First Sea Lord in 1904 he lost no time in furthering plans for the construction of an 'all big gun' battleship that had been germinating in his mind. With ruthless energy he drove designers and constructors into such feverish activity that, in February 1905, he proudly witnessed the launching of *Dreadnought* by King Edward VII and enthusiastically proclaimed her to be the largest, fastest and most powerful ship ever built. Ten months later this remarkable ship finished her trials and went into service and, in doing so, aroused interest, and consternation, in naval circles all over the world.

Dreadnought certainly had superior power in that she could bring eight of her 12″ guns to bear with devastating effect against the four 12″ guns of her most modern predecessors. She was also the first battleship to be equipped with steam turbines which gave her a 2½ knot margin of speed over every existing rival.

The action of the Admiralty in building *Dreadnought* was heavily criticised on grounds that the introduction of such a revolutionary capital ship had, at a stroke, reduced Britain's numerical superiority over other nations since all navies, including that of Germany, would henceforth start from scratch in a race to build up 'Dreadnought' fleets.

Jacky Fisher, in no way deterred, stood firm in his aggressive contention that battleships, like heavy-weights, had to give and take punishment and that his super-ship with the power to hit hard, the speed to outmanoeuvre and armour protection comparable to that of her immediate forbears would make all pre-Dreadnoughts – 'Too weak to fight and too slow to run away'.

He countered criticism by forecasting that Great Britain with a flying start could maintain numerical superiority over other nations and cajoled and bullied the Government into a massive battleship building programme.

The First Sea Lord's forecast had been accurate and, by 1913, we had a main fleet of twenty improved 'Dreadnoughts', nine Battle Cruisers and a further thirteen capital ships in various stages of construction.

The eight ships of our 2nd Battle Squadron assembled together for the first time were the latest and most powerful additions to the Home Fleet. We felt pride in this superiority and looked down on the eight pre-Dreadnoughts in our company.

'Hit first, hit hard and keep on hitting,' was one of the dynamic maxims inherited from Jacky Fisher and, in 1914, there was much discussion on methods of controlling the fire of the large calibre guns in battleships. In *Orion* our 75 ton guns, in their armoured twin-gunned revolving turrets, were elevated and trained on to their target by powerful hydraulic machinery which could be operated, with surprising delicacy, by Gunlayers and Trainers who, through their individual telescopes, could focus on the enemy and keep the guns pointed with precision. These key men were directed on to their target and given the appropriate elevation for the guns by the Control Officer far above them up the foremast from which high position he was better able to observe the 'fall of shot' in relation to the enemy and make the necessary corrections for 'line' and 'range' to achieve hits.

Gunnery efficiency depended to a great extent on the Gunlayer's accuracy in fixing the cross wires in his telescope bang on the target at the moment he pulled the trigger to fire the gun. Under ideal conditions this was not too difficult for a trained man, but when the ship rolled and pitched in a seaway and the target was too distant for clear observation the Gunlayer and Trainer working in harmony had to be exceptionally skilled in their operations. Full scale practices were comparatively rare for it was a costly matter to fire these great guns and, in consequence, Gunlayers were given frequent exercise on synthetic training devices.

From time to time full calibre practice shoots at towed targets were arranged and the results, analysed with scrupulous intensity, aroused considerable competitive elation or despondency. My first experience of 'battle practice' occurred when we were selected for a full calibre firing in Lyme Bay. This was more than a routine exercise because our target was the *Empress of India*, an old battleship due for scrapping, which the Admiralty had decided to use as a guinea pig to study the effect of high explosive projectiles on an armoured ship. After considerable pounding, the poor old lady sank under a pall of smoke into a sailor's' grave. I saw little of this execution because I was entombed below armour at my place in the Transmitting Station, the nerve centre of the gun control system. The centre piece in this holy of holies, crammed with instruments, was a 'Fire control table' served by the Schoolmaster as priest-in-charge attended by Bandsmen acolytes. This mystical apparatus was known as the 'Argo clock' which our

Captain, who had invented an even more magical table, deprecatingly dubbed 'This clap-trap machinery".

Being a crack gunnery ship we were constantly exercised at our Action Stations and I spent long periods closeted with Schoolie in the Transmitting Station during which he tutored me on the principles of gun control. He was a kindly man and a mathematician of a quality far above my meagre resources, but he took infinite trouble in trimming his explanations down to my level, so that I grasped the purpose of our central function. He explained that when the fighting range of the guns was short the Gunlayers and Trainers had a good view of their target but now that the large modern guns could fire at ranges of six to eight miles, or even more, the accuracy of laying and training the guns had necessarily deteriorated. The Gun Control Officer, purposely placed in the foretop, had a better view of the target but the Gunlayers from their lower positions, could see little of the distant enemy. This problem led to the thought that if every movement of a lofty 'directing' telescope could be precisely transmitted to the guns in their turrets a 'Director layer' could keep an eye on the target and all the other gunlayers and trainers by watching receiving instruments could follow his motions and thereby overcome the disabilities of obscure vision.

This, in a nutshell, was the principle of 'Director firing' and I was assured that when the necessary gear had been fitted the whole practice of gunnery would be spectacularly improved. *Thunderer* was the only ship in our squadron so far fitted with an experimental 'Director' but plans were in hand to install this revolutionary equipment in all Dreadnought battleships.*

The fire control table helped to solve the problem of establishing the accurate range of a distant enemy. Battleships carried a number of range-finders and under fair conditions efficient rangetakers could be depended upon to be reasonably accurate in their readings but, as ranges increased, observation of the target became ever more difficult and this, coupled with the movement of the ship in rough weather and vibrations set up by high speed, inevitably introduced marginal errors in the ranges reported to the

* In fact only six battleships were fitted with Directors when the war started in August, 1914.

gun control organisation. The solution was found by collecting the reports from all range finders in a transmitting station where the readings of each could be plotted on the Fire Control Table to work out the mean range, so that, by following the trend of the graph, it was possible to establish the rate in yards per minute at which one was closing or opening from the enemy.

It was fascinating to see on the plot, as on a camera obscura, images of outside happenings graphically portrayed.

Jammed with the Marines like sardines in our metal compartment, tucked away in the bowels of the ship, linked by instruments and telephones to the Control Officer and the guns, it was exciting to be in the hub of activity. We felt a fellow feeling with Jonah in the belly of the whale, unable to do much about the navigation but acutely aware of big things going on outside.

*   *   *

The spring and early summer weather in 1914 happened to be particularly brilliant and as the Home Fleet spent much of the time at anchor there was an orgy of spit and polish as ships vied with each other to excel in beauty. This passive, but not idle, period in harbour was occasioned by a variation in the customary annual programme. Normally at this time of year the Fleet would have been in the North Sea on summer manoeuvres, but, in 1914, the Admiralty decided that a 'Test mobilization' would be an effective way of showing the Navy's readiness for war and, in consequence, the Home Fleet had a stand easy while awaiting a culminating demonstration of sea power at a Review of the entire Fleet by the King.

Rapid mobilization meant in effect that the ships in the Reserve Fleet, normally partially manned, had to be fully commissioned and made ready for immediate active service. This entailed complex administration and the purpose of the 'mobilization' was to check the efficiency of plans to bring the Navy up to full strength in the shortest possible time. Mobilization began on 10 July and, a day or so later, the Home Fleet sailed for Portsmouth to join the now fully commissioned ships of the Reserve Fleet awaiting us at Spithead.

Never before had such a mighty fleet been assembled. More

than two hundred ships in ten lines stretched from Southsea to Southampton Water and this visible evidence of Britannia's continued capacity to rule the waves aroused national enthusiasm. We were all conscious of the sense of historical occasion and felt pride in playing a part, however insignificant, in wielding Britain's sure shield. Being in full commission we had little to do in making ready beyond slapping on new coats of paint and expending extra elbow grease on our burnished brightwork. But for the ships of the Reserve Fleet it was a different matter and their appearance of outward well-being masked exhaustion of scratch crews weary from days of toiling against the clock to bring their unfamiliar vessels to a state of readiness by the appointed day.

Befitting our modern status the ships of the 2nd Battle Squadron * were stationed in proximity to *Iron Duke*, the newly commissioned Fleet flagship at the head of the line. In this pride of place we were in the hub of public interest and continuously circled by paddle steamers and harbour craft listing alarmingly as flag-waving patriots surged from side to side to cheer their fancy. Though the great ships were the centre of attraction this Review presented for the first time the progenitors of instruments of warfare that would, in years to come, revolutionize naval action and, eventually, drive the leviathans into obsolescence.

Few noticed a little clutch of sea-planes riding at their buoys and those who did had scant appreciation of their latent potency; five groups of fragile aircraft whose 100 h.p. engines could barely lift them into fledgling flight. The Royal Naval Air Service had just been formed and as these pioneers made their bow they were greeted with the applause due to those who risk their necks and their crank machines were dismissed as toys of little significance. It was only five years since Bleriot had blazed the trail by staggering over the Straits of Dover and although the early aviators were making giant strides the concept of the aeroplane as a practical weapon of war was confined to a handful of visionaries. Naval pundits of the time turned towards the development of the airship and its possible use for reconnaisance. The Review was graced by four non-rigid dirigibles which to everyone's open mouthed

* *King George V* (V.A.); *Centurion*; *Ajax*; *Audacious*; *Orion* (R.A.); *Monarch*; *Conqueror*; *Thunderer*.

surprise floated serenely above us at an unprecedented speed of 80 knots – downwind. Public naivety was epitomized by *The Times* correspondent who, in reporting the first flight of a seaplane over the Fleet at night, wrote: 'On Friday evening one heard a harsh buzzing and realized with a shock that somewhere 800 feet above someone was observing. That was all, but it gave one an uncomfortable feeling indeed.'

To the North of the Fleet a flotilla of small submarines lay unobtrusively at anchor giving, despite their somewhat sinister appearance, little suggestion of menace to the overwhelming strength of the assembled Armada. The Submarine Service was barely ten years old and few outside a closed circle of specialists knew anything about the capabilities of this new arm of the Service. It is true that Submarines had taken part in recent Fleet manoeuvres but their exercises had been so circumscribed by restrictions to safeguard their safety that their real potency was not appreciated and was, therefore, discounted. Though forced to recognize the presence of the submarines in their midst the main body of naval opinion in the Fleet relegated this rather obnoxious new weapon to the rôle of harbour defence.

Throughout that weekend of perfect weather the beaches teemed with indefatigable sightseers sharing, at a distance, our pomp and circumstance and delighting in a searchlight display laid on for their benefit.

I was on watch on the Sunday evening when the sound of a twenty-one gun salute heralded the arrival of the King at the South railway jetty and in the distance I saw a Union flag break out at the masthead of the Royal yacht *Victoria and Albert* as an indication that the Admiral of the Fleet had assumed command.

On Monday, 20 July a falling glass presaged a depression. From an early hour ships had been preparing for sea and had unmoored and shortened in cables in readiness for departure. Sharp at the appointed time *Victoria and Albert* passed the Point at Portsmouth flying the signal for the Fleet to weigh and take station astern. As she steamed across the head of our lines her two buff funnels, white upperworks, clipper bow and stump bowsprit lent a bright touch of Victoriana to an otherwise sombre panorama of dark grey ships forming up to follow in her wake. It had been planned, so we were told, for the King to accompany the Fleet to sea for manoeuvres, but the Irish crisis and the turmoil in Europe following on the assassination of the Archduke Ferdinand at Sarajevo necessitated his urgent return to London and, in consequence, the Royal yacht came to an anchor near the Nab with the Royal Standard standing out stiffly in the rising wind.

Headed by *Iron Duke*, wearing the flag of Sir George Callaghan, the Commander-in-Chief, the Fleet of fifty-seven battleships and battle cruisers and one hundred and fifty attendant cruisers and destroyers steamed past the *Victoria and Albert* in single line. As each ship approached the saluting point the entire side was manned by the ship's company. The red tunics of the Royal Marine Light Infantry made a brilliant splash of colour on the fo'c'sle in contrast to the ranks of blue and gold abaft them. It was a full dress affair with officers in cocked hats, epaulets and swords. The seamen, in No. 1 rig, wore their sennet hats, the round straw headgear used on ceremonial and tropical occasions. They were known colloquially as 'Benjies' and were roundly cursed because their bulk and fragility was ill suited to crude life on a crowded mess deck.

Being sixth in line we had not long to wait for our turn. Rigged out in a bum freezer with a dirk at my side I stood on the draughty deck to the rear of the Foretopmen lining the starboard rail with crossed hands. I was inattentive to the possibility of calamity until an Ordinary Seaman directly in front of me made a wild clutch at his benjy. He missed, and to our joint dismay we watched the offending hat skim away like a miniature flying saucer. The incident did not pass unnoticed and I was stung into action by a bellow from the bridge – 'Get that man to hell out of it and close ranks'. The miserable culprit muttering 'It was me chin strap parted' was hustled out of sight and, in the nick of time, our serried symmetry was restored as we came abreast the Royal yacht.

With carefully rehearsed synchrony the whole company uncovered to give the ceremonial three cheers to His Majesty, whose slight figure could be seen returning our salute on a monkey's island above the bridge of the *Victoria and Albert*. In a matter of minutes it was all over and we increased speed and hurried out into the murky Channel for tactical exercises. Two days later the ships of the Reserve Fleet, flushed with valedictory signals of congratulation on their demeanour, parted company and set course for their Home ports and the Home Fleet in its entirety returned to Portland.

*　　*　　*

One of the more entertaining facets of our Admiral was that his passion for manly pursuits embraced active motor cycling. The incongruity of such an austere figure aboard a bike stimulated irreverent conjecture as to his prowess, for motor cycles were not yet the sleek and trouble-free machines that they later became. But Sir Robert was a man of indomitable disposition. Pottering about country lanes in a cloud of dust was not his idea of sport, nothing less than a race from London to Edinburgh, a hazardous and exhausting trial in those days, would satisfy his thirst for adventure. To our incredulous surprise we heard that he led the field at Carlisle and, had it not been for a dark night encounter with a cow cruising reprehensibly without navigation lights, he was well on the way to victory. As it was he returned crisp as a biscuit and adorned with sticking plaster to be received with respectful admiration as his crumpled machine was hoisted inboard for refit.

In keeping with his view that anything he could do ought to be done better by the young gentlemen, Sir Robert had directed, to the Bloke's suppressed disgust, that Gunroom officers should be encouraged to add motor cycling to their repertoire and that they should be given permission to embark their machines if they so desired. This unique privilege was too good to miss and, in common with several of my messmates, I became the proud part owner of a highly temperamental 4 stroke machine. This prodigy could, at a pinch, work up to 30 m.p.h. on the level but, if faced with an incline, was prone to drop to a pushing speed of 1 m.p.h. 28 July, being a halcyon day, enticed three of us to make a club run to the hinterland and our journey, spiced with sundry mechanical distractions, fetched up on a hillock on the far side of

Dorchester. We lay in the bright sun drowsily absorbing the blissful scents and peace of the countryside and idly philosophizing on the merits of life until lengthening shadows signalled recall. Stepping into the boat at Weymouth pier we little knew that we would not again set foot on land for half a year.

Back on board we found the ship in turmoil and that night 8 bells tolled the advent of a new era. Thereafter nothing was to be the same again. Contact with the sweet scented shore had been severed by secret orders to make ready for sea and prepare for war.

CHAPTER VIII

War and Scapa Flow

ON leaving harbour the Fleet rounded Portland Bill and set course to the south west. Speculative rumours buzzed like wasps as we steamed slowly towards the broad Atlantic. Years of naval rivalry had conditioned us to view Germany as our potential enemy but if war was in the offing why were we steaming away to the south-west?

At noon the corner of the curtain was lifted to give us a glimpse of our destiny. Signals from the Flagship reformed the Fleet and, headed by the Commander-in-Chief in *Iron Duke*, we turned to an easterly course. Bugles sounded 'Clear lower deck' and the Captain standing on the after capstan addressed his attentive company. We learned that German troop movements threatened an attack on France and that the British Government, alerted by this possibility, were taking preliminary steps to bring the nation to a state of readiness. To forestall sudden offensive action by the German Navy the Home Fleet was being concentrated at its planned war station and in fulfilment of orders from the Admiralty we were now on passage to Scapa Flow in the Orkneys. The threat of active hostilities was so imminent that the C.-in-C. had directed that all ships should prepare for action at short notice.

This news had vast implications for each and every one of us. It was many years since the Navy was last at war and time had whittled away those with active fighting experience and, in any case, historical experience would be of little value since we were now wielding modern weapons the might of which had not yet been tested in battle. Our concept of action was based on theoretical calculations rather than reality.

We steamed slowly up Channel to pass through the Dover Straits in the dark. 'General Quarters' was sounded off, the armament was checked and live ammunition was made ready for use. A general signal warned the Fleet to take measures to reduce fire risk and this led to an orgy of destruction as ships were purged of inflammable fittings. Wooden decks, doors, lockers, carpets, pianos, in fact anything remotely combustible, went overboard to litter the sea with flotsam. My precious motor-bike was an inevitable casualty and I mournfully assisted its obsequies in the vicinity of the Varne Lightship.

With all ships darkened we traversed the narrows on a moonless night. The Downs were crowded with shipping and, although squadrons were manoeuvred to avoid traffic, many a merchant captain must have gripped his bridge rail in alarm at the dim sight of sinister shapes sliding silently past.

Dawn found us well out in the North Sea and, having survived the night without hostile encounter, the Fleet took its finger off the trigger and returned to mundane cleaning routines with a sense of anti-climax.

The arrival at Scapa Flow on 31 July was somewhat disappointing. To the vast majority of us this northern base was unfamiliar ground and we gazed with curiosity at our new home, which seemed remote and inhospitable as we looked in vain for signs of life on the grassy, treeless islands surrounding the landlocked anchorage.

As we moored a covey of waiting colliers weighed anchor to replenish our bunkers and in a steady drizzle we set about the grimy labour of coaling ship, an evolution that was to become depressingly familiar in the months to come. Two days later we were at sea again on the first of countless sweeps to the south east.

Before the days of regular broadcasting news travelled at the speed of the postal service and in our northern fortress we were cut off from an up-to-date ration of current events. Enough trickled through by wireless to warn that the international situation was deteriorating. We were, therefore, not unprepared for the

Admiralty's signal 'Commence hostilities against Germany', which was transmitted to all ships at midnight on 4 August. At the critical moment I had just started the middle watch as Officer of Quarters in a 4″ gun casemate and a picture of sleepy guns' crews sipping scalding cocoa and discussing the portents in the dim glow of blue night action lighting is firmly etched in my memory.

The next day the battleships split up in pairs for independent gunnery practices and, with *Thunderer* in company, we were about to stream a target for a sub-calibre shoot * when proceedings were temporarily halted by a diminutive sailing trawler fouling the range. By the cut of her jib she appeared to be a foreigner and on investigation we discovered that she was of German origin. The little ship, alarmed by our majestic approach, went about and sailed off on the other tack. Irritated by this evasion we sent a 4″ practice shell whistling over her masthead at which she went to panic stations and her sails came down at the rush. This, possibly the first contact with the 'enemy' in the war, was exciting and I was thrilled to hear the pipe 'Away First cutter' and to be ordered by the Bloke to board and report back by signal.

I climbed on board, feeling self-consciously warlike with revolver in hand. The small crew of the *Aue* were terrified by this apparition; they had no wireless and knew nothing of the war and, as they spoke no English, I had difficulty in conveying the astonishing fact that they had to bundle their belongings into the cutter and abandon their ship. I passed several crans of fresh fish into the boat which we later sold on board and gave the proceeds to the despondent fishermen to mitigate the tedium of their internment. *Thunderer* then took our prize in tow and, opening out to a range of six miles, we carried out a full calibre practice shoot and sank the little ship with our third salvo.

The next day we returned to harbour and, for the first time, anchored in what was to be our customary berth in the months ahead. Scapa Flow lies about six miles beyond the north-east coast of Scotland separated from the mainland by the Pentland

* The placing of a small calibre gun within the barrel of a larger weapon so that gun control could be exercised without the expenditure of heavy ammunition.

Firth, a channel with a reputation as one of the world's most evil seaways. The tide sweeps through this narrow gorge at speeds of up to ten knots and when, as frequently happens in these northern latitudes, a gale fights for supremacy against an opposing stream it sets up a confused sea that is notorious for its spite. It was in these waters that a battleship passing the 'Merrymen of Mey', where water overfalls a declivity on the sea's bottom, dropped her bows forty feet into a whirlpool and shipped green water that stove in her bridge structure many feet above the water line.

The Flow itself is an eighty square mile stretch of water bounded to the north by Kirkwall Island and to the south by a semi-circle of smaller islands. Despite the fierceness of the current in the adjacent Pentland Firth the anchorage in the Flow is curiously free from tidal streams. The encircling cluster of islands act as a breakwater against the ocean swell but, being low lying, they give little protection against the wind which, in winter months, blows with ferocity. Between the islands there are five entrance channels, four of which are narrow and tortuous. The fifth, Hoxa Sound, opens out to the south and, being broader, this was the main channel chosen for passage to and from the Flow. The anchorage selected for the heavier ships of the Fleet lay abreast the island of Flotta, a low stretch of land on the port hand of the entrance through Hoxa. Destroyers and lighter ships were berthed in Long Hope, a more sheltered inlet three miles away to the westward. The area between the Fleet anchorage and Kirkwall Island was extensively used for gunnery and torpedo exercises. At the beginning of the war the base offered little beyond sheltered water for colliers to come alongside for re-fuelling, but the demands from constantly seagoing ships became so pressing that elaborate facilities had to be built up to cope with their urgent requirements.

On returning to harbour the Fleet was somewhat shocked by a signal announcing that Sir John Jellicoe had taken over command of the 'Grand Fleet'. His predecessor, Sir George Callaghan, had brought us to our war station, and it had been tacitly assumed that he would lead us in battle. To the vast majority of us the name Jellicoe meant little at that time beyond the fact that he had a notable Gunnery reputation. We were not to know that he had been secretly designated for the highest sea command on the outbreak of war. The sudden deposition of our Commander-in-Chief smacked of unfair treatment and universal sympathy was felt for Sir George as he silently departed into the shades.

Jellicoe himself objected to the abrupt action which was forced upon him and offered his services as Second-in-Command, but Their Lordships were adamant and within a few hours of the opening of hostilities Jellicoe's flag was hoisted in *Iron Duke*. He took over a great miscellany of ships gathered together from various sources and lacking the ordered discipline of unified command.

At a time of crisis, demanding readiness for battle at short notice, he had to weld disparate ships, squadrons and flotillas into a composite instrument with the power to bring maximum force to bear in a wide variety of situations. Jellicoe had been prominent as one of the architects of Admiral Fisher's great concepts and he brought to his awesome task a profound technical understanding of modern weapons and unique vision of things to come.

British maritime strategy aimed to bring Germany to subjection by cutting the enemy's sea lines of communication with the outside world, while retaining freedom of passage for our own merchant fleet. Blockade was the keystone of our naval strategy and, in confining our enemy, we were greatly helped by the geographical fact that the British Isles lay athwart Germany's trade routes. The distant blockade which was operated throughout the Great War did not, of course, deny Germany access to the North Sea and the Baltic, but the ships of the enemy, to gain the open seas, were forced to run the gauntlet of the Straits of Dover or to make a detour far to the north round the Shetlands.

The Navy quickly closed the southern exit by laying extensive minefields and barred the northern passage with patrolling cruisers backed by the might of the Grand Fleet based in a good strategic position at Scapa Flow. From the outset these measures were effective to the extent that, apart from a few ships raiding the ocean trade routes, the blockade became absolute and German merchant shipping disappeared from the seven seas.

The enemy was fully alive to the danger of economic strangulation. The German Navy aimed to break the cordon by defeating the British Fleet but, in pursuing this objective, was inhibited by inferiority in the number of heavy guns that could be deployed against the massive British battle line. It was anticipated that the pressure of the blockade would force the German Fleet into action and, despite their lack of parity in numbers, that they would challenge our supremacy and seek battle.

The enemy was in a position to choose an advantageous time and place for action, whereas the Grand Fleet had to be ready to engage at any time at short notice. From the beginning Admiral Jellicoe was faced with the stupendous task of keeping the wide area of the North Sea under constant surveillance while disposing his heavy ships in such a way that he could appear in superior strength if the enemy made a forceful sortie.

In the early months of the war a general fleet action was confidently expected. As a nation the German people were not imbued with the concept of maritime strategy and tended to relegate the German Navy to a secondary role. Though the blockade became increasingly irksome its effect on the economy, in the early stages, was not sufficiently critical to justify desperate counter measures and the Germans relied on their army to win the war before the stranglehold of the blockade became serious.

The German Admirals were prohibited by the Kaiser himself from taking offensive action that would risk defeat of the High Seas Fleet in pitched battle and, frustrated, they fell back on a policy of attrition by under-water warfare until the day when they could meet the British on more equal terms. In 1914 this was a viable policy because at the end of that year Jellicoe had but seventeen Dreadnought battleships at his disposal to meet sixteen German counterparts. Thereafter the odds worsened for the German Navy as ships of the pre-war building programmes came into service and joined the Grand Fleet. In adopting a more or less defensive policy the Kaiser's Navy presented Jellicoe with the traditional problem of forcing action on an enemy bent on evasion. The Germans were fully conscious of the strategic advantage of keeping their fleet in being, albeit in their harbours, for, as long as it remained intact, it constituted a potential threat and imposed strain on British resources which, in itself, was advantageous to the German cause.

At the outbreak of war all the Dreadnought battleships of the Grand Fleet were coal-burning and the Fleet as a whole was capable of a full power speed of 21 knots. This maximum could, however, only be maintained for a short time and when engaged on urgent business the Fleet cruised at nineteen knots, a speed that could be held for longer periods. Even at this lower speed the coal consumption was heavy and the state of ships' bunkers was a constant and worrying preoccupation.

In *Orion*, a typical battleship of the Grand Fleet, we had to keep sixteen of our eighteen boilers fired to provide steam for nineteen knots and, at this speed, we consumed 350 tons of coal each day to cover approximately 500 miles, a distance roughly equivalent to that from Scapa Flow to Wilhelmshaven. Except in dire emergency stocks of coal remaining were never allowed to drop below 25 per cent of our full stowage of 3,000 tons and this restricted our operating range to six days' steaming. All operations had to be planned to keep within this limit and four or five days represented a typical sweep to the south-east. On return to base the battleships alone required thousands of tons of coal and at least twenty colliers had to be on call immediately the Fleet anchored.

Later generations, to whom refuelling means little more than watching a Chief Stoker wield a wheel spanner, have good reason to be thankful that they were spared the arduous discomfort of coaling ship. Arrival in harbour, after days of watch keeping at sea meant hours of hard labour for all hands hoisting in and stowing 1,800-odd tons of Welsh steam coal, followed by more hours cleaning off a coating of black dust which perversely penetrated into every conceivable crevice. The time taken depended to some extent on the workability of the collier allocated to us and there was general grousing if, as often happened, we were unfortunate enough to suffer an ancient, rust-streaked vessel with narrow hatches and wheezing winches with barely strength to hoist the laden bags of coal. The cargo arrived in bulk in the colliers' holds, where gangs of seamen shovelled coal into 2 cwt canvas bags which were lifted in hoists of ten by a winch-powered whip and dumped on the upper deck to be trundled away on trolleys and tipped down chutes. Down below, in stifling dust, stokers trimmed the bunkers. The art in rapid working lay in keeping all the collier's winches hard at it the whole time.

The Bloke was particularly ubiquitous on these occasions, and there were ructions if his prowling eye caught sight of a whip hanging idly down a hold. On one occasion he stood, racked by impatience, watching the bows on approach of an unkempt collier whose captain, after several attempts, had failed to berth in a seamanlike manner. Clapping his megaphone to his bristling beard the Bloke bellowed, 'If only you'd put your bloody helm hard-a-starboard and go full ahead you'd get alongside.' The mate of the collier, a lank unlovely figure with a drooping mandarin moustache, leant over his fo'c'sle rail and, spitting a stream of yellow tobacco juice into the dwindling space between the ships, retaliated with 'Yerss. An' if only yore aunt 'ad 'ad a bloody black beard she'd 'ave bin yore uncle.' It was the only time I saw the Bloke discomfited. Snatching his cap from his head he hurled it at his 'doggie' off whom it ricocheted down an open coal chute. With a wintry smile he snapped, 'Salve my cap,' and darted into limbo to chase up skrimshankers.

When the war started there were few in the Fleet who fully appreciated the dangers inherent in underwater warfare and, though it was recognized that submarines might be encountered near enemy harbours, it was generally assumed that they were incapable of venturing further afield and certainly not as far as our northern base. Unconscious of the threat of hidden menace in our home waters we went about our business as if it did not exist. Within days we were shaken out of this state of euphoria.

On 8 August, in a position to the north of the Orkneys *Orion* was steaming at slow speed preparatory to a gunnery exercise when *Monarch*, with whom we were in company hoisted an urgent signal 'Submarine in sight' and opened up a sharp fusilade with her secondary armament. Excitement was intensified by a report that a torpedo track had crossed our wake. The Admiral, never one to suffer fools gladly, promptly quelled hallucinatory fantasies with a signal to 'Cease fire and proceed with exercise' and the incident faded into insignificance.

In fact the capacities of the German U-boats had been grossly underestimated. The enemy had 28 operational submarines, many of which were quite capable of offensive operations in the North Sea. The Commander-in-Chief, who was one of the few who had foreseen the threat from U-boats, was acutely aware of the possibility of submarine attacks on ships at sea and his apprehensions were rudely confirmed when *Aboukir*, an old cruiser patrolling the Dogger Bank area, was torpedoed by a German submarine. Unmindful of danger her sister ships, *Hogue* and *Cressy*, stopped to pick up survivors and were in turn sunk with great loss of life by the same submarine.

These realities shocked the Fleet and, to counter the threat, all ships were ordered to zig-zag at high speed when at sea. Admiral Jellicoe was equally concerned by lack of defence against submarine or torpedo-boat attacks on the Fleet in harbour. Scapa Flow had long been envisaged as the main base in the event of war with Germany, but the building up of the Fleet had been so costly that Admiralty demands for extra money to provide defences for East coast harbours had been shelved from year to year and misguided parsimony resulted in the Fleet being virtually defenceless against attack in harbour.

It had been assumed that the navigational hazards of the Pentland Firth constituted sufficient defence against submarine attacks within Scapa Flow. The Commander-in-Chief found this argument entirely unconvincing and entered into a long and sometimes acrimonious battle with the Admiralty insisting that harbour defence must be given priority. He believed that the Grand Fleet was safer at sea than in harbour.

The heavy ships were equipped with gear to hang a curtain of chain mail in the water a few feet away from their sides. This net defence was designed to arrest and explode an attacking torpedo at a safe distance away from the vulnerable compartments of the ship. Nets were only effective when the ship was at rest, for stress on the gear when steaming, and the fact that the curtain would not hang vertically when under way, precluded their use at sea. The gear for manipulating nets cluttered the upper deck with winches and a complicated cat's cradle of steel wires and the recurring business of rigging nets out and brailing them in again was an unmitigated nuisance.

Soon it was decided that closing the five entrances to Scapa Flow with block ships and anti-submarine nets patrolled by trawlers covered by shore-based artillery would give effective protection to the anchorage. It took some months to rig permanent defences and, in the meantime, the ships of our squadron were detailed to make and lay temporary nets across Hoy Sound, the north western entrance to the Flow. When in harbour I spent all daylight hours in the launch with the Boatswain and a party of seamen riggers shackling wire-meshed nets to jackstays stretched between moored buoys. It was something of a relief to break off from this seemingly endless work and go to sea. Everyone was on the alert for an attack on the Fleet at anchor and hardly a day passed without someone sighting something suspicious. This, inevitably, raised the temperature for, as some wit said, 'The sighting of a submarine in the anchorage produced the same sort of excitement as would a snake in a drawing room.'

On 1 September the whole Fleet indulged in what became known as 'The first battle of Scapa'. A cruiser suddenly opened fire on a 'submarine periscope'. The repercussions were spectacular. All ships raised steam and the sun was blotted out by a pall of black coal smoke. Small craft were sent to scour the waters and a flotilla of destroyers, which happened to be passing, steamed wildly between the lines of battleships as they busily prepared for sea. At the height of the excitement I chanced to be on the quarter-deck and, inadvertently crossed the bows of the Bloke, who curtly bundled me into a picquet boat with orders to 'Go, boy, and sink the bloody submarine.'

So, with the Petty Officer Coxswain at my side, I took the wheel and set off at full speed to join the melée of milling craft. Some time later, after several narrow escapes from collision, we began to wonder what we would do if we actually saw a periscope.

The Stoker P.O., an ardent spectator with head and shoulders protruding from the hatch over his engine room, passed up a coal hammer with the useful suggestion that 'It might come in 'andy to smash 'is bleedin' eyeglass.'

The Coxswain, catching sight of a whiskered seal that dived

at our approach, muttered 'There 'e goes, the little bastard, goin' down to give 'em the tip.'

In the gathering dusk, the Grand Fleet hurried out of harbour to seek the relative safety of the open sea. The alarm, whether true or false, served to crystallize conviction that the continued use of an undefended base imposed unwarranted risk and Admiral Jellicoe, after a day or so at sea, shepherded us into Loch Ewe. This harbour, being on the north-west coast of Scotland and 130 miles beyond the Orkneys, was considered to be beyond submarine range.

In October we returned to our main base, and the scares continued. Tide rips, flotsam and seals triggered off a series of alarms which culminated in the 'Second battle of Scapa'. The Commander-in-Chief, to emphasize his disquiet, withdrew his Dreadnoughts to Lough Swilly on the north coast of Ireland, well out of range of attack, but 300 miles away from the North Sea.

Ironically this excursion to safer waters led to a tragic loss. On 27 October the eight ships of our Battle Squadron were exercising tactical manoeuvres to the north of the Irish coast. As the sun rose above a clear horizon *Audacious*, sister of our flagship *King George V*, hauled out of line and stopped, reporting that she had been incapacitated by a violent explosion.

At first it was assumed that she had been hit by a torpedo and the Vice-Admiral, with the lesson of *Aboukir*, *Hogue* and *Cressy* fresh in mind, scattered his ships to clear the area and called for tugs to assist *Audacious*. The stricken ship was taken in tow but she was badly hurt and, during the night, she succumbed and sank, fortunately without loss of life.

Subsequently it was established that *Audacious* had hit one of a small line of mines that had been laid by a German ship which had slipped through the blockade to lay her destructive cargo on the trade route from the Atlantic to the Irish Sea. The *Olympic*, a large White Star liner crowded with passengers from America, passed close to the sinking *Audacious*, but by good fortune she continued her voyage unscathed.

The loss of one of our most modern and powerful Dreadnoughts reduced our already slender margin of battle line superiority over the High Seas Fleet, and endeavours were made to deceive the enemy by constructing a dummy *Audacious* by building up a superstructure on the hull of a merchant ship.

Early in November, under pressure from the Admiralty, who felt that the C.-in-C. was being unduly anxious, we returned yet again to Scapa to find the permanent defences at last taking shape. Admiral Jellicoe's contention that his base had been insecure was vindicated when a trawler patrolling the main Hoxa entrance actually sighted and rammed a German submarine. Had it not been for the recently laid barrier net, she might have dived into the Flow and torpedoed ships at anchor. The rammed submarine managed to escape but she was badly damaged and subsequently foundered in the Pentland Firth.

CHAPTER IX

Grand Fleet

THE domestic pattern of our lives changed as we adjusted to the conditions of war service. Endeavours were made to maintain our accustomed peacetime routine and standards but the pressures of constant sea-going, coaling, self-refitting and novel extraneous duties absorbed so much of our available manpower that ceremonial and spit and polish had to go by the board. A few remnants were preserved. The hoisting of colours in the morning was still a 'guard and band' affair and, as the numbers of our allies grew, the playing of anthems became a musical marathon. Morning prayers survived, though the congregation dwindled under the pressure of secular demands and these brief periods of spiritual reflection touched even conscript worshippers. The words of the familiar prayer, 'Preserve us from the dangers of the sea and from the violence of the enemy that we may return in safety to enjoy the blessings of the land with the fruits of our labours', took on a new significance.

In one respect formal drill was intensified. Our Captain believed in the old adage that practice makes perfect and the whole ship's company were closed up at their action stations for an hour a day exercising battle procedures. The idea was to make certain that men would react automatically when distracted in action and undoubtedly the daily exercise had the desired effect.

We suffered many changes in personnel as the expanding Navy drained away our trained men for service elsewhere. Inevitably this affected general efficiency and the dilution tended to sap at the morale of a ship's company that had settled down in communal strength. Against this the incentive of active service and opportunities for personal development in the less hidebound atmosphere built up our collective spirit.

Physical separation from the shore and other ships developed more intimate relationships and we found unsuspected affinities. But, with the best part of a thousand men cooped up on board, the stock of jokes and yarns began to wear thin. Garbled information in the newspapers gave us something to chew over but we were more interested in what we were doing and why, and what was in store for us next week. Solid information on such topics was scarce. The Admiral and the Captain were the august dispensers of knowledge, but so little trickled out from the cuddy in those days of olympian detachment that we had to fall back on such sources as the cook's mate, that traditional distributor of 'stop-press' snippets, who was never at a loss for juicy prophecy. The Captain came under close and critical scrutiny. His utterances were carefully garnered and canvassed in every corner of the ship and his behaviour from day to day acted as a barometer in forecasting our fortunes.

Sir Robert belonged to a generation that held fast to the belief that smartness of appearance and fighting efficiency were indivisible, and he could not bring himself to stomach laxity from the peace-time standards of cleanliness and order to which he was accustomed.

The *Orion* class were peculiar in that the quarter-deck was amidships instead of being right aft on the upper deck in the traditional position. In normal times this was no inconvenience, the Admiral could mount the starboard gangway and cross a spotless deck to his adjacent quarters. But lying in an open anchorage in war time, with nets rigged out against torpedo attack, precluded the use of a midship gangway and we had, perforce, to make and fit an accommodation ladder over the stern of the ship abaft the net defence. This meant that arriving notabilities, to reach the quarter-deck, had to traverse a length of deck which was, in fact, the only space which the ship's company could use for a breath of fresh air. Inevitably, this after-deck was frequented by uncouth figures taking advantage of a stand easy to have a 'draw and a spit' and, despite panic measures to clean up their residue when the barge was seen to be approaching, there always seemed to be the odd fag end to trigger off the Admiral's acid comment. This invariably needled the Captain into crimson anger which he subsequently relieved by blasting off at the watchkeepers. I remember a day when, as Midshipman of the Watch, I had spotted the barge afar and having chivvied the side-boys into a frenzied scurry round the deck, I stood with the Officer of the Watch at the after ladder waiting to greet the great man when we were startled by a deep, resonant rumble from our approaching Captain who, brandishing his telescope, proclaimed 'Mis-tah Co-ook; Mis-tah Co-ook, are you aware Sir, that you are standing knee deep in matches?'

In the autumn our amiable Gunroom fraternity was disrupted when the six senior Midshipmen, after weeks of hectic self-examination, presented themselves to a Seamanship Board from which they emerged with the golden stripe of commissioned rank. Their subsequent departure left a gap and, like the guests at the Mad Hatter's tea party, we juniors moved into their warm seats.

I was elevated to command of the 2nd picquet boat, a 52-foot carvel-built craft with a speed, if pushed, approaching ten knots. Up forrard, down in the fore peak, we stowed an anchor and a jumble of gear in seat lockers. This glory hole was the crew's preserve and it served as our second-class passenger accommodation. A compartment amidships housed a coal-fired boiler and a push-and-pull reciprocating engine. Abaft this a cabin, with a wooden canopy to shield against the weather, was flanked with cushioned seats, tastefully covered in white duck with blue piping, made with loving care by the stern sheet man from materials paid for with bursting pride by the Midshipman of the boat.

On deck the engine and boiler room was covered over by a metal casing pierced by a hatch through which the black face of the stokey boy was prone to appear at inopportune moments. Bang amidships the funnel, that noble feature of the old time steam boats, belched smuts and sparks from its highly polished, flared brass top.

We were frequently away for long hours at a stretch and grew accustomed to dossing down to snatch a nap and cooking an improvised meal of bacon and bangers on a shovel in the stoke-hold.

Picquet boats were fun to handle and, in common with other Midshipmen in the Fleet, I endeavoured to manoeuvre my command with flair and panache, to sweep up to my destination at high speed, to judge distance to a hair's breadth and to go full astern and bring to with a gentleness that would not crack an egg.

From time to time we took our turn as Duty Steam Boat which meant that we were attached to the Flagship for a day running errands for the Staff. I found this a pleasant break and, between trips, it was engaging to yarn in a strange Gunroom and pick up intriguing backstairs gossip.

The picquet boats of the Fleet were sore pressed and kept on the go until the weather conditions deteriorated to the pitch when even hard driving Commanders reluctantly ordered plunging boats alongside to be hoisted inboard by the main derrick.

In time the stress on ship's boats became so arduous in the winter weather that fishing drifters were commandeered and attached to battleships to ease the strain.

The months slipped past and the first flush of optimism that the war would be over by Christmas gave way to the sober realization that peace was not, perhaps, just round the corner. The days shortened, winter gales lashed us with depressing ferocity and recreation for thousands of men in the Fleet became a real problem. Though there was no lack of work to keep men busy it became increasingly obvious that change of scene and opportunities for exercise were necessary to counter the debilitating effects of close confinement.

For the officers conditions were tolerable, but the majority on the crowded mess deck had no room to swing a cat and virtually nothing to ameliorate the tedium of off-duty hours.

Not much could be done immediately but, looking to the future, ships were detailed to send working parties to the Isle of Flotta to convert virgin turf into playing fields. *Orion* was given the task of constructing a stone pier and, when weather permitted, I towed the pinnace to the shore at dawn with a bunch of amateur civil engineers to collect rocks and build a very creditable landing place for the boats of the Fleet.

From these small beginnings Flotta eventually blossomed into a recreational centre with football grounds, a canteen and a small golf course on which Admiral Jellicoe had the right of way.

At the outset of the war there were difficulties in supplying fresh provisions for the hundreds of crews so suddenly assembled at Scapa Flow and, until a comprehensive victualling organization had been built up, the quality of food fell short of normal standards. It was Pepys who wrote 'seamen love their bellies above all else . . . and any abatement in the quantity or agreeableness of the victuals is to discourage and provoke them at the tenderest point'. The truth of his statement echoed across the centuries. There were no wet canteens and ships' companies did not take kindly to enforced temperance.

Though the majority of the men accepted the necessity for severence from social life with good grace the maintenance of prompt communication with their families was an essential factor in preserving peace of mind. At the beginning an erratic postal service disrupted links with home and aggravated the sense of isolation. Even the little necessities of life, such as writing paper or tooth paste, were hard to come by.

In the course of time *Imperieuse*, an ancient cruiser, was anchored in Long Hope to operate as a depot and terminal station for the reception of men in transit to and from the Fleet. Within her chaotic interior harassed officers set up a general post office and ran a transport service of drifters feeding the four corners of the Flow. Hard by the Fleet repair ships *Cyclops* and *Assistance* worked round the clock trying to keep pace with a constant stream of defective equipment sent over by ships for refitting. Then a shopping precinct was organized in *Borodino*, a chartered merchant ship employed in delivering stores to the ships of the Fleet. This shop, run by the Army and Navy Stores, was well stocked with everything from collar studs to monkey jackets. Later the *Ghourko*, another store ship, was fitted out with a theatre in her hold and all the facilities for staging entertainment. This proved to be a popular innovation and there was always a queue for the 'Ghourko Palace of Varieties' to berth alongside to give ships' 'funny parties' scope for their histrionic talents.

Until the playing fields on Flotta were commissioned there was little chance for physical exercise and to make good this short-coming all available hands doubled round the upper deck each morning led by our Admiral who, as he came round on each circuit, barked at the Bandmaster to brisk up the tempo.

But these formal capers were deemed to be insufficient for the 'young gentlemen' whose physical welfare was, as always, close to the Admiral's heart. He cleared the furniture from his two large day cabins and each evening held a sweaty salon for our compulsory benefit. Under his beady eye we ran, jumped, wrestled and fought to the point of breathless nausea. Boxing was always the *plat du jour* and we quickly learned to simulate intense activity in some less harmful sport to avoid the dire experience of three rounds with our host. He was a fighter of the old school, no crouching stance for him, bullet head well up, lithe on his toes and with a left as swift as a serpent's tongue. Having set two of us sparring our ring-master would double into the farther cabin to stir things up, which offered a brief interlude for painless shadow boxing. Manoeuvring to keep the connecting door in sight was a subtle skill giving the tactically fortunate contestant early warning of the Admiral's reappearance and, by swiftly open-ing fire, earn a rewarding 'Well done boy! You've got the range, hit again – harder!'

On 15 December we had just finished coaling after an uneventful trip towards Norway when we were alerted by an immediate signal to 'raise steam with all despatch'. That afternoon six of the ships of our Second Battle Squadron in company with light cruisers and destroyers slipped out into the North Sea to a rendez-vous off Cromarty with Vice-Admiral Beatty and four of his battle-cruisers. Throughout the night our force, under the com-mand of Vice-Admiral Warrender in *King George V*, steamed to the southward making for a position about 120 miles east of Flamborough Head where we were due to rendezvous shortly after daylight with light cruisers and destroyers from the Harwich striking force. Apart from the Admirals we were all completely in the dark that anything untoward was afoot. Before dawn on 16 December we were roused by brassy bugles sounding off 'General Quarters' and, in some excitement, we hastened to our action stations and cleared away the guns.

In fact, behind the scenes, big events portended. The Admiralty, having got wind that the German battle-cruisers were preparing for a possible raid on the British coast their Lordships had ordered the Commander-in-Chief to place his battle-cruisers in a strategical spot in the centre of the North Sea from which they would be in a good position to intercept the enemy. In the belief that Admiral Hipper and his five battle-cruisers would be making a lone and unsupported dash across the North Sea, the Admiralty were confident that Beatty and his battle-cruisers athwart the path of retreat would be able to cope with the situation, but, to be on the safe side, the C.-in-C. had directed the Second Battle Squadron to reinforce the British strength. Unknown to the Admiralty, Admiral von Ingenohl, with the whole of the High Seas Fleet in company, had left harbour in great secrecy and early in the morning on 16 December he was making way westward in support of Hipper's battle-cruisers which, at that time, were 100 miles ahead approaching the Yorkshire coast.

As things turned out the courses of the High Seas Fleet steaming westwards and the British force moving south were converging. At 5 a.m., in pitch darkness, some British destroyers, way out on our port bow, made contact and had a sharp brush with German torpedo-boats which were part of the advanced screen operating ahead of the High Seas Fleet. This unexpected small ship action had triggered off the alarm and sent us rushing to action stations.

Neither side were in a position to grasp the significance of the encounter. Admiral Warrender, acting on his intelligence that the German battle-cruisers, if at sea, would be well away to the westward assumed that his destroyers had made chance contact with some isolated unit and he continued south towards his dawn rendezvous. He had no idea that his ships were in a perilous position almost within gun range of the entire High Seas Fleet. Admiral von Ingenohl, on receiving reports that his torpedo-boats were engaged with British light forces, jumped to the partially correct conclusion that he had encountered the Grand Fleet. To avoid action with a superior force he hauled away to the east and left Hipper to find his unsupported way home as best he could. What von Ingenohl did not appreciate was that he was being presented with the very situation for which the German High Command had been praying – opportunity for the High Seas Fleet in strength to overwhelm an isolated part of the Grand Fleet. His decision to retreat before he knew what he was up against was bitterly criticized in Germany.

Daylight and a clear horizon gave us a pause to fall out for breakfast. We soon closed up again, however, when our Admiral had a signal reporting that the German battle-cruisers were bombarding Scarborough, Hartlepool and Whitby. Knowing the position of the enemy, and anticipating correctly that Hipper would retire through a known gap in the offshore minefields, we set off to the westward at full speed to catch him as he emerged from a twenty-mile-wide channel of uninfested water.

I was at that time allocated for training to one of the 13.5″ turrets. We spent the whole of that forenoon at action stations and the Captain kept us on our toes by passing messages through the transmitting station warning us to be prepared for instant action. The guns' crews were visibly excited at the prospect of battle. After a time one of the Gunlayers, a very stolid Chief Petty Officer, stood up and with careful deliberation blew up his rubber lifebelt, an act which drew sniggers from younger members of his crew and comment to the effect that Chiefy was windy and contemplating a swim ashore. The Gunlayer, unperturbed, sat down on his improvised rubber cushion and restored his status quo by proclaiming 'It gets a bit 'ard on the arse sittin' about all morning.'

The weather, which had been bright and clear, gradually deteriorated during the forenoon and by 11.30 am we were steaming into a slight head sea under lowering clouds and rain squalls which reduced visibility to a bare two miles.

Admiral Beatty in *Lion* with superior speed had pushed on ahead and our battle-cruisers were some twenty miles away to the north-west. We learned later that at this time Hipper and his battle-cruisers were no more than forty miles ahead of Beatty and that the two battle-cruiser forces were approaching each other at a closing speed of forty-five knots. At this critical point

Southampton and *Nottingham,* two cruisers screening ahead of *Lion,* sighted and engaged three of Hipper's scouting cruisers operating forty miles ahead of their admiral. In the low visibility the action was short and inconclusive but the enemy cruisers were deflected from their easterly course and forced to make a detour to the south which, as it happened, led them directly towards Admiral Warrender and his six battleships.

In the turret, at 12.15 p.m., we had a sudden alert and, following directions from the transmitting station, the guns were trained onto a bearing on the starboard beam. As the turret swept round I was with the Officer of Quarters looking through a slit in the observation hood on the top of the turret. An imperative order to 'load' brought me down to the platform at the rear of the guns but not before I had a split second view of three faint shadows in the mist about two miles away and steering an opposite course. I had actually sighted the enemy. I gripped the rail in tense excitement and braced myself against the thundering explosion that would force the massive gun to hurtle to the rear in recoil.

But we waited in vain. That dim glimpse was all that was seen by the Gunnery Officer in the fore-top, and before he could give the order to open fire the vague shapes had faded from sight behind a grey curtain of falling rain.

Admiral Warrender turned our squadron in pursuit. But by the time we had swung round to an easterly course the enemy was well away and seen no more.

This chance contact was, in every respect, unfortunate. The German cruisers quickly realized that they were in the presence of a formidable line of battleships and promptly reported to Hipper who, appreciating that he was making straight for units of the Grand Fleet, steered away to the north and, outflanking the British forces, made good his escape and reached Germany unscathed.

This near conflict was the first occasion in the North Sea when heavy ships came within an ace of confrontation and it aroused much speculation afloat and ashore.

For our part we returned to Scapa in a mood of frustration that we had been cheated by the vagaries of weather. The press cashed in with querulous headlines demanding reasons why the invincible British Navy had not shielded innocent citizens in the stricken seaside towns from the ravages of 'baby-killing murderers'.

The Germans made capital out of the Imperial Navy's spirited initiative in striking at the heart of Britain and returning in triumph without loss.

Time proved that both sides had their share of good fortune on that December day. Admiral Warrender with our detached squadron all but blundered into the entire High Seas Fleet and it was lucky for us that von Ingenohl shied off at a shadow and retired. Hipper, too, was lucky in getting a chance warning which enabled him to skirt round the jaws of an ominous trap.

History records that this episode reinforced Admiral Jellicoe's belief in the doctrine of 'concentration of force' and thereafter the Grand Fleet operated as a closely integrated body.

* * *

In the large Grand Fleet community each ship was an island and its company tended to develop the characteristics of villagers.

We felt some relationship with our Squadron mates with whom we shared experiences but even this link was tenuous. We lived our lives and they lived theirs and there was not much mixing.

Certain ships wore an aura of distinction created by outstanding performance or notorious reputation. Flagships, in particular, were endowed with mystical properties because they housed the arbiters of fortune.

Admirals had a built-in public image, being heralded by bugles and piped on to pedestals for all to see. But beneath the panoply of office they were men with individual personalities exercising their command and spreading their influence in diverse ways. Some wielded authority with a rod of strict discipline, aloof, professionally correct and cool in manner. Others used a bold and convincing presence to create an atmosphere of vigour and dash. Some were insensitive in their communications, others had a happy knack of phrasing signals conveying sympathetic understanding. A few diffused the radiance of warm relationship upon all with whom they came in contact, an attribute which spread like oil on troubled waters. Admiral Jellicoe was such a man.

It so happened that *Orion* was out of action for a fortnight with turbine trouble. Conscious of our incapacity the ship's company slumped in depression as the engine room staff laboured to put things right. We were in this fractious frame of mind when a signal announced an immediate visit by the Commander-in-Chief.

I was Midshipman of the Watch when the great man drew alongside. I shall never forget the small figure of the Admiral springing up the accommodation ladder with the agility of a robin to stand, alert and smiling, to acknowledge our salute. Hardly any of us had seen the C.-in-C. before and our attitude was one of respectful curiosity.

With professional acuity he talked technicalities in the engine room, had a word and friendly greeting for all and sundry, briskly toured the mess decks, visited the galley and inspected the seamen on the upper deck. A short visit, unrehearsed and informal, but it made a striking impact on the ship's company.

Though Admiral Jellicoe had not the presence of Beatty, with cap a-cockbill and three-buttoned monkey jacket, he nevertheless gave an immediate impression of knowledge, judgement and, above all, of human understanding. He had only spoken to a handful of men in *Orion* but he had been seen by many and he left a wave of confidence in his wake. There was not one of us, thereafter, could look at the towering bridge structure of *Iron Duke* leading the Fleet without picturing the slight figure of our Commander-in-Chief standing at the compass and shouldering his awesome responsibilities on our behalf.

Christmas came and went with its traditional break in routine. The Captain's parade round decorated messes led by the youngest boy rigged out in a Commander's monkey jacket, and blind eyes turned to the impropriety of convivial 'sippers' as men shared their illicit stocks of saved-up rum rations. As sixteen bells* struck on New Year's Eve the thoughts of everyone turned on the hope that as the enemy had so recently been active he would venture again and that 1915 would witness the trial of strength that would end our vigil and the war. We had not long to wait for our expectations, in part, to be realized. On 15 January Hipper's battle-cruisers made another sortie and Admiral Beatty success-

* Eight bells for the old year and eight bells for the new.

fully brought them to action off the Dogger Bank and, in a general chase, the *Blücher*, the rearmost ship in the German line, was mortally hit and within close sight of the leading British ships rolled over and sank with great loss of life.

The inconclusive outcome of this action was disappointing, and consequently criticized, but to us the battle was a heartening harbinger of promising events to come. At the time *Orion* was at sea with the Grand Fleet in support of our battle-cruisers but, though Admiral Jellicoe pressed on at maximum speed, we were a full 150 miles to the northward when Hipper, with a flying start, made good his escape to the east.

We were back in harbour and had finished coaling when the battle-cruiser force arrived and the Fleet manned ship and cheered the victors as they came up to their anchorage.

I was one of a volunteer party sent over to lend a hand in coaling *Southampton*. This cruiser, wearing the broad pendant of Commodore Goodenough, had played an active part in the battle and I was thrilled to see the Commodore himself leading his exhilarated company in their labours. When it was all over and our party stood shivering on the quarter-deck waiting for the boat to take us home we had a message of invitation to the cuddy where, black as a nigger minstrel, 'Barge' Goodenough whacked out drinks all round as a gesture of appreciation for our volunteer help. This was typical of the man whose character combined strict dedication to the highest principles of service with an unusual flair for unconventional initiative which he was to demonstrate in action later in the war.

Having become a senior midshipman I was temporarily attached to the Engineer Commander for a month's training in engineering. They were a hard-worked lot down below and it was fascinating to be in that vital centre of power which, all too often, was taken for granted.

I stood watch with the Engineers and was impressed by their absorbed concentration on the sweet running of the machinery in their charge. I tried my clumsy hand at firing a boiler and learned, the hard way, to respect the stokers' skilled economy of effort and developed a lasting admiration for the black squad who, out of sight and unsung, sweated their guts out to provide steam for the ever-hungry turbines.

I next spent a month under the Torpedo Officer working in the submerged torpedo flat. Here the tempo was quieter and I was lucky enough to hitch myself on to a Torpedo Gunner's Mate who had the gift of practical instruction. Under his enthusiastic eye I stripped a complete 21" torpedo down to the last screw until the steel deck was strewn with a miscellany of curious and unfamiliar bits and pieces. The subsequent assembly and testing of the torpedo, in which my mentor offered minimum guidance, gave me an intimate understanding of the anatomy of a 'tin fish' which stood me in good stead in later years.

Then followed a month's signal instruction and I found life on the signal bridge amongst the 'bunting tossers' utterly absorbing. Communications were limited to signals by flag, semaphore and flashing morse code by a hand-worked lattice shutter in front of an arc lamp. Wireless telegraphy, though fitted in all ships, was comparatively new and uncertain in behaviour and it was seldom used for transmission of manoeuvring signals.

The Signalmen, beyond all others, had to be continuously alert and clear-eyed. They worked in full view of the Admiral and Captain and, by the very nature of their function, any slackness or slipshod performance was blazoned for all to see and condemn.

The Grand Fleet under way was an unforgettable sight. The vast concourse of forbidding dark grey ships in disciplined pattern kept station on the 'Guide of the Fleet' and manoeuvred as a single body. When at sea the Fleet was formed in a 'Cruising Order' designed to keep ships concentrated during the approach leading up to tactical contact with the enemy, at which vital moment the capital ships were ordered by signal to take up 'Battle-line' formation preparatory to instant action. This battle formation, comprising all battleships in a single line, was based upon a tradition of naval war that force should be concentrated to enable the maximum possible number of heavy guns in each capital ship to bear upon her opposite number in the enemy line.

The main armament turrets in the improved Dreadnought battleships were mounted on the centre line, an arrangement designed to engage the full armament. Though the turrets could sweep round in wide arcs on either side, it was not possible to fire the full complement of guns on bearings ahead or astern because intervening bridge structures on the upper deck masked the line of fire. This restriction confined full broadsides to bearings from the bow to the quarter, known colloquially as 'A arcs'. Since the enemy was similarly restricted and, as Admirals on both sides sought to keep their 'A arcs' open, it followed that in a Fleet engagement the two battle lines tended to steer courses roughly parallel to each other, in which situation all ships were theoretically in a position to pound away at their opponents with the full weight of their armament. This situation did not always obtain and an Admiral in a position to take the initiative endeavoured to manoeuvre his battle-line so that all his guns could attack an enemy whose arcs of fire were restricted. The copy-book example of this tactical move envisaged an Admiral laying his battle-line athwart the line of advance of his opponent, in which favourable position all his ships might direct devastating full broadsides against an enemy whose power to reply was severely limited. This classical movement, bringing tremendous advantage to the successful exponent, was known as 'Crossing the enemy's T', and we learnt from the Navigator, who lectured to us on the 'Battle Instructions' that this manoeuvre was the main objective in our Commander-in-Chief's tactical handling of the Fleet in battle.

The battleships of the Grand Fleet were organized in Squadrons of eight ships, split into two Divisions. At sea in 'cruising order' these Divisions of four ships in line ahead were stationed in columns about one-and-a-half miles apart. This concentrated the full strength of the Fleet within a rectangle with a front of some seven miles and a depth of a mile and a half and, in such close formation, all ships were within reasonable visual signalling distance of the Commander-in-Chief whose flagship, *Iron Duke*, normally led the central column. This greatly facilitated the handling of a fleet of such large proportions and the flexible column formation lent itself to rapid deployment into battle-line at the critical moment.

To give warning of an approaching enemy a number of cruisers were stationed about twenty miles ahead of the Battle Fleet and spread across the line of advance at visibility distance apart. These sensitive antennae, covering a seventy-mile front on a clear day, carried responsibility for probing as far as practicable into hostile formations and keeping the Commander-in-Chief informed on the position of the enemy. The battle-cruisers, operating as a separate fleet with its own reconnaissance cruisers, were stationed yet further ahead to make use of their high speed and large-calibre armament to force their way through and, having made contact with the enemy battle-fleet, to feint and lure the German Admiral towards the Grand Fleet.

From a vantage point on the bridge, seeing and understanding the significance of the fleeting signals, I marvelled at the parade ground precision of manoeuvring ships and the beauty of twenty or more battleships executing the stately movements of a tactical quadrille.

As a Senior Midshipman I had been promoted to an action station as assistant 'Officer of Quarters' in 'B' turret under a Lieutenant-Commander of amiable and chatty disposition. The interior of the gun-house was dominated by the breeches of the two massive 13.5" guns projecting over wells to allow for elevation of the guns to an angle of 20° above the horizontal.

Shut off by thick armour we spent many hours in cramped seclusion, blind to the outside world but acutely on the *qui vive* for orders relayed by jerking pointers on our receiving instruments. We tested equipment, practised breakdown drills and burnished steel and brass to gleaming perfection. The guns' crews tended to grow bored by daily repetition of dry exercises and we welcomed opportunities to fire the guns in a practice shoot.

On such occasions the gun-house was gripped in frozen quietness broken only by the tick of active instruments and the hiss of surging water in hydraulic rams as the operators followed the Director. The great breeches of the guns rose and fell in time with the roll of the ship and one felt a slight swinging movement as the Trainer gently adjusted his bearing. Although expected one was unprepared for the awesome climax when the gun erupted in obedience to the stimulus of a distant trigger. Deafened by the roar of discharge one felt the turret lurch under the shock as the great 75-ton mass heaved back against the restraining force of the recoil mechanism which, miraculously, subdued the violence in a few feet and slowly thrust the gun forward to its 'run-out' position. To the accompaniment of hoarse orders and responses fresh ammunition rattled up from the depths and, within moments, a switch was made to signal to the Director Layer that the gun was once more loaded and ready to fire.

As war experience was sifted and analysed the fitness and fighting qualities of Admirals in command of Squadrons, most of whom had been appointed before active service, came under review resulting in some shuffling of the pack to bring the aces to the forefront. Our Admiral, whose physical fitness was a byword and whose pugnacious qualities were widely esteemed, was appointed to command a squadron of armoured cruisers and, in the early summer, he shifted his Flag to *Defence*. When he was piped over the side for the last time the ship's company watched his departure with mixed feelings of regret at the loss of a spirited and patently courageous leader and relief that the hawk was going to hover over someone else's field. As one of them muttered 'Cor, them chatty* *Defence*'s 'ad better 'ave a quick scrub round, the pore bleeders don't know what's coming to 'em.'

For me it was a sad occasion. In the Gunroom we knew that the Admiral, despite his partiality for chasing Midshipmen, was genuinely interested in our upbringing and we were sorry to see him go.

He certainly left the imprint of his high standards on the ship. A few days after his departure a scornful seagull, soaring over the quarter-deck, let fly and dropped his card on the sacred planking alongside the Marine Corporal of the Watch who, shocked by this sacrilege, shook his fist and cried, 'Buzz off you bastard – you wouldn't 'ave dared do that in Sir Robert's day.'

* Ships manned from Chatham were popularly supposed to be less disciplined than those manned from Portsmouth and Devonport. The expression 'Chatty and happy' implied a company happy to wallow in a slovenly ship.

CHAPTER X

Destroyers

ABOUT a year after the outbreak of war the Captain sent for me. This sudden summons aroused interest in the Gunroom and, since none of us had guilt-free consciences, I was given gratuitous commiseration as I set off to face an ordeal.

I entered the presence with foreboding to be told by the Captain that 'Their Lordships' had approved a recommendation made by him that I should be offered a permanent commission in the Navy.

'Wha-at, Mistah O-rah-m, is your inclination in this mattah?' Taken aback I wallowed in a welter of emotions. Gathering stern way I was backing out of the cabin stammering my thanks and gratification when I was brought up all standing by his deep voice booming, 'Come to an anchor boy and join me in a glass of marsalah wine.' As he ceremoniously drank to my future he opened up a benevolent facet of his character which, I must confess, I had not suspected. I returned to the Gunroom in a glow and, warming the bell,* anticipated my new status, which entitled me to drink spirits, by standing gins all round to my astonished messmates.

This development altered the whole course of my life and I began to take stock and wonder what the future held for me. I could see that before long I would be appointed elsewhere, an

---

* To strike the bell shortly before the end of a watch. That is to anticipate a coming event.

exciting but slightly daunting prospect as my whole experience of the Navy had been within a single ship.

I had to bide my time but, in due course, the Admiralty confirmed my promotion to Sub-Lieutenant and I can remember few more pleasurable sensations than looking, in privacy, at my single gold stripe gleaming with promise.

A month later I was ordered, at short notice, to pack seagoing gear in readiness to join a ship called *Glen Isla* on 'special service'. It was all very hush-hush and in a state of curious expectancy I set off in the picquet boat to Long Hope where, to my dismay, we drew alongside a disreputable little merchant ship, dejected and deserted. Climbing the ricketty gangway I met my new Commanding Officer, a Lieutenant Commander seconded from *Thunderer*, who greeted me with 'Ah! Sub, you're the first arrival. Get your gear stowed away and come up to my cabin on the bridge.'

Being first on the scene I appropriated the least noisome of the dirty cabins and reported to the Captain who was poring over a grubby set of ship's drawings. He was a stocky, broad-shouldered man, friendly but taciturn and, like a lighthouse, given to dark silences alternating with flashes of crisp wisdom.

From staccato snatches I gathered that *Glen Isla* was one of the first 'Q ships' – whatever they were – and that, on the following day dockyard workmen would start on structural alterations, prior to fitting our four six-pounder guns, two on each side of the 'tween deck. The First Lieutenant, from *Conqueror*, had been delayed but would be joining us shortly with our crew of 30 from that ship. In the meantime I was to find my way round and prepare for reception of the ship's company. We talked well into the gloaming and, with the aid of a bottle of whisky, planned a campaign.

The German U-boats had recently developed an annoying habit of making a surface approach to small merchant ships, which were not worth the expenditure of a torpedo, and after ordering their defenceless crews to take to the boats were sinking their quarry by gunfire. Reports from survivors indicated that the submarines, confident that their victims could not hit back, were prone to go about their dirty business in leisurely fashion and this opened up the idea of snaring them with a decoy. The first of these Q ships was a trawler fitted with a gun on deck masked by a fishing net ostensibly hung up to dry. Frequenting off-shore fishing waters she had duped and bagged a U-boat and the Admiralty, encouraged by this success, had decided to convert more ships.

Essentially a Q ship had to present an appearance of sweet innocence until the moment to strike and, in striking, had to destroy because an escaping U-boat would blow the gaff and prejudice the whole scheme.

Glen Isla looked innocent enough. No U-boat Captain worth his salt would have considered that such a plaintive little ship creeping about at eight knots, with a tall, thin smoke stack sticking up like an exclamation mark, deserved more than the couple of shells necessary to send her aching bones to the bottom. But her outward show was designed for deception. The dockyard mateys had cut rectangular holes in the ship's sides and covered these with flap doors which could be dropped down to reveal our armament manned by trained guns' crews with itchy fingers on the triggers. Everything depended on maintaining our inoffensive appearance until the Captain, by surreptitious manoeuvring, had brought us to a sure kill position. With *Glen Isla*'s limited capabilities this might take time and, to bridge this gap, it was planned for the First Lieutenant with six carefully rehearsed sailors to make a rush for the life-boat where they would put on an act giving semblance of frightened frenzy without, however, lowering the boat too far to a position in which it would foul the guns. In the meantime, as Officer of Quarters, I was to be stationed on the gun deck at the receiving end of a voice pipe to take orders from the Captain through an intermediary figure lying out of sight on the bridge deck.

The First Lieutenant and the crew duly arrived and we set about the business of making ourselves comfortable, a task which involved a thorough scrub-round and liberal use of disinfectant. Number One, a recently promoted Lieutenant, was a wild Irishman, with an infectious gaiety. The leading role in the cast playing the 'panic stations' comedy with the life-boat was right up his street.

The crew, once they had shaken down, entered into the spirit of the enterprise, which smacked strongly of a *Boy's Own Paper* adventure, with delighted enthusiasm especially when our motley party was whacked out with cloth caps and rough civilian clothing. We sprouted immature beards and taught the hands to slouch about the upper deck in the unhurried fashion appropriate to a decrepit coaster on passage.

It was planned for us to patrol under the 'red duster'* but, to fulfil the terms of international law, we kept a white ensign bent on for display at the moment of opening fire. We also kept uniform caps in easy reach to put on in the event of disaster to ward off the risk of being shot as pirates if captured.

Left very much to our own devices we worked up our drills, carried out practice shoots at a floating barrel in the Flow and eventually set sail.

Our maiden patrol was peaceful in the extreme. In calm weather we trailed our coat along the coast towards Aberdeen and sighted nothing except a floating mine which, in pretence that it was a submarine, we attacked with bravado and sent to the bottom.

And then, as suddenly as it had started, our adventure evaporated. On returning to harbour we found the Fleet preparing for sea and, in obedience to an urgent signal, we bundled the *Conquerors* back to their ship and, disappointed, we left our *Glen Isla* swinging forlornly round her anchor to be picked up later by a new crew on its way up from Chatham.

As the war progressed an increasing number of Q ships were brought into service which, in the following eighteen months, sank seven U-boats in exchange for the loss of four of their own number. Thereafter the Germans grew windy and by remaining submerged and firing torpedoes without warning they sank no less than 27 decoys. History records that the Q ship idea paid good dividends. They bagged eleven U-boats, a figure that represented seven per cent of the total number of German submarines destroyed.

Back in *Orion* I reported to the Bloke who, after peremptory instruction to 'Scrape that disgusting yellow fungus from your chin,' told me that I would be leaving the ship on our return to

* The red ensign worn by British merchant ships.

harbour. Hurrying to the Captain's Office I was given an official appointment to H.M.S. *Earnest*, directing me to 'repair on board that vessel at Immingham forthwith'.

Flipping through 'Jane's Fighting Ships', I found that I was destined to join a destroyer of a type known as 30-knotters, armed with a single twelve-pounder gun and two small torpedo tubes. Her photograph showed that she had a low turtle back bow and four rather dominant funnels belching black coal smoke. A small ship, fifteen years old at that time, which is long in the tooth for a warship and, in comparison with the more modern Grand Fleet destroyers, she was clearly past her prime.

But, as always when about to take up a new appointment, one puts on rose coloured spectacles which can transform even elderly geese into swans.

With growing impatience, I waited for the day of departure which, when it came, had an element of melancholy. Despite enthusiasm for new pastures it is a wrench to leave a ship which, by sheer intimacy, has grown to be a part of oneself. *Orion* had been a happy ship for me and I felt downcast, and perhaps outcast, as I took a parting look at her familiar outline. But next morning, rattling past Invergordon on the Highland Railway, I was filled with a splendid sense of emancipation and excitement at the prospect of taking on First Lieutenant's responsibilities.

It was bliss to be travelling through the heather-covered Highlands. For nearly a year I had hardly set foot on shore and my senses quickened to forgotten sights, smells and sounds.

The Humber is an unprepossessing river and Immingham Dock on the south bank of the estuary sadly unattractive – a wet basin, a dry dock and a few dreary industrial buildings set down in isolation in a flat, featureless landscape contaminated by an overpowering stench of dead fish from a nearby bone meal factory.

Immingham has a big rise and fall of tide and it is only possible to enter the basin during short periods either side of high water. When I arrived it was low water and I found the little *Earnest*, having come in from patrol, crouching 30 feet down clinging to the piles of the approach pier, waiting for the tide to rise sufficiently for the lock gates to be opened to allow passage to her harbour berth in the basin. She had a long wait – and so did I – and it was 4.0 a.m. before she crept in and secured.

In the dim light of dawn I stepped on board and met the Captain coming aft along the deck dressed in a grubby duffle coat and leather sea boots. Though obviously tired he was cheerful in his greeting and suggested that I should turn in till breakfast time. With the aid of a lugubrious steward I lumped my gear down a small circular hatch to a diminutive cabin and without bothering to undress stretched out on my bunk to be awakened at eight bells with a cup of dark brown, lukewarm tea. With breakfast and hot coffee inside me and warmed by a gleam of sunshine on deck I sent for my principal assistant.

The Coxswain in a destroyer helps the First Lieutenant to discharge his responsibility for running the ship, maintaining discipline and looking after the general welfare of the ship's company. A good Coxswain can work wonders and is a veritable treasure – mine was a pain in the neck. I gathered that he was an old destroyer hand and, as I soon discovered, he was up to all the tricks. He told me that he had been in *Earnest* since the beginning of the war; that we had a complement of 60 and that they were a poor lot; that we were due to start coaling from a railway truck in half an hour; that he had everything in hand and I could rely on him to run things Bristol fashion. This last I doubted for he had a shifty eye and smelt of stale rum. I told him to carry on and climbed down into the Captain's cabin, a cramped little space right aft with barely room for a table, armchair and a bunk.

My new 'owner'* was a Lieutenant, Royal Naval Reserve, who had been serving until recently as Second Officer in a P and O liner. He had a fresh complexion, an ingenuous, confiding nature and an air of indeterminate authority which veered from indecision to brusque command with the suddenness of a shift of wind in a line squall. His prior experience of the Navy had been limited to two periods of a month's training in battleships and, though he held an Extra Master's Certificate and was a good seaman, he was somewhat green and naïve on naval matters and rather out of his depth as Captain of a ship of war. I felt rather

* A nickname for a Commanding Officer, indicating his ownership of all he surveyed.

green myself when I realized the full extent of my responsibilities but, though ten years my senior, my Captain seemed to welcome my naval experience, such as it was, and we quickly settled down to a happy and trusting relationship. He told me that as one of the units of the Local Defence Flotilla we patrolled a beat from Middlesbrough to the Wash keeping our eyes open for anything untoward. Our puny armament inhibited bold measures but there was always the possibility that we might attack a submarine on the surface and, if we chanced upon something bigger than ourselves, our 30-knot speed could keep us out of trouble until we had made our enemy report.

The Commanding Officer of our flotilla, who had an office in Immingham was, so I was told, a blood-and-thunder, old Navy type, who ran the flotilla with crusty impatience. He was regarded with awe and the sound of his tapping walking stick as he roamed the docks had the same effect as the signal 'enemy in sight'.

I went on deck and, finding the ship enveloped in coal dust, made a tour of inspection. The '30-knotters' were slim ships, about 213 feet in length and with a beam of 21 feet. To attain their speed they were lightly built, and a large section amidships was taken up with engine and boiler rooms leaving very little space at either end for accommodating the men under the turtle back fo'c'sle and the officers in small tank-like compartments aft.

Coming from a battleship which, despite the rigours of war was kept remarkably clean and efficient, I was disgusted by the unkempt and disorderly appearance of my new ship. Dirt everywhere, gear strewn about, rust-streaked paintwork and the hands drifting about in a state that would have quickly landed them in the rattle* in a big ship. I did not then realize the difficulties in keeping a small ship in good order and jumped to the conclusion that a drastic shake-up was an urgent necessity. In this I was absolutely right but it took several months to achieve any noticeable improvement. The ship's company, good enough men in themselves, were a mixed bunch of reservists and H.O.s† the former swinging their weight about and bullying the latter who, rather naturally, dragged their feet in resentment. Clearly discipline, what

* Arraigned on a charge as a defaulter.
† Men recruited from civilian life for 'Hostilities only' service.

there was of it, had been slackly administered and I realized that I was in for a rough passage.

I shared the Wardroom with the Gunner and the Warrant Engineer. These two stalwarts who, in my eyes, were venerable old gentlemen, were splendid messmates who cheerfully jollied me along and with great tact restrained me from trying to go too fast round awkward corners. Our little tin box of a mess was hardly comfortable but in cold weather it was cosy round the coal stove and companionable round the small table yarning and grumbling at the shocking food served up by our doleful steward. At sea the Gunner and I kept watch and watch* on the bridge, occasionally relieved by the Captain when he felt magnanimous.

Our patrols up and down the coast were singularly devoid of interest. We spent our time chasing coasters back into the swept channels from which they strayed with sturdy independence. We exchanged signals with minesweepers plodding along at their never-ending and hazardous toil. We kept our eyes skinned for the High Seas Fleet and any unusual activity.

The bridge was very small, much exposed and ill-fitted for accurate navigation, which was always a problem in waters strewn with shoals and minefields and subject to thick weather. Watchkeeping was pleasant enough in calm conditions, but in foul weather the ship was a little bitch, cavorting about like a puppy and pushing her nose, and the bridge, slap into a head sea instead of riding over it. She was astonishingly flexible and many a time my breakfast cup of coffee was all but emptied by the sheer lateral movement of her stern. We became accustomed to her lively habits, but a four-hour watch in a north-easterly gale off Flamborough Head was no picnic.

On one such day I came off watch and, throwing off my soaked oilskin, jammed myself into a corner of the Wardroom to counter the violent movement. The steward poked his unshaven face through the door and I demanded bacon and eggs and plenty of them. He was a dreary man made surly by his hate of the sea. A butcher by trade he had no leanings towards the culinary arts. I waited a quarter of an hour and, in growing impatience, banged on the trap hatch which he flung open growling 'Orl right, orl

* Four hours on and four off duty.

right – I'm doing me best.' Ten more minutes passed and he staggered in to dump a plate of cold 'fanny adams'* in front of me at which I expostulated, 'Where are my eggs?' With baleful sadness he sighed, 'That's your lot. I can keep the bloody fire in the grate, an' I can keep the bloody fryin' pan on the fire, but wot I carnt do is keep the bloody eggs in the fryin' pan.'

As I had realized at the outset I was faced with a difficult job in pulling the ship's company together. I had been brought up on the notion that 'a strict ship is a happy ship' but, at first, I was not very apt in applying this maxim. With memories of the disciplinary effects of the parade ground I started by copying the techniques of Gunnery Instructors. But this method, though effective in a gunnery environment, was sadly inappropriate in handling a small destroyer's company unacquainted with, or strongly antagonistic to, strict command. I had to learn that discipline in a small ship is based more upon willing observance of an accepted code of behaviour than upon meticulous drill, shouted orders and enforced obedience.

My trouble was that there was no code of behaviour and my immature efforts to make tentative reforms were inexorably scotched by the craft of a few old sweats. The Coxswain, on whom I had to rely, was the central figure in the ring of saboteurs.

To my face he was elaborately subservient but out of sight I suspected, with good reason, that he was a master of malpractice. If I jumped on him to tighten things up he retaliated by bringing innocent men before me as defaulters on trumped up charges, whereas I knew that the real culprits were to be found among a clique of Coxswain's pets. He put on a show of bland co-operation and, behind the scenes, used his guile to circumvent my authority. I had months of uphill struggle with this devious man and it was not until he overstepped himself in a little matter of smuggling duty free tobacco ashore that we were able to bring him to justice before Captain 'D',† who made short shrift and in blistering terms disrated the now cringing creep of a man to

* Corned beef.
† Short title for the Officer Commanding a group of Destroyers, Submarines, etc., e.g.:
Captain D 13 = Captain Commanding XIII Destroyer flotilla.
Commander S 13 = Commander Commanding XIII Submarine flotilla.

Able Seaman. To my relief he was then drafted away and, with the removal of the principal source of infection, the morale of the ship's company improved out of all recognition and my authority became less precarious.

The handling of men, even in well-ordered surroundings, is a tricky business and to be thrown in the deep end is a salutory experience for a young officer. It was a shock to find that in my official status there was a bigger gulf between the ship's company and myself than I had bargained for. To my sailors I was now 'Jimmy the One' and although I tried to play the part with confidence I was conscious that in their eyes I was 'Jimmy in short trousers' and I felt somewhat exposed in this curtailed rig. There were times when I was puzzled and distressed by what seemed to me to be an irritating lack of spirit, but time and closer acquaintance bridged the gap and I realized that apparent bloody-mindedness was no more than the matelot's traditional way of protesting against a dull task and a stroppy Sub Lieutenant. Mine was a maturing job and though I suffered growing pains I learned that a position of privilege has to be paid for and that carrying the can is hard work.

Our work was certainly tedious. Unprofitable days flogging the ocean in all weathers alternated with spells in a base devoid of amenities or diversions. Occasional time off for boiler cleaning enabled us to sample the delights of Grimsby, which lay at the end of a long cold pilgrimage in a tram-railway.

The Grimsby area gained the dubious distinction of being the first place in Britain to suffer an air raid. The Germans found that the Humber estuary could be picked out at night from the air and, during 1915, Zeppelins made a number of sporadic sorties over local towns. While one of these attacks was in progress I happened to be spending the evening with some soldier friends in a small defence encampment in a field on the outskirts of Cleethorpes. The sentry, in some excitement, burst in upon us and, with jars of beer in hand, we ran out of the hut to gaze in awe at the long silver shape of a dirigible floating serenely over our heads and plainly visible in the clear moonlit sky.

As a gesture my grabby* friends fired a Lewis gun, which was

* Sailors' nickname for soldiers.

all they had handy at the moment, but as the enemy was flying high, this was totally ineffective. With a faint drone of engines the Zeppelin moved up river. It was not until the next day that I heard the airship had dropped a small bomb on Cleethorpes which, by ill chance, killed a number of soldiers in a chapel in which they were billeted. There being nothing more to see we had gone back to the hut and our talk turned on the war. My host was a Captain in an infantry regiment serving temporarily at Cleethorpes while recuperating after a long spell in France. His two young subalterns, with the bloom of youth still on their hairless chins, listened open mouthed to sickening tales of trench life, as indeed I did myself. Though fascinated by the horror of these first hand experiences I was shocked by my friend's callous attitude. I returned on board next day with a feeling of relief that in the war at sea we seldom, if ever, met our enemy face to face.

Since very little occurred to leaven our days of dull patrolling I began to fear that I was in a backwater and became restive. I missed the sense of urgent purpose to which I had become accustomed in the Grand Fleet and felt growing anxiety that I was in danger of missing the tide.

Taking advantage of a week in dry dock I went to London and braved the Admiralty. This, my first visit to that aloof establishment, was something of an adventure and as I zig-zagged through the dingy corridors of power it was borne in upon me that I was sticking my neck out on a foolhardy mission. A Dickensian clerk ushered me into the office of a languid Commander who, stifling a yawn, asked my bidding. 'Humph!' he said, 'The importance of being in *Earnest* is not enough – is that it? What's wrong with your glamorous 30-knotter?' Assuring him that all was well with that fine but ancient vessel I ventured a timid desire for an appointment to something a bit more modern. Closing his eyes the oracle ruminated. Awakening some time later, astonished that he still had my company, he brought our conference to a close with 'All right, Sub, I'll see what I can do.'

He did, in fact, do me proud and a few weeks later I was electrified by an official appointment to one of a brand new flotilla of destroyers attached to the battle-cruiser fleet based on the Firth of Forth. Too full of excitement to feel any qualms of regret in deserting the faithful *Earnest* I travelled north to Edinburgh.

On an early spring morning in 1916 I joined H.M.S. *Obdurate* lying at a buoy under the shadow of the great Forth Bridge. In midstream, only a few cables away, *Lion* and her battle-cruiser consorts lay quietly at their moorings, their great bulk dominating all but the vast structure of the Bridge itself. The anchorage, which is comparatively narrow at that point, was crammed with the ships of Admiral Beatty's command.

The 13th Destroyer Flotilla comprised sixteen newly-commissioned ships of a standard class evolved from pre-war experience and embodying the fruits of sound practical foresight. They were cleverly designed and became renowned for their reliable sea-keeping performance under stress. In all, no less than 85 of this class of destroyer were built and they bore the brunt of three years' exacting war service in the North Sea.

They were all similar in appearance and performance, with raised fo'c'sle, low bridge, three funnels, an overall length of 265 feet and 1,000 tons displacement. Swift, powerful ships with a full speed of 34 knots and armed with three 4″ guns and four revolving above-water torpedo tubes. Their boilers had been designed for low consumption of oil fuel at moderate speeds which enabled them to cover 2,500 miles at an economical speed of fifteen knots.

In my eyes *Obdurate* was the acme of perfection and as I stepped on board she seemed surprisingly large; she was after all twice the tonnage of *Earnest*, and I was immediately impressed by her clean and shipshape appearance. The Wardroom, into which I was ushered by the Quartermaster, ran across the full beam of the ship and was bigger than my expectations. Though fitted out with the familiar Service pattern mahogany furniture, black and green carpet and yellow silk lamp shades, it seemed, nevertheless, to be the last word in elegant comfort.

From the depths of a leather armchair I took wary stock of my new messmates through an hospitable, and roseate, glass of pink gin. They seemed reasonable enough and I soon relaxed. We were a small quartet, First Lieutenant, Torpedo Gunner, Chief Engineer and myself.

Number One, tall, blond and intrepid, was a polished product of the new Navy. Trained to a strong sense of active duty he took the responsibilities of his office seriously and, having a leaning towards gunnery methods, he ran the ship with meticulous care for detail. He kept the ship's company on the hop and, although they groused at times, he soon had them worked up to a fair state of war efficiency. In the Torpedo Gunner we had a chip off the old block, a man of solid practical worth and typical of those who justly earned the tribute that the Warrant Officers were the backbone of the Navy. The Commissioned Engineer, sallow from years of immurement in machinery spaces, was a quietly spoken Scotsman with an edge to his canny comment on men and events. Years of experience as an Artificer in destroyers had developed a depth of resource and he relished mechanical conundrums that called for improvisation.

At sea we hardly met because when off watch we were making up for lost time in our bunks, but in harbour the mess was alive with cheerful argument, shop and flotilla gossip.

The Captain, Lieutenant-Commander C. Hulton Sams, was something of a solitary and, though he messed with us, spent much of his time when in harbour in the seclusion of his own cabin, to which I was initially summoned for scrutiny.

Turning from his small desk he transfixed me with a steely stare and looked me over in silence. He gave no inkling of what he made of his new Sub-Lieutenant. For my part I encountered a somewhat forbidding personality. As he rose to shake my hand I was conscious of suppressed strength, a coiled spring of a man, deceptively quiescent but charged with latent action. A stocky figure with a red weather-beaten face, strictly economical in speech and spartan in habit. He was, as I soon discovered, a dedicated destroyer man with scant regard for the big ship Navy and well content with his life in small ships. A fine seaman, he was scrupulously efficient and modest to the point of self-effacement. All this was not immediately apparent at our first meeting and I was disconcerted by his curt utterances and his habit of pushing his lower lip forward which, as it turned out, merely meant that he was concentrating in thought. I need not have worried. Despite his austere manner the Captain took me in hand with patient kindness and under his firm rule I picked up a packet of practical knowledge.

I was particularly delighted that day to take over a cabin of my own. I had previously slept in a glorified dog kennel and a scruffy one at that; here I had a palace in comparison and as I stowed my gear I revelled in all its 50 square foot spaciousness.

That afternoon we were ordered to raise steam and later I took charge on the fo'c'sle while the hands unshackled the cable and rove the slip wire. With the last of the light we slipped from the buoy and as the Captain worked the engines and I felt the vibrant deck beneath my feet I sensed an ambience of urgent vitality as the Fleet got under way.

Within minutes we moved into our place in a long line of destroyers and, following the cruiser *Champion*, the leader of our flotilla, under the Forth Bridge we steamed eastwards through the 'gate' into the dark waters of the North Sea.

Taking over as Officer of the Watch at midnight I was awed by my unfamiliar surroundings and, truth to tell, apprehensive. Though I had gained useful, if rather happy-go-lucky, watch-keeping experience in *Earnest* I was not accustomed to working with a flotilla and the responsibility of being in solitary charge on the bridge amid an unseen concourse of darkened ships steaming at 25 knots on a pitch black night was daunting. I temporarily lost sight of my next ahead and, in a panic, increased speed. As I strained my anxious eyes and thankfully picked up her faint blue stern light I was conscious of a shadowy figure with that ominously protruding lip silhouetted against the dim light of the compass binnacle. The presence of the Captain, though slightly unnerving, was remarkably consoling and, in the weeks to come, the way in which he always seemed to materialize at moments of crisis was quite uncanny.

He normally left me to find my own salvation and seldom uttered, but when he did he took over with crisp decisiveness and, calamity averted, immediately put the ship back in my charge. This was practical training at its best and I quickly gained confidence.

The battle-cruisers were organized in two squadrons comprising *Lion, Queen Mary, Princess Royal, Tiger*; and *Invincible, Indefatigable, New Zealand* respectively. The former, popularly known as the 'big cats', were great ships of 27,000 tons, armed with eight 13.5″ guns and designed for a full-out speed of 32 knots. At that time they were all coal-burning and all four ships had been commissioned in the two years immediately prior to the outbreak of war. To achieve their phenomenally high speed the designers had had to cut down weight and, in consequence, they carried lighter armour protection and mounted fewer guns than the Dreadnought battleships but could outstrip the speed of the Grand Fleet by no less than ten knots. The 'cats' squadron were magnificent ships, vastly impressive in size and performance and the pride of the Navy. Their precursors, the Second Battle Cruiser Squadron, were rather smaller ships mounting eight 12″ guns and about five knots slower than their bigger sisters. The battle-cruisers were accompanied by eight scouting Light Cruisers and two destroyer flotillas making a total of 49 ships in all.

Vice-Admiral Beatty, who normally wore his flag in *Lion*, was a man of striking character with a reputation for dash and bold action. His influence permeated all the ships of his command. The battle-cruiser force as a whole were inspired by a conviction that they were a *corps d'élite*. They had been tested in action and knew that it was their destiny to play an important part in the forefront in any major contact with the enemy which might develop in the months ahead.

Every one of our excursions to sea was charged with dynamic possibilities and, though most turned out to be frustratingly devoid of incident, we set off on each sweep with high expectation. I had plenty to occupy my time. At sea I spent eight out of the twenty-four hours on the windswept bridge as Officer of the Watch and, as 'navigator', recorded the ship's movements.

In harbour I was responsible for the fore part of the ship, looked after half the seamen and made myself generally useful to the First Lieutenant. But every spare minute I could snatch was spent in the chart house trying to make headway against a never ending torrent of 'Notices to Mariners' giving up-to-date information on navigational hazards, restrictions and prohibitions, all of which had to be transcribed on to the voluminous sets of charts and 'Sailing Directions' which we carried. I also worked as secretary to the Captain, mustered confidential books and burrowed into 'operation orders' to ferret out their impact on our flotilla. All this kept me in the stream of current events and, although matters of strategy were not passed down to our level, it was intriguing to follow the tactical aspects of Fleet operations.

In 'Action' I was stationed on the fo'c'sle as Officer of Quarters in charge of the foremost of our three guns. This was a 4″ Q.F.* gun in which the cordite propellant was enclosed in a brass cylinder which, on being thrust into the gun, tripped a spring that automatically pushed a steel block laterally across to seal the breech, thus cutting down the time required for reloading. The whole apparatus, including loading, was worked by hand and my crew of eight had to sweat to keep up a high rate of fire. By big ship standards our system of gun control was primitive in the extreme, just a voice pipe connection to the bridge through which we were directed on to our target and, given a rough estimation of range and deflection, leaving the Officers of Quarters to do the best they could in local control. There were few opportunities for target practice and, although we worked up the guns' crews to reasonable loading agility, chances of exercising control procedures were so minimal that we were somewhat dubious about our ability to hit a haystack beyond point blank range.

This shortcoming in training affected all ships in the Fleet and under the stress of war conditions destroyers, in particular, were kept on the go to such an extent that they could rarely be spared for stereotyped armament exercises.

There was quite a high proportion of long service ratings in our 80-strong ship's company and we were able to absorb the relatively small number of H.O.s into our general activities without too much difficulty though, from their point of view, particularly those who on arrival in their first ship felt lost, seasick and woebegone, it was hard going.

The destroyers working with the Fleet had a double function in battle. Primarily they had to work up to a position on the bow of the enemy's heavy ships to deliver a torpedo attack and secondly to use their guns to frustrate hostile torpedo-boats from attacking our capital ships. At other times destroyers were normally used to screen heavy ships from the risk of attack by enemy submarines.

* Quick firing.

The scale of German submarine warfare was building up and causing grave anxiety. Though submarines of that time had limited effectiveness, measures to counter their menace were virtually non-existent. Under-water detection devices had not been invented and a submerged submarine was invisible in every sense of the word unless she betrayed her presence by accidentally breaking surface or by showing too much periscope. It is true that their torpedoes left a trail of bubbles in their wake which could be seen by a sharp look-out, but a ship had to be alert and quick on the helm to alter course in time to 'comb' the tracks of approaching torpedoes to avoid disaster.

The purpose of the destroyer screen, spread on a broad semi-circle ahead and on the bows of ships under escort, was to harass the submarine as it manoeuvred into an attacking position, to take quick advantage by pouncing into attack if the submarine disclosed its presence; and to signal early warning if a submarine or its torpedo tracks were sighted.

The weapons available for submarine destruction were the 'ram', the gun and the depth charge. If a flustered submarine was foolish enough to break surface in a position close ahead there might be a chance to ram and destroy, but such opportunities were rare. Gunfire was only effective if the submarine's vulnerable hull was in sight long enough to bring guns to bear and, as a rule, this method was only successful at point blank range.

Depth charges, canisters of high explosives dropped over the side and triggered into detonation by the pressure of the sea water at a predetermined depth, could be lethal if, and only if, the explosion was very close to the submarine. In the complete absence of submarine detection apparatus the dropping of depth charges was haphazard and positive results were infrequent.

To be attacked by depth charges was unnerving to submarine crews and the knowledge that careless behaviour might bring down a rain of violent explosions certainly encouraged U-boat captains to keep their heads down and, in doing so, forfeit chances of careful periscope observation.

Destroyers were fitted with inclined troughs on the after deck loaded with depth charges which when set free rolled over the stern into the sea. The release mechanism could be operated from the bridge so that the Officer of the Watch could choose his moment but, in selecting the critical second, he had nothing but his eye to aid him in sensing when his stern was over the hidden enemy.

The Officer of the Watch in a screening destroyer, in addition to his normal responsibility for the handling and safety of his ship, had to maintain his correct position on the screen and at all times be prepared to react swiftly in emergency.

After initial misgivings I came to enjoy watchkeeping. The battle-cruisers invariably crashed about the ocean at high speed and it was thrilling to stand at the compass in charge of a lithe, swift ship constantly alert for instant action. The sensation of speed was intensified by outflung bow waves and throbbing vibrations of power. The ship, in the imagination, was a living, wilful creature intent on cleaving an arrow-straight furrow and temperamentally heeling far over in protest when deflected under helm.

The surrounding sea was studded with the ships of the Fleet disposed in the pattern of the reigning cruising order, each ship immobile in relation to the other but all betraying haste by white water at their stems and fretted smoke streaming from their funnels. *Lion*, the focal centre of our moving circle, ever pressing forward with a bone in her teeth, was seldom without signal flags at the yard arms and the eye was irresistibly drawn in her direction on the look-out for orders compelling immediate obedience.

Station-keeping in fine weather was not too difficult; it was largely a matter of anticipation and making small adjustments to course and speed before one dropped glaringly out of position. But foul weather with the ship punching into a head sea and the bridge swept by heavy spray was a different matter.

I remember being smartly whipped in at the end of a dirty morning watch. After three and a half hours of wet misery I was counting the minutes to eight bells and relief. Throughout my watch we had been steaming at 27 knots into the teeth of a rising gale, the weather was worsening and we were shipping green water over the fo'c'sle. The ship was bumping heavily and quivering from stem to stern each time she thrust her forefoot into a head sea. Out on the starboard quarter the battle-cruisers, headed by *Lion,* were storming along with occasional white spray whipped up by the wind over their bows.

Peering ahead to judge how the ship was taking it I took a vicious blast of all but solid water slap in the face and, blear-eyed, went to the lurching compass to take a snap bearing of the flagship. I realized that I was out of my proper station but was reluctant to subject the ship to greater stress by increasing speed. Sticking my head under the canvas flap of the chart table I dripped pools of water as I marked our estimated 8 a.m. position on the chart for the benefit of my relief.

I had just decided to call the Captain when the signalman reported, '*Lion* is flying signal addressed to us Sir, – "You are astern of station".' Wiping my drenched binoculars I checked up and, sure enough, there were our distinguishing pendants flying superior to a condemnatory hoist of flags. Telling the signalman to acknowledge I rang down to the engine room ordering a tentative increase of one knot.

Then, just as the Captain in response to my call, climbed up the ladder on to the bridge, we saw another string of coloured bunting, the ultimate ignominy, 'Indicate name of Officer of the Watch.' In acute embarrassment I told the signalman to blazon my personal shame when the Captain intervened, 'Make a reply. Your 0746. Commanding Officer. Stop. Regret poor station keeping ship is making heavy weather at present speed.'

It was this readiness by the Captain to shield his subordinates by always accepting his overall responsibility that earned our respect and made him such an endearing character. To me he vouchsafed no more than, 'Once is enough. Next time call me sooner.'

The threat of submarine attack was ever present and life on the screen was usually full of incident. Hardly an hour of daylight passed without someone seeing the feather of a periscope in a breaking wave or sinister intent in a school of porpoises.

Alarms and evasive manoeuvres were commonplace, each one creating temporary diversion and bringing Admirals and Captains in haste to their bridges to sort things out and restore the cavalcade to serried order.

The destroyers of the Great War had inherited a tradition of seamanlike smartness in manoeuvre and it was a maxim that all orders had to be obeyed with the utmost expedition. This lesson was rammed home to me one dark night. We were stationed on the bow of a cruiser with orders to take station astern when the light failed. At the end of twilight I reduced to slow speed and waited until I could see the dim shape of the big ship before edging in to follow in her wake. I was congratulating myself on the comfortable way in which I had taken up my new station when the Captain, disembodied in the gloom, punctured my euphoria. 'Destroyers ordered to change station,' he snapped, 'always, repeat always, increase speed. Never let me catch you creeping about at slow speed again.'

The 13th Flotilla was organized for its function in battle into four Divisions each under the control of a Commander. *Obdurate* was Sub-Divisional leader in the 1st Division with *Moresby* as her battle companion.

Working together bonded the Flotilla in a camaraderie enriched by good-natured rivalry which frequently found expression in an exchange of signalled back-chat between ships. The current vogue at that time was to convey sardonic comments in the form of biblical quotations. Every ship kept a Bible handy and bridge personnel grew expert in a battle of instant wit with the odds in favour of the originator who could choose his moment to score off the respondent, who was at a disadvantage in having to hasten through the concordance to find a biting retort.

We lost a game one day when our Divisional Commander, finding us slow in answering a signal, whacked in 'Proverbs. 6.9.'* This caught us with our trousers down and we could do no better than 'Habakkuk. 3.2.'†

On another occasion *Moresby*, who had dropped astern, was cracking on speed to catch up and, in doing so, emitted a cloud of funnel smoke which, in an oil fired ship, indicated carelessness in the boiler room. This was a heaven sent opportunity for us to signal 'Solomon. 3.6',‡ which as a matter of fact, was rather

* How long wilt thou sleep O sluggard when wilt thou arise out of thy sleep.
† O Lord I have heard thy speech . . . in wrath remember mercy.
‡ Who is this that cometh out of the wilderness like pillars of smoke.

a chestnut and I think honours went to our stable mate who replied 'Psalm 74.1'*

With the coming of summer the lengthening days gave more time for exercising and having carried out a couple of shoots and fired practice torpedoes we felt worked up and ready for anything.

* O God why hast thou cast us off forever, why doth thine anger smoke against the sheep of thy pasture.

CHAPTER XI

Jutland—Day

THE memories of those who took part in the Battle of Jutland are ineradicable.

The confrontation of the two great fleets had been long awaited and when the time came the Grand Fleet entered the arena with high prospect of an annihilating victory. In the event the fog of war, chance and strange coincidence bedevilled the antagonists and the outcome was indecisive. Both sides announced victory and the rival claims sparked off controversy that echoes down the years. But, despite subsequent argument, Jutland was an occasion of intense action and high drama to the 105,000 officers and men who met in battle 80 miles off the coast of Denmark on the afternoon of the 31 May, 1916. In this great conflict 250 ships manoeuvred at high speed for twelve hours and it is not surprising that the course of the action was confusing in the extreme. The vast majority of the participants had no more than a strictly local view and only a handful of senior officers were able to grasp the bare elements of the tactical situation. Even the two Commanders-in-Chief were so starved of information that they had to make most of their momentous decisions without concrete knowledge of events beyond the range of their personal vision. It took years of patient study to build a coherent picture of the battle in all its complexity and it would be idle to traverse a field that has been so exhaustively surveyed.

But, however complex, historical happenings are but an aggregate of individual records and experiences. My part in the adventures of an insignificant unit is no more than a small piece in a vast and colourful jigsaw.

The setting of the stage for this great encounter had been in progress since the outset of war. By 1916 Admiral Jellicoe, recognizing that the High Seas Fleet would not seek a pitched battle against the concentrated power of the Grand Fleet, tried from time to time to entice his enemy into a trap which, he well knew, would have to be set in the south-eastern corner of the North Sea in waters that were extensively mined.

He organized sorties by apparently unsupported light forces and took steps to counter any German reaction with overwhelming might, hoping that his advanced ships, having made contact with a superior enemy, would feint and flee and by so doing draw their pursuers towards the Grand Fleet massed below the horizon. In setting these traps he was greatly helped by the Admiralty Intelligence organization which, by monitoring German wireless traffic, was able to report unusual activity and, by the use of direction finding techniques, could establish the approximate position of transmitting ships. Furthermore, he had an inestimable advantage in being made privy to the gist of many German signals which the cryptographers, by breaking enemy codes, were able to decipher. This early warning enabled Jellicoe to get his fleet to sea and well to the southward whenever a German sortie was anticipated.

Admiral Scheer, the German Commander-in-Chief, had a problem of a different colour. In following his Government's policy of attrition he strove to take advantage of any relaxation of concentration by the British so that he might pounce upon and destroy any detached units of the Grand Fleet that ventured within striking distance. He was careful to stage his actions in areas which permitted a quick withdrawal to shelter behind minefields before the appearance of the British fleet in full battle array.

When mounting operations both sides planned to draw their opponents into waters where ships would be menaced by submarines or newly laid minefields.

The German tip-and-run bombardments of Yarmouth, Lowestoft and Scarborough had been designed to arouse British public opinion into demanding that the Navy's 'sure shield' should protect them from such raids and pressure was brought to bear on the Admiralty to base some heavy ships farther south to guard against the possibility of further sporadic attacks on defenceless seaside towns. Jellicoe resolutely refused to comply on grounds that, apart from Scapa Flow, there were no defended bases on the East Coast which could accommodate, and cater for the needs of, the full strength of the Grand Fleet. He contended that the battle-cruiser force based on the Firth of Forth was the maximum degree of dispersion that he could countenance.

In May both sides were considering operations to attain their respective objectives. The Germans planned a sortie to bombard Sunderland which, being farther north than hitherto, was deemed to be more likely to draw Beatty and his battle-cruisers into action before the main body of the Grand Fleet could intervene. As an innovation Scheer planned to use Zeppelin airships for reconnaissance on his northern flank. Failing suitable weather for airship operation an alternative sortie was planned in which German cruisers would show themselves in the vicinity of the Skagerrak in the hope that Beatty would dash eastwards from the Firth of Forth to fall into the jaws of the supporting High Seas Fleet before the slower battleships from Scapa Flow could come to their succour. Knowing that his actions would bring the British to sea Admiral Scheer, on the 17 May, stationed sixteen 'U-boat' submarines on patrol off the Scottish coast to report and attack ships leaving the Firth of Forth and the Orkneys. It so happened that the weather was unsuitable for the Zeppelins and it was not until the end of the month that the Sunderland raid was cancelled and preparations were made for the alternative sally north to the Skagerrak.

On the British side Jellicoe planned a penetration by light cruisers into the Skagerrak on 2 June supported by the Grand Fleet waiting out of sight in the hope that the bait would attract the High Seas Fleet. Both Commanders-in-Chief were set upon operations in the same area at approximately the same time but, despite this coincidence, the reconnaissance of those days was so limited that even so their courses might not have crossed. But chance played a card that altered the situation dramatically.

At noon on 30 May the Admiralty, detecting an increase in

German wireless activity, warned Jellicoe at Scapa Flow that there were signs that the German fleet was preparing for sea and, later that day, the Grand Fleet was ordered to make a sweep to the south-east. Jellicoe made plans to concentrate his force in a position 80 miles off the southern tip of Norway to counter an anticipated move by Scheer in that direction. By midnight the Grand Fleet was clear of harbour and *Lion* and the battle-cruisers were at sea steering eastwards across the North Sea. Two hours later Scheer in the battleship *Friedrich der Grosse* and Hipper, the Admiral commanding the German battle-cruiser force, wearing his flag in *Lutzow*, led their ships to sea from Wilhelmshaven to begin their sortie towards the Skagerrak. Throughout the night the opposing fleets steamed at economical speed on converging courses – Scheer making his way to the north, Jellicoe sweeping to the south-east.

Early in the morning of 31 May the Operations Division in the Admiralty asked the monitoring staff to check the position of Scheer's flagship and were told that the direction of the German C.-in-C.'s wireless transmissions indicated that he was still in harbour in the Jade River. This important intelligence was promptly passed to Jellicoe.

But the Admiralty had been duped by Scheer who, to conceal his movements, had made a habit of transferring his call sign to a shore station when he went to sea. The effect of this trick was that Jellicoe and Beatty steamed on through the night under the mistaken impression that their enemy was still in harbour. Despite this Jellicoe decided to continue his sweep and ordered Beatty, who was some 70 miles to the south, to carry on his easterly course until 2 p.m. when, if nothing had been sighted, he was to turn north and bring his battle-cruisers to join company with the Grand Fleet.

I had the afternoon watch on that day of summer sunshine, peacefully keeping station two miles on the port beam of *Lion* leading *Princess Royal, Queen Mary, Tiger, New Zealand* and *Indefatigable* on a leisurely amble at fifteen knots across a calm sea. Though slightly hazy the visibility was reasonably good and five miles away to the north-west we could see the 5th Battle Squadron – *Barham, Valiant, Warspite* and *Malaya*, the most

H M Destroyer "Earnest"

10. HM submarine C34 entering Blockhouse Creek. (Page 187)

11. A 'V' class submarine at Barrow. (Page 195)

modern and powerful battleships in the Fleet – stationed in a
position to give close support to Beatty's faster but less heavily
armoured battle-cruisers. Beyond the visible horizon twelve
scouting light cruisers were spread on an arc from east to south.
The cruiser *Champion* and eighteen destroyers of our 13th Flotilla
and attached 10th Flotilla were in company with the battle-cruisers
and *Fearless* and nine destroyers of the 1st Flotilla screened the
5th Battle Squadron.

The *Barham* and her sister ships were not normal stable-mates
of ours; it so happened that they had been temporarily attached
to Beatty's command in replacement for three of his battle-cruisers
which were at Scapa Flow for gunnery exercises. This chance sub-
stitution had significant consequences later in the day.

There was little to do and I leaned over the bridge rail envying
a cluster of prone sailors enjoying a make and mend 'caulk'. We
knew nothing of the intelligence reports that had set us in motion
but Beatty had made a general signal announcing his intention to
alter course at 2.15 p.m. to rendezvous with the Grand Fleet 70
miles to the north. As the hour approached a string of flags in *Lion*
ordered a redisposition of the screening destroyers preparatory
to the change in direction. As the big ships swung round to the
northward I called the Captain and we lugubriously voiced our
frustration as we turned homewards at the end of yet another un-
productive excursion.

Chance then stepped in and played the opening gambit in
what was to prove to be an historical conflict.

At 2.15 p.m. the light cruiser *Galatea*, scouting twenty miles to
the east, was about to alter course to the north to conform to
Beatty's movement when she sighted a Danish merchant ship hull
down to the eastward blowing off steam. This aroused interest and,
with *Phaeton* in company, she steamed on for a closer look and
in doing so surprised a German cruiser and two torpedo-boats
engaged in a similar investigation. Within minutes they were in
action and *Galatea* was hit by a shell which failed to explode. This
did not hinder the transmission of an urgent signal at 2.25 reporting 'Enemy in sight.' (A)* *Galatea* then sighted smoke to the

* The lettered notations in this and the succeeding chapter refer to the
relative positions of ships on Diagrams I and II – pp. 150 and 162.

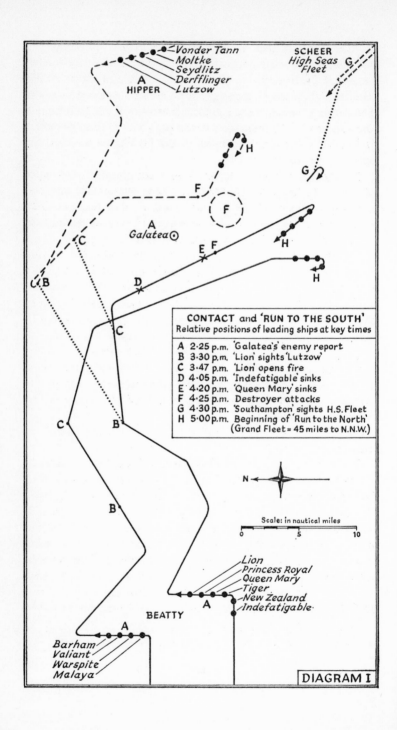

Von der Tann
Moltke
Seydlitz
Derfflinger
Lützow

A
HIPPER

SCHEER
High Seas
Fleet   G

H

F

G

A
Galatea ⊙

E F

F

H

H

C

B

C
B

D

C

B

CONTACT and 'RUN TO THE SOUTH'
Relative positions of leading ships at key times

A 2·25 p.m. 'Galatea's enemy report
B 3·30 p.m. 'Lion' sights 'Lutzow'
C 3·47 p.m. 'Lion' opens fire
D 4·05 p.m. 'Indefatigable' sinks
E 4·20 p.m. 'Queen Mary' sinks
F 4·25 p.m. Destroyer attacks
G 4·30 p.m. 'Southampton' sights H.S. Fleet
H 5·00 p.m. Beginning of 'Run to the North'
         (Grand Fleet = 45 miles to N.N.W.)

C

B

N

Scale: in nautical miles
0   5   10

Lion
Princess Royal
Queen Mary
Tiger
New Zealand
Indefatigable

A

BEATTY

A

Barham
Valiant
Warspite
Malaya

DIAGRAM I

east and turned away to draw the enemy towards Beatty. The German ships which she had encountered were, in fact, scouts operating to the west of Hipper's battle-cruisers which, at that time, were 80 miles off the coast of Jutland steaming north 50 miles in advance of Scheer and the entire High Seas Fleet.

The receipt of enemy reports electrified both sides. Hipper in *Lutzow*, with *Derfflinger, Seydlitz, Moltke, von der Tann*, four light cruisers and torpedo-boats in company, completely unaware that British heavy ships were in the offing, obeyed the old sea tradition and steered towards the gunfire to give support to his light forces.

Beatty, with a huntsman's spontaneous reaction, immediately turned toward's *Galatea*'s reported position of the enemy and ordered all his ships to raise steam for full speed.

For an hour *Lion* and *Lutzow* converged, both Admirals alerted but in ignorance that their rivals were in the vicinity.

Beatty, though still under the impression that the High Seas Fleet was in harbour and that he had only light forces to contend with, was taking no chances and ordered *Champion* to gather her pack of destroyers at their action station ahead of the hurrying battle-cruisers. As the big ships worked up speed it took us time to gain our new station ahead of *Lion* steaming magnificently at 28 knots. We were now in a state of preparedness, the guns and torpedo tubes ready, the ship cleared for action, and the vibration of the hull as we cracked on at full speed matched our feelings of urgency and high excitement. The Captain took over on the bridge while I tried to keep record of our many alterations of course as the flotilla of eighteen destroyers made haste to form up on *Champion* in the van of the battle-cruisers. *Barham* and her supporting force of battleships having less speed were just in sight about eight miles astern doing their utmost to catch up.

At 3.30 Hipper's flagship, *Lutzow*, was sighted fourteen miles on the starboard bow steering north-west. (B) Beatty promptly altered course to the eastward to bar the enemy from his base. On his side, Hipper, sighting the British at approximately the same time and recognizing that he was in contact with Beatty's battle-cruiser force, made an immediate turn to the south-east to

151

lure his unsuspecting foe towards the High Seas Fleet 50 miles away to the southward.

It is significant that Hipper did not sight the four *Barham* class battleships which, from his view point, were below the horizon and, assuming that Beatty was operating on his own, decided to engage while leading his unsupported antagonist to destruction. Had he realized the presence of capital ships he would have drawn the conclusion that the Grand Fleet was in the offing and would have warned Scheer who, in all probability, would have withdrawn rather than risk pitched battle with a superior fleet. Beatty, seeing his opponent turn to the south-east, quickly appreciated that he was being led towards the High Seas Fleet and, in fulfilment of his prime function to make contact and report the position of the enemy battle fleet to Jellicoe, he formed line of battle.

The two battle-cruiser forces were now rapidly converging. Five minutes later they had closed to a range of eight miles (C) and Beatty led his ships round to south-south-east and opened fire. This began a phase of the battle which was subsequently called the 'run to the south', a 40-minute period of heavy engagement between the two lines of battle-cruisers on approximately parallel courses.

The sudden switch to the south-south-east threw the destroyers out of station. We had been assembled ahead of *Lion* but the rapid 70° turn to starboard left us trailing and there was a mad scramble to regain our battle station in the van. Most of our flotilla mates steamed up the disengaged side of our battle-cruisers, but *Obdurate* and *Morris* found themselves on the engaged side and as we crept up between the battle lines we were much inhibited by the necessity to moderate our speed so that excessive funnel smoke would not obscure the big ships' view of the enemy. Throughout this opening stage of fierce action we were in the front row of the stalls, one might almost say in the orchestra pit, and the clamour was awe inspiring.

I had by now taken up my station at the fo'c'sle gun and as we were not then in action there was time to watch developments. A mile to starboard *Lion* and her five consorts in line ahead crashed along at full speed, high spray at their bows and volumes of black smoke pouring from their tall funnels in visible evidence of sweating 'black squads' feeding hungry boilers. All gun turrets were trained in our direction and the great guns at high elevation belched bright flame and yellow smoke as they fired over our heads.

Six miles away to port we could see the five German battle-cruisers showing indistinctly against a sombre background of haze and smoke illumined with orange spurts of light at the muzzles of their rapidly firing guns. Their opening salvoes were short and, being in the direct line of fire, we were straddled several times by the towering splashes of falling shells. But we were not their target and as the enemy quickly corrected to a hitting range his projectiles roared overhead and left us unscathed.

Standing with my gun's crew on the open fo'c'sle I felt peculiarly exposed and curbed an urge to seek spurious shelter on the disengaged side of the gun mounting. Instincts of self-preservation were, however, quickly submerged by waves of intense excitement set up by the sheer magnitude of passing events.

At the outset the German fire was accurate and as our ships showed up clearly against an afternoon horizon the enemy achieved swift and punishing results. Within ten minutes of opening fire both sides had found the range and the two flagships drew first blood by hitting each other at more or less the same instant. I was watching *Lion* at the moment when a heavy shell hit her midship turret. From a mile away all we could see was a burst of light brighter than the flash of her gunfire and a column of billowing smoke. It was not until later that we heard that the flame caused by the exploding shell penetrated down the trunk of the turret and that disaster was narrowly averted by the dying act of the Major of Marines who, by flooding the magazine and sacrificing the crew, saved *Lion* from total destruction. The *Lutzow* was less severely damaged and both flagships maintained hot fire. Within minutes my sleeve was pulled by one of the gun's crew drawing my attention to *Indefatigable*, the last ship in the British line which, enveloped in smoke, had hauled out to starboard. (D) To our horror we saw her hit again and, shattered by a violent explosion, the great ship rolled over and sank in two minutes taking with her all but two of her complement of 1,017 officers and men.

In the face of this tragic loss Beatty opened the range and, to ease the pressure, ordered the destroyers in to the attack. *Champion* had by this time gathered her pack in a position ahead of *Lion* and as we saw our sixteen flotilla mates streaming across towards the enemy we cracked on to full speed to join the hunt.

At this stage, the very crux of the battle, events built up in rapid succession to a crescendo of action. As we pressed on ahead a crisp word from the bridge prompted me to bring my awe-struck gun's crew to a state of proper concentration on their job in hand. This done I glanced out on the starboard quarter at the line of big ships steadily pounding at the distant enemy. Even as I looked the *Queen Mary*, the third ship in the line, was struck by a plunging salvo. (E)

A glaring red flash, the sound of a gigantic explosion, smoke towering three times the height of her mast, and the 27,000-ton ship, which a moment before had been proudly steaming at 25 knots with all guns blazing defiance, had disappeared from view. The stark reality was too stupendous to take in. One felt involved in the occult, a trick in which a conjuror's black pall lifted to reveal – nothing. Only twenty of her 1,266 crew survived to be picked up later by a passing destroyer.

It was at this point that Beatty, witnessing the loss from the bridge of *Lion*, made the classic comment quoted by his Flag Captain, 'There seems to be something wrong with our bloody ships today,' and promptly made a signal to his four remaining ships to alter course towards the enemy. In taking this seemingly rash decision he was, in fact, fortified by the knowledge that *Barham* and her squadron, by cutting corners, were catching up and, from a position astern had brought their 15″ guns to bear and were harassing *Moltke* and *von de Tann* at the rear of the German line.

Hipper too was hard pressed and, although his five ships were still in action, two had been severely mauled and the remainder had suffered battle damage. Like Beatty he felt the need for easement and ordered the cruiser *Regensburg* to launch fifteen German torpedo-boats into an attack on the British line.

The function of destroyers in battle was to make for a position on the bow of the enemy and, having closed to a feasible range, to turn and fire their torpedoes. The purpose of this attack was to reduce the enemy's fire power by forcing him to turn away or run the risk of being hit and disabled by torpedoes. Destroyers had a secondary function in breaking up similar attacks by enemy torpedo-boats.

By sheer coincidence the hounds on both sides had been unleashed simultaneously to steam at full speed into a fierce melée between the lines. (F) The opposing forces were evenly matched and their combat was spectacular, highly exciting and chaotic – 30 ships at 30 knots weaving about in a restricted area striving to find a way through to a torpedo firing position and hotly engaged in frustrating enemy craft. The approaching German torpedo-boats with gushing funnels, high bow waves and sterns well tucked down in foaming wakes looked sinister and menacing. I remember feeling that they were a pack of wolves that must, at all costs, be killed.

The sea was calm but churned into disturbance by the dashing ships. The sun shone fitfully through smoke which the light wind did little to clear.

At the fo'c'sle gun we waited expectantly for the Captain's order and, with a sense of relief opened rapid fire at the leading ship of the advancing pack. In a matter of minutes we were caught up in a maelstrom of whirling ships as we swerved and jockeyed for a break-through position. We were under helm most of the time, the ship heeling as she spun. Events moved far too quickly for stereotyped gun control procedure and we let fly at anything hostile that came within our arc of fire. It became a personal affair, and I have a vivid recollection of the sweating Trainer cursing as he strove to change his point of aim from ship to ship as I tried to seize fleeting opportunities.

Quite apart from the difficulty in making split second decisions on friend or foe our legitimate enemies swept past at aggregate speeds of up to 60 knots and there was scant time to make a wild guess at range and deflection and get the gun pointed and fired before the chance passed and we were frantically trying to focus on a new target. It was quite impossible to pick out one's own fall of shot in a sea pocked with shell splashes, nor was there time to correct the range had we been able to do so. We fired many rounds at more or less point blank range but had no idea if any found their mark though several bright flashes gave hope that we had inflicted punishment. We discovered, subsequently, that we had been hit by two shells one of which, passing under my gun, punched neat holes on either side of the mess deck but, fortunately failed to explode.

In the heat of swift action senses become keyed up by the high tempo and feeling for time is lost. I would have been at a loss to say if we had been engaged for minutes or hours. Crowding incidents made it seem an eternity and yet the period of action passed in a flash. In fact the dog fight had lasted barely fifteen minutes when *Lion* hoisted the destroyer recall and we dutifully broke off to come to heel.

At the outset of this action we had not quite caught up with the main body of the flotilla when it went into the attack and were too far back to reach a torpedo firing position on the bow of the enemy. But several of our flotilla were more fortunately placed in being further ahead. *Nestor*, leading *Nicator* and *Nomad*, managed to penetrate to a good position about two and a half miles on the bow of *Lutzow* and, under heavy gun fire from the big ship's secondary armament, swung round and fired three torpedoes which achieved the desired effect in making Hipper turn away.

Nestor (Commander Bingham) attacked once again and fired four more torpedoes. This time the range was closed to one and three-quarter miles and as the three destroyers turned to retire *Nestor* was hit in the boiler room and badly disabled. Signalling to *Nicator* to make good her escape Commander Bingham, with great gallantry, fired his remaining torpedo in the few minutes before his ship, under a rain of shells, settled by the stern and sank. Not far away *Nomad*, who had also been severely damaged by gun fire, struggled on at slow speed and managed to loose off her torpedoes in the moments before she succumbed, rolled over and disappeared.* Yet another group led by *Petard*, disregarding the

* 152 men from *Nestor* and *Nomad* were subsequently picked up by the enemy and taken to Germany as prisoners of war. Commander Bingham, who was one of the survivors, was awarded the Victoria Cross.

'Destroyer recall' signal, turned back towards the enemy and successfully torpedoed, and damaged, the battle-cruiser *Seydlitz*.

The attack by the German torpedo-boats was abortive. Frustrated in their efforts to break through they fired a few torpedoes at long range but the British heavy ships saw the torpedo tracks and took avoiding action. Two enemy torpedo-boats were sunk by gunfire in the general skirmish between the battle lines.

Absorbed in our own affairs during this hectic period we were blind to extraneous events and, on returning from the attack, we were surprised to see *Lion* reverse direction and turn to a northerly course.

While the destroyer action had been developing the four ships of the 2nd Light Cruiser Squadron, in fulfilling their function as scouts, had moved to a position several miles in advance of Admiral Beatty in *Lion*.

Just before 4.30 p.m. Commodore Goodenough, wearing his broad pendant in *Southampton*, still under the impression that the High Seas Fleet were in harbour, was astonished to see unmistakable battleships on the horizon. (G) Fully alive to the vital significance of this sighting he promptly sent an urgent signal to Admiral Jellicoe: 'Enemy battle fleet bearing south-east. Enemy's course north. My position 56° 34′ N 60° 20′ E.'*

Pressing on to have a closer look at the German ships the cruisers came under devastating fire and the Commodore was forced to retire but not before he had confirmed that he was in fact in the presence of the entire High Seas Fleet in single line hurrying to support Hipper's hard-pressed battle-cruisers. *Southampton*, swinging round, sent off an amplifying report and, under heavy fire, zig-zagged away to the north-west. By constantly jinking towards the shell splashes the four light cruisers foxed the German gun control officers and miraculously escaped damage as they withdrew to safety.

In the meantime Hipper, thankful that he had achieved his purpose in leading his opponent into the jaws of death, turned his battle-cruisers to the north to take up his appointed position in the van of the advancing High Seas Fleet. Beatty too, by sighting and

* This position is approximately 70 miles NNW from Horn's Reef Light Vessel.

reporting his contact with the enemy's battle fleet, had fulfilled his primary function and, no doubt with an equal sense of relief, turned to a northerly course to lure the unsuspecting Scheer towards Jellicoe and the Grand Fleet, at that time 45 miles away to the Nor-nor-west.

At this juncture the 5th Battle Squadron came thundering up. *Barham*, still hotly engaged with Hipper's ships, had not seen Beatty's signal to turn and, in consequence, swept past *Lion* on an opposite course and, as they did so, sighted Scheer's leading battleships fourteen miles away on the port bow. Quickly appreciating the reason for Beatty's sudden turn the four battleships hastened to follow suit and altered course in succession to the north. By the time this manoeuvre was completed *Barham* was three miles astern of *Lion* and under heavy fire from the High Seas Fleet. (H) Settled on their new course the battleships were in a good position to give support to Beatty and the fire from their 15″ guns inflicted damage on *Lutzow, Derfflinger* and two of the leading German battleships. With their superior speed *Barham* and her consorts drew ahead and out of gun range. Scheer, observing this apparent flight and convinced that he had an isolated British squadron in his power, made the signal 'General chase' and the High Seas Fleet pressed on at their maximum speed in an endeavour to re-engage. For the best part of an hour the antagonists hastened northwards, darkening the sky with dense clouds of coal smoke. From time to time *Lion* and *Barham* closed the range to punish Hipper whose squadron, nine miles ahead of Scheer, was by this time decidedly groggy. *Lutzow, Seydlitz, von der Tann* and *Derfflinger* had suffered damage and only *Moltke* was fighting fit.

The destroyers on returning from their attack and finding themselves well astern of the battle-cruisers, joined company with *Barham* and her squadron. We had occasional glimpses of the High Seas Fleet but in the haze and smoke could see little more than blurred shapes pricked by orange flashes. As we steamed north on the disengaged side of Barham this phase of the battle became relatively quiet. In a brief stand-easy I went to the bridge to report while the Captain took stock of our situation. From a material point of view our damage was not serious, the Chief reported that all was well in his department, and we had suffered no casualties. From what we had seen we were able to appreciate the picture and with the High Seas Fleet breathing down our necks we knew that when we made junction with Jellicoe a general fleet action would develop.

We plotted our reckoning on the chart and calculated that as the two fleets must be approaching each other at over 40 knots we would not have long to wait for the clash of power.

CHAPTER XII

Jutland—Night

THROUGHOUT that afternoon the Grand Fleet had been steadily advancing to the south-east. Admiral Jellicoe, alerted by *Galatea*'s original sighting and Beatty's report that he was engaged with Hipper's advanced forces, increased the speed of the Fleet to twenty knots.

Just after 4.30 p.m. the situation was dramatically changed by receipt of *Southampton*'s report that she was in contact with the High Seas Fleet. The Commander-in-Chief, appreciating that Beatty was in all probability leading the enemy in his direction, assumed that he was about to engage the High Seas Fleet at its full strength,* and made an immediate general signal 'Enemy battle fleet is coming north. Fleet action is imminent.'

Jellicoe had 24 Dreadnought battleships, three battle-cruisers, eight armoured cruisers, eleven light cruisers and 50 destroyers in company with him at sea on that day. The Grand Fleet battle-ships were disposed in a cruising order of six columns of four ships covering a wing-to-wing front of five miles. They were pre-ceded by a line of armoured cruisers spread athwart the line of advance. Ahead of these scouts Rear-Admiral Hood with his three *Invincible* class battle-cruisers hastened to Beatty's aid.†

Jellicoe lacked specific information on the movements of the

---

* In fact the High Seas Fleet comprised sixteen Dreadnoughts, six pre-Dreadnoughts and five battle-cruisers.
† These were the battle-cruisers *Invincible*, *Inflexible* and *Indomitable* that had been temporarily detached to Scapa Flow for gunnery exercises.

enemy during the 'run to the North' and although he could calculate the approximate time of contact he could not foresee in what direction he would eventually sight the ships of the High Seas Fleet. Lacking this essential knowledge he was faced with a vexing problem in deciding upon the best way to form his Fleet into the most advantageous battle line before the moment of actual combat. Everything would depend upon his vital decision and until he knew the certain position of the enemy relative to himself he was not able to make the all-important 'Deployment' signal. As the sands of time ran out he waited, in vain, for amplifying reports from his battle-cruiser force. Still he stood on, waiting for positive information on which to act. The visibility had deteriorated but it was slightly clearer to the southward than elsewhere. One can readily imagine the tension on the Admiral's bridge in *Iron Duke*, leading the left central column as the vast concourse of ships swept on towards the invisible enemy, straining upon the start and awaiting only the executive signal.

Deployment and formation of the battle line would take a quarter of an hour. Every second's delay increased the risk of being caught in the act of deployment by an enemy already in battle array. Still Jellicoe bided his time.

At last, just before 6.0 p.m. *Marlborough*, leading the starboard wing column, saw gun flashes and reported that she had sighted *Lion* and her squadron six miles distant on her starboard bow. (K) This was disturbing news as Jellicoe had been expecting to sight Beatty right ahead but it was at least concrete evidence on which to act. But where was the High Seas Fleet relative to Beatty?

For a few moments the Commander-in-Chief stood alone at the compass summing up the situation. It was Churchill who said that Jellicoe was the only man who could lose the war in an afternoon. This was the moment of truth. Quietly he turned and ordered Deployment on his port wing column and signalled *King George V*, the designated leader of the battle line, to steer southeast-by-east. As the signal flags fluttered down, the leading ships of columns simultaneously altered course 90° to port and, followed by the ships in their several columns, the Fleet formed into a long single line. As the battleships reached the critical point of the deployment each turned successively without further signal

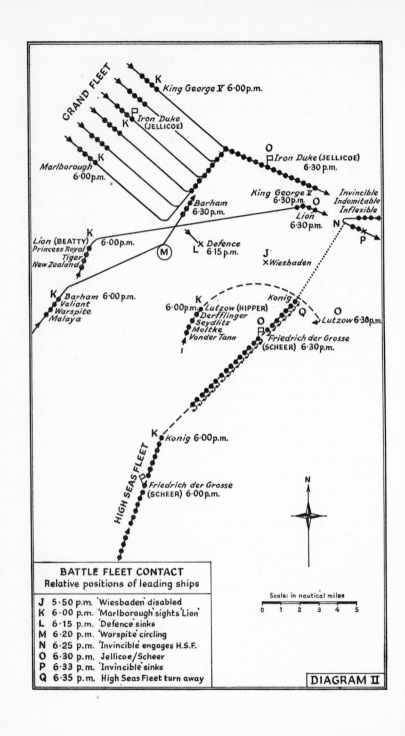

GRAND FLEET

K King George V 6.00 p.m.

K Iron Duke (JELLICOE)

O Iron Duke (JELLICOE) 6.30 p.m.

Marlborough 6.00 p.m. K

Barham 6.30 p.m.

King George V 6.30 p.m. O

Invincible Indomitable Inflexible

Lion 6.30 p.m.

N

K Lion (BEATTY) 6.00 p.m.
Princess Royal
Tiger
New Zealand

× Defence 6.15 p.m. L

M

× P

K Barham 6.00 p.m.
Valiant
Warspite
Malaya

J × Wiesbaden

K 6.00 p.m. Lutzow (HIPPER)
Derfflinger
Seydlitz
Moltke
Von der Tann

Konig
Q

O Lutzow 6.30 p.m.

O Friedrich der Grosse (SCHEER) 6.30 p.m.

I

K Konig 6.00 p.m.

HIGH SEAS FLEET

Friedrich der Grosse (SCHEER) 6.00 p.m.

N

BATTLE FLEET CONTACT
Relative positions of leading ships

J	5·50 p.m.	'Wiesbaden disabled
K	6·00 p.m.	'Marlborough sights Lion'
L	6·15 p.m.	'Defence sinks
M	6·20 p.m.	'Warspite circling
N	6·25 p.m.	'Invincible engages H.S.F.
O	6·30 p.m.	Jellicoe/Scheer
P	6·33 p.m.	'Invincible sinks
Q	6·35 p.m.	High Seas Fleet turn away

Scale: in nautical miles
0 1 2 3 4 5

DIAGRAM II

and followed in the wake of *King George V*. This deployment manoeuvre, brilliantly executed and timed to perfection, was completed by 6.35 p.m. when *Agincourt*, the last ship, turned to take up her station at the rear of the seven-mile line of 24 Dreadnought battleships with their 220 great broadside guns trained to starboard and ready for instant action.

Beatty, on making contact with the Grand Fleet, led his battle-cruisers at full speed across the front of the deploying battleships to take up their traditional station ahead of *King George V* in the van. In doing so he edged to the eastwards and skilfully prevented Hipper in *Lutzow* from sighting the Grand Fleet.

And what of Scheer? For the past hour he had been striving to bring the force of his fleet to bear on Beatty's isolated ships. Incredibly he was unaware of the trap into which he was steering. Just before 6.30 Beatty's encircling movement to the eastward was observed and, as the smoke of his headlong passage drifted clear, Scheer and his staff on the bridge of *Friedrich der Grosse* saw the unmistakable outlines of capital ships, and realized the full horror of their bitter situation. (O) In a great arc from north-east to north-west the serried might of the British menaced the very existence of the High Seas Fleet. The jaws of the trap were about to spring. At the very outset of battle Scheer was shocked by the knowledge that he had been outmanoeuvred, that his T had been crossed, and that nothing short of a miracle could extricate his fleet from annihilation. Escape was his only recourse.

I was still on the bridge with the Captain when we made first contact with the Grand Fleet. *Champion* and her destroyers were in close company with *Barham* and her 5th Battle Squadron when we sighted the armoured cruisers *Defence, Warrior* and *Black Prince* in their scouting position five miles ahead of *Marlborough*. We saw them cut across Beatty's bows steaming at top speed towards the head of the German line firing at the blazing wreck of the enemy cruiser *Wiesbaden*.* (J) At the masthead of *Defence* I caught sight of the flag of Sir Robert Arbuthnot, my Admiral of pre-war days, and remember thinking how typical it was of his

---

* *Wiesbaden* was critically disabled and a sitting target for all who passed. She survived the onslaught but sank with all hands during the night.

gallant and pugilistic spirit to spring from his corner and press into close quarters regardless of the consequences. But he was up against a heavyweight and, minutes later, his lightly armoured cruisers came under fierce fire from Scheer's leading battleships. Crushed by a rain of heavy shells *Defence* was rent apart and sank. (L) I was appalled. There were no survivors. *Warrior*, disabled, struggled slowly westwards endeavouring to move out of gun range. *Black Prince* withdrew without suffering serious damage.

We were then involved in a curious incident. *Barham*, on sighting the deploying Grand Fleet, made an alteration of course to station her squadron at the rear of the battle line. In executing this manoeuvre *Warspite*'s helm jammed with the result that she circled before control of steering was regained. (M) The High Seas Fleet were coming up fast from the southward and *Warspite*'s gyration carried her within six miles of Scheer's leading ships. This accidental manoeuvre had the effect of drawing the enemy's fire from the unfortunate *Warrior* who was given breathing space to struggle out of range.* As *Warspite* came sweeping round the destroyers had to stampede to avoid her. We were re-assembling when we were caught up in a scrimmage with the light forces of the Grand Fleet as they hurried down from the north-west athwart our course. Surrounded by a forest of shell splashes a great confluence of cruisers and destroyers twisted and weaved to avoid collision. For ten hectic minutes confusion reigned and the fact that there were no disasters is a tribute to cool heads as Captains sorted themselves out. With good reason this spectacular meeting was christened 'Windy corner'. When our flotilla had collected itself *Champion* led us up the disengaged side of the Grand Fleet. At 6.30 we were abreast the rear battleships and had a long way to go to catch up with *Lion* who, at this time, was seven miles away leading the battle line.

From then on we had little idea as to the progress of the battle. The stage was set and crammed with actors and from our position in the back row of the supporting cast we had no more than fragmentary local glimpses of the main drama.

* *Warrior* was subsequently taken in tow but foundered the following morning.

12. The wardroom of K6. The author is seated, centre. (Page 239)

13. K6. The Captain in his cabin. (Page 239)

14. A 'K' class submarine steaming at speed on the surface. (Page 217)

15. HMS *Queen Elizabeth* wearing the flag of Admiral Beatty. (Page 243)

Scheer on the bridge of *Friedrich der Grosse*, the eighth ship in the German line, was in a terrible dilemma. *König* and his leading ships were under concentrated fire from eleven of the British battleships and his single line formation prevented effective retaliation because the guns of the main body of the High Seas Fleet were masked by the ships ahead. Second by second the position worsened. Only drastic action could stave off disaster. Signalling his torpedo-boats in to the attack the German C.-in-C. ordered an immediate 'Battle turn away', a well-practised manoeuvre in which the ships of his fleet turned together on to an opposite course. (Q) Despite the distraction of battle the heavy ships swung round without confusion while the light forces forged ahead into the attack laying a smoke screen to hide the turn-about from the British. This manoeuvre was successful.

Jellicoe, under threat of a developing torpedo attack, was, for vital moments, unaware that behind the smoke screen, Scheer was slipping away to the westward. When he realized that he was no longer in contact Jellicoe altered the course of the Grand Fleet from south-east to south to maintain a position between the retiring enemy and his base.

At this stage both Commanders-in-Chief lacked positive information about the location of their adversaries. Though Scheer had gained temporary easement he was in an unenviable position. He knew that his way to safety was barred by a superior force and he could not afford to add miles to his homeward journey by an excursion out into the North Sea. He reasoned that Jellicoe would assume that he was making an escape to the south-west and that the Grand Fleet would press on to the southward. With this in mind Scheer decided that, with luck, he could slip in astern of the British and make towards Horns Reef at maximum speed. Once again he turned about and set course to the east.

But his plan was thwarted by the ubiquitous Commodore Goodenough who, scouting for the vanished enemy, observed the German alteration of course and promptly reported to Jellicoe.

The High Seas Fleet, still in single line, moved eastwards. Shortly after 7.0 p.m. Hipper's battle-cruisers and Scheer's leading battleships came under heavy fire. Far from slipping away unnoticed behind the British Scheer found that he was heading straight for the Grand Fleet battle line. His T was crossed again. He could see little of his enemy against a darkening eastern horizon and, by the volume of fire, it was evident that the German fleet was clearly silhouetted against the setting sun. Recognizing that his position was untenable Scheer took the only action possible and ordered another turn away. This time the manoeuvre was confused and, after some narrow escapes from collision, the High Seas Fleet in some disorder fled once more on a westerly course.

To cover his retreat Scheer, in desperation, signalled his battle-cruisers to 'Charge the enemy. Ram.' But Hipper's valiant squadron was by now virtually incapable of offensive action. *Seydlitz* was flooded forward and down by the bow; *von de Tann*'s heavy guns were out of action; *Derfflinger* was a shambles with over 50 dead and *Moltke* had been hit repeatedly by heavy shells. *Lutzow*, in a sinking condition, had withdrawn from the line and Hipper, at this critical moment, was embarking in a torpedo-boat to shift his flag to *Derfflinger*. As the remnants of the German battle-cruisers formed up for their 'Death ride' Scheer had second thoughts, cancelled his suicidal order and told his hard-pressed ships to follow in the wake of the retreating High Seas Fleet. He did not, however, recall his light forces and a swarm of torpedo-boats trailing dense clouds of funnel smoke charged ahead to make a determined attack on the British battleships.

Jellicoe, who had always said that he would make a temporary turn away to minimize the risk inherent in such an attack, ordered his Divisional Admirals to take avoiding action, a manoeuvre which successfully countered the German thrust. A number of torpedoes crossed the British line but only one found its mark.* With the passing of the threat Jellicoe resumed his southerly course but, by that time, the enemy was again lost to view behind a smoke screen laid by the retiring torpedo-boats. With only a few hours of dwindling daylight in hand the two fleets were out of touch and the respective Commanders-in-Chief, both unwilling to court the gamble of a night encounter between capital ships,

* *Marlborough* was hit by a single torpedo but was not severely disabled.

decided to use the short hours of summer darkness to gain positions of advantage.

Jellicoe, who knew the enemy was to the westward, manoeuvred to keep between the High Seas Fleet and its base and planned to resume action at dawn. Scheer, intent on avoiding action, had a choice of three routes of escape – to the north-east towards the Baltic, to the southward down the western side of the extensive Heligoland Bight minefields, or south-easterly towards the swept channels 30 miles to the south of the Horns Reef light vessel. He chose the third as being the most direct, and therefore the quickest, way of seeking protection behind mined waters. He recognized the possibility of chance encounter during the hours of darkness but took a calculated risk in the expectation that he could be beyond Horns Reef and nearing safety shortly after dawn.

In the waning hours of daylight we followed *Champion* as she made her way up the disengaged side of the British battle line. We knew nothing of what was going on in the main arena beyond our vision, but from occasional bursts of fire we knew that the fleets were in intermittent action. At one stage we passed the wreck of a big ship, her visible bow and stern incongruously pointing at the sky, and we cheered wildly at this evidence of success. It was not until much later that we learned that we had seen the shattered relic of *Invincible* who, thrusting ahead of the Grand Fleet, had engaged *Lutzow* in a fierce combat (N) in which both ships were destined to suffer mortal damage. (P) Only six of a large ship's company were saved from *Invincible*, including the Gunnery Officer, who miraculously stepped from the foretop into the sea as his ship, split in half by a magazine explosion, sank beneath him.

There was little for us to do at this time and the Captain took advantage of the lull to send the ship's company below to snatch a meal. The First Lieutenant and the Chief went on a tour of inspection to look for trouble and I, with sandwich and dividers in hand, pored over the chart in a vain endeavour to work out our position. It was a case of making bricks without straw because the Captain had been far too pre-occupied to jot down our many changes of course and speed. The pages of the navigator's note book, which I had hopefully left on the chart table, were virginally blank. However, navigation was not in the forefront of our problems at that moment and drawing an optimistic circle on the chart and marking it '2030 (approx.)' I asked the Captain what we were doing. His answer was terse and to the point – 'Following father.'

We heard later that there had been several contacts with enemy ships but in the failing light and deteriorating visibility these resolved into no more than sporadic bursts of fire in brief intervals before targets faded in the gloaming.

At 9 p.m. we noticed that the Grand Fleet ships were manoeuvring into a new formation. They were, in fact, taking up a night cruising order of three columns of eight ships in each. We reduced speed and as the dusk merged into darkness the big ships moved beyond our vision.

Back at action stations my gun's crew speculated on what the night had in store for us. The Gunner and his crew clustered round the torpedo tubes checking, for the hundredth time, that the 'fish' were ready for instant action. The outlines of adjacent ships melted into the darkness until the eye had no focus but the shaded blue stern light of *Champion*. It was a night when overcast clouds absorb all vestige of starlight and the eye can make no horizon distinction between sea and sky.

Jellicoe, having gathered his fleet in compact formation, pondered on Scheer's escape routes. He discarded the route to the north-east and calculated that the High Seas Fleet, in its endeavour to avoid action, would probably run to the southward outside the minefields and make best speed towards the Ems River. He could not dismiss the possibility that Scheer might take the shorter route and steer straight for Horns Reef. He decided to make for a strategical point to cover both possibilities and planned to be 30 miles to the west of Horns Reef by dawn. To make sure he kept ahead of the Germans he ordered a speed of advance of seventeen knots, which was slightly in excess of Scheer's estimated capability. He knew that the main body of the High Seas Fleet was somewhere out to the westward but beyond this he could only guess what the enemy would do during the short hours of darkness. To guard against the chance that Scheer might risk a night encounter in a desperate endeavour to reach the shelter of the secret swept channels through the Horns Reef minefields in the shortest possible time, Jellicoe ordered his 70 destroyers and their six leaders to tail astern to give warning should the enemy sneak to the eastwards behind the Grand Fleet. Having disposed his ships in formations spreading nine miles back from *Iron Duke*, the Commander-in-Chief awaited the dawn confident that if Scheer took the western or eastern routes the Grand Fleet would be ahead and in a position to intercept.

By 10 p.m. his 140 ships were in their night formation. Captains braced themselves for four hours' vigil with scalding cups of cocoa.

At this hour Scheer, having set his head for Horns Reef at a speed of sixteen knots, was barely ten miles to the west of Jellicoe and the two great fleets steamed south-south-east on more or less parallel but slightly converging courses.

Beatty and his battle-cruisers, who had taken up a position thirteen miles on the starboard bow of *Iron Duke*, were at this time no more than five miles in advance of *Westfalen* leading the German battle line.

As the night wore on the Grand Fleet drew slowly ahead and, on their converging course the High Seas Fleet crept ever closer to the rear of the British battleship formation. Scheer, whose cruisers had reported the approximate position of the Grand Fleet, persisted on his course in the expectation that he would pass undetected behind his unseen enemy.

The destroyers were quite unaware of the broader tactical picture. We knew that the Grand Fleet was somewhere ahead and, as we plodded along behind *Champion* with *Moresby*, *Petard* and the remaining ships of the flotilla following in our wake, we guessed that destroyers of other flotillas would be in company. In fact, although we did not know it at the time, we were in the centre of six lines of destroyers following their leaders in close formation. It was eerie on the fo'c'sle, the quietness broken only by the hiss of the bow wave and the faint hum of the distant boiler room fans. Despite the summer calm it grew cold and the gun's crew, having long since expended their stock of speculative comment, lapsed into muffled mutterings. We had no inkling of the trend of future events beyond a conviction that the dawn would herald a resumption of battle. At one time we heard the sound of gunfire on the starboard quarter but it was too far away to distinguish what was happening.*

Suddenly the night was split open by brilliant flashes of fire two miles on our starboard beam. We heard gunfire, several violent explosions and saw a British destroyer silhouetted in the glare of a searchlight. In the darkness, punctuated by blinding light, it was quite impossible to size up the situation and, though we had glimpses of moving ships, we could not distinguish friend from foe. We brought our guns to bear but saw no identifiable target at which to fire. In a short time the commotion subsided and we resumed our southerly course. Days later we learned that we had witnessed the vital moment when the leading ships of the German battle line, crossing the wake of the Grand Fleet, encountered the 4th Destroyer Flotilla.

Tipperary led her ships into attack and their torpedoes sank the German cruiser *Rostock* and a torpedo-boat. In the confusion the British destroyer *Spitfire* rammed the battleship *Nassau*, but though she suffered damage from gunfire and a buckled bow, the crippled ship survived and was able to limp back to harbour. The gallant 4th Flotilla was decimated. *Tipperary*, *Ardent*, *Fortune* and *Sparrowhawk* were sunk and the remaining ships were scattered in the darkness.† The armoured cruiser *Black Prince* was also sunk at this time. She was following the battle fleet to the south, was caught up in the fight, came under heavy fire from the German battleship *Thuringen* and was destroyed.

Though the pyrotechnics of this brisk action were seen by all the ships in the vicinity, including the rear ships of the Grand Fleet, it was generally assumed that they were occasioned by brushes between British destroyers and enemy torpedo-boats. Few ships, mostly those in the disorganized 4th Flotilla, had actually identified German heavy ships and, in the event, nobody reported this vital information to the Commander-in-Chief. This was a cardinal omission. Jellicoe, in ignorance that the High Seas Fleet had

* It transpired that this was *Southampton* and *Dublin* sinking the German cruiser *Frauenlob*.

† History records that in the confusion of this night encounter the German cruiser *Elbing* was accidentally rammed and sunk by the battleship *Posen*.

crossed his stern, continued on his southerly course still convinced that Scheer was somewhere out to the westward.

We steamed on through the night unaware that in the darkness the tail of our line had accidentally lost contact. At 12.30 we saw another skirmish on our starboard quarter as the rump of our flotilla led by *Petard* came under fire from heavy ships of the High Seas Fleet. In this brief and inconclusive engagement *Turbulent* was sunk by gunfire.

Shortly after 2 a.m. the sky began to brighten in the east. The whole German fleet had by now crossed the track of the Grand Fleet and had only 40 miles to go to relative safety in the swept channels. *Faulknor* and sixteen destroyers of the 12th Flotilla barred their way. Captain Stirling, sighting a line of big ships in the dim light of early dawn, led his flotilla into an attack in which seventeen torpedoes were fired and the battleship *Pommern* was sunk. Captain Stirling, alone among all those who had witnessed the various actions of the night, reported the presence of enemy battleships. By sheer mischance his urgent signal coincided with jamming by a German wireless station and failed to get through to *Iron Duke*. This was a cruel turn of fate for, had Jellicoe received this signal, he would have appreciated the situation and could, even at that late stage, have intercepted Scheer near Horns Reef.

It was still dim twilight when *Champion*, hearing the sound of gunfire, altered towards the scene of *Faulknor*'s action. *Obdurate* and *Moresby*, the sole remnants of the flotilla, followed in her wake as she increased to full speed. At 2.30 a.m. we caught a glimpse of four large shadowy shapes looming against the still dark western horizon. *Champion*, thinking we had overtaken the rear ships of the Grand Fleet, turned away to avoid confusion. *Moresby*, our next astern, was not so sure, and, continuing on a closing course, identified four 'Deutschland' class battleships. As she swung round to retire *Moresby* fired a torpedo and we distinctly heard the noise of detonation as it hit and sank an enemy torpedo-boat. Despite *Moresby*'s aggressive action *Champion* remained convinced that the ghostly forms we had seen were friendly and remained silent. Once again, and for the last time, Jellicoe was left in ignorance of the passage of big ships across his stern.

Growing daylight revealed a cheerless morning of lowering clouds and the beginnings of a freshening wind. The visibility was poor, barely two miles, and our grey surroundings were reflected in the strained faces of the gun's crew as they flapped duffle-coated arms to drive out the chill. Night action is an unnerving experience and although we had not been personally involved we had had ample evidence that swift and terrible events could have engulfed us at any moment. Our eyes were bloodshot with the strain of peering into the darkness and it was a relief to feel that now there would be some warning, however brief, of threatening onslaught. Twelve hours of tension had been wearing and wearying and though not dispirited we viewed the coming day with sombre sobriety.

Encircled as we were by poor visibility there was little to see except the familiar form of *Champion* and, to our surprise, two strangers – *Maenad* and *Marksman* – survivors from the 12th Flotilla who, lost in the confusion of their attack had unwittingly joined our curtailed company.

At 2.45 a.m. in obedience to a general signal from the Commander-in-Chief, we altered course to north and *Champion* set about the difficult task of gathering her flock. An hour later we were galvanized by the sight of four German torpedo-boats emerging out of the pallid mist about one and a half miles away steering an opposite course. The enemy was on the alert and both sides opened fire simultaneously. I well remember the exhilaration of this sudden action. The crew drilled with the precision of automata and the gun grew hot as we pumped out shells in rapid succession. Over and above the cacophony I heard the Signalman's shrill warning 'Torpedo on port bow' and caught sight of a faint line disfiguring the sea. As we heeled under helm I ran to the bow and, fascinated by this deadly menace, watched the bubbling track streak close ahead of our stem and run away to limbo. *Champion* too had taken avoiding action and by the time we had braced up to resume action the enemy had disengaged and moved beyond our visibility. It was a brief and exciting incident and, so we discovered later, it was the ultimate clash with the enemy in this historic battle. When, after the war, the German archives were studied, it was learned that these four torpedo-boats were hurrying to their base with 1,250 survivors picked up from the stricken *Lutzow* which, mortally wounded by *Invincible*, succumbed and died in the night.

We re-formed and steering north retraced our path over waters traversed during the dark hours. Investigating an oil slick we sighted bodies jerked into simulated life by the restless sea. Amidst this pathetic flotsam we detected vital movement and, drawing closer, found two oil-soaked survivors from *Ardent* who, in their extremity, had barely strength to call for help. We lowered a whaler and brought them to warm bunks, but they were in a sorry plight and were destined to spend weeks in hospital.

As *Moresby* and *Maenad*, in the near vicinity stopped to rescue eleven of *Fortune's* crew we were overtaken by *Iron Duke* and directed to rejoin *Lion* which we had not seen since the embroilment at 'Windy corner'. The poor visibility persisted and we soon came to the conclusion that chance of further engagement had faded and that we were, in fact, sweeping over the field of action to pick up wounded stragglers.

As we took up our position on the battle-cruiser screen it was difficult to adjust to the realization that the long-awaited fleet action was over. A sense of immediacy still hovered on the edge of consciousness and it seemed almost unnatural to fall out from action stations and relax into normal routine existence.

At noon *Lion* called for reports on fuel and, as we had not had time to top up before leaving harbour, our margin was considered to be too small for comfort and we were told to make our own way back to the Firth of Forth at economical speed. Within minutes the battle-cruisers melted into the drifting mist and we felt a distinct sense of relief in being alone on an empty sea.

CHAPTER XIII

Post Jutland

HOMEWARD bound on our own we were faced with a problem of navigation. Having virtually no record of our courses and speeds during the battle it was idle to try and calculate our position and there was no gainsaying the fact that we were lost. The wind had freshened and scurrying clouds masked the sun from observation. The Captain pondered the chart and mumbling 'My guess is as good as anybody's' drew a large circle and prodding it with his finger said, 'The rocks are a long way off – steer west and let me know if it gets thick.' With this parting injunction he left the bridge for the first time for twenty-four hours.

We were not alone in our dilemma. Later that afternoon I sighted a cruiser and signalled 'Can you give me position please?' To which polite enquiry he flashed back 'Scotland bears west.' And he was wrong. When we eventually made landfall we found that we had been on a parallel of latitude south of the Border.

The ship that afternoon was cocooned in monastic silence. The long hours of watchfulness had taken their toll and apart from a few watchkeepers every man jack got his head down. On the bridge I kept on the move to stave off drowsiness and counted the minutes to eight bells and relief. At long last the First Lieutenant, rejuvenated by an hour's caulk, climbed the bridge ladder and breezily discussed his programme for getting shipshape. Among his items was the problem of unloading my fo'c'sle gun.

When we had ceased fire earlier that day a nose-fused lyddite shell was in the gun and, as it was a somewhat cumbrous matter to eject such a projectile, he decided that the easiest way of emptying the gun was to fire it. Having warned the Captain I piped the gun's crew to muster and a few minutes later Petty Officer Tait, the Gunlayer, hailed from the fo'c'sle and was told the object of the exercise. He had an Able Seaman with him and between them they laid and trained the gun out on the bow and, without waiting for the remainder of the gun's crew, he reported that he was ready. The First Lieutenant, satisfied that the range was clear, gave the order to 'Fire' and together we leant over the bridge rail as the Gunlayer closed up to his position at the left of the gun. As he pulled the trigger there was an explosion and, to our horror, we saw the gun burst just abaft the trunnion. The severed rear part of the gun was blown back by the force of the explosion and the breech block flying in our direction hit, and all but penetrated, the protective mattress surrounding the bridge. We hurried to the fo'c'sle to find the Gunlayer dead and the Able Seaman lacerated and unconscious.

Rousing the hands we bedded down the wounded man on the Wardroom settee. There was not much we could do for him beyond quenching his pain with morphine, but he survived and, later, recovered in hospital. The body of the dead man was laid in the tiller flat, one of the few unoccupied spaces in the ship.

The Wardroom that evening, neglected for two days, was in disorder, the stove was out and it was stuffily cold. Our talk at supper, punctuated by faint groans from the wounded man as the ship rolled, was desultory.

The gun accident shocked the whole company. It was cruelly paradoxical that after battle without casualty we should suffer loss by misadventure and the cause of the accident gave rise to much argument. There seemed to be no reason why a perfectly normal gun, which only a few hours earlier had functioned in an exemplary manner, should suddenly erupt.

Afterwards inspecting ordnance experts found a flaw in the barrel of the gun and considered that when the gun cooled after the heat generated in action the barrel shrank gripping the driving band of the shell with more than normal intensity so that the force of the exploding cordite, instead of driving the shell out of the muzzle, found a path of lesser resistance through the flaw in the barrel of the gun.

We steamed on through the night and, with thankfulness, picked up the beam of St. Abbs Head Lighthouse which, providentially, had been put in operation during those dark hours to guide returning ships. The wind moderated and on a bright clear morning we stopped off May Island, lying athwart the entrance to the Firth of Forth, to commit Petty Officer Tait to the deep. As the limp body, sewn up in his hammock with fire bars at his feet, sank into the green water trailing a stream of valedictory bubbles I felt a keen sense of deprivation at the silent departure of this stalwart man whose gay and imperturbable spirit had done so much to bind our gun's crew into a resolute team.

A burial at sea is impressive in its simplicity. It is a practical occasion unencumbered by funereal trappings and formal obsequies. The throbbing life of the ship has a continuity that is but briefly halted and quietly resumed. A messmate is remembered but not mourned, he slips over the side and a transient silence is broken by the distant clang of an engine room telegraph and the swash of speeding propellors. It is all as natural as the sea itself and the symbol DD* in the log is but a synonym of an entry recording the draft of a time-expired man to his home port.

As we steamed up the Firth of Forth the ship's company, refreshed by rest, were inspirited by a sense of the Fleet's achievement. We had participated in a great naval action in which the enemy, under cover of darkness and poor visibility, had chosen to seek harbour rather than fight to a conclusion. We were in no doubt about the outcome and, truth to tell, somewhat pleased with ourselves, so were baffled when workers on the Forth Bridge shouted at us as we passed under the great arch on the way to our buoy. We thought at first that their gesticulations indicated welcome and were disconcerted when we came within earshot to realize we were being subjected to unmistakeable abuse.† It was

* Discharged dead.
† Similar criticism even went to the extent that ship-yard workers jeered sailors when they were landed from the battleship *Marlborough* at Newcastle.

not until we read the papers that we fathomed the cause of this discourtesy.

The press had picked up rumours of a Fleet action and clamoured for details. The Admiralty, pending the arrival of Admiral Jellicoe's dispatch, had only a fragmentary picture built upon information gathered from intercepted wireless signals.

Scheer, with less distance to cover, arrived in harbour early on 1 June and promptly claimed a victory for the High Seas Fleet adding a reasonably accurate list of British ships sunk. He carefully forebore mention of the full tally of German losses and damage. Within hours this spectacular news swept round the world.

The Grand Fleet did not reach Scapa Flow until the next day and, in the meantime, the Admiralty were under extreme pressure and in their dilemma issued a deplorable communiqué which, virtually, did no more than confirm the German story that we had lost three battle-cruisers, three armoured cruisers and eight destroyers. Some days later, after receipt of Jellicoe's report, a second statement giving a more balanced picture was issued but by this time the British people, profoundly shocked by a spate of querulous criticism in the papers, had come to believe that their battle fleet had been battered and that they stood defenceless against invasion.

In fact the British won a strategical advantage at Jutland that proved to be a major factor in securing ultimate victory. The High Seas Fleet, despite the vainglorious German claim, hardly ventured abroad for the rest of the war and, in 1918, the crews of German battleships mutinied when ordered to sea for an offensive sortie.

But the seeds of doubt sown by the Admiralty's original communiqué flourished and it was a long time before the man in the street realized the true significance of the battle. The apparently inconclusive outcome of the action stimulated critics into an agonizing analysis of tactics which, unfortunately, crystallised into a Jellicoe versus Beatty controversy. In the Fleet those of us who had witnessed the actual conditions under which Jutland was fought grew increasingly irritated by academic arguments which failed to take proper cognizance of the problems facing the man on the spot.

My most immediate task on arrival in harbour was to gather material for the Captain's official report and, having diligently garnered reams for his approval, I took my offering to his cabin. Silently, with lip protruding, he scanned my effusion to the last word. 'Hum,' he said, 'bit mountainous isn't it? I doubt if the C.-in-C. wants a book from everyone.' Then, in keeping with his modest reticence, he took up his pen and wrote a report which, had there been a competition, would have won a prize for brevity. Paraphrased – but only slightly – it placed on record that we had engaged enemy torpedo-boats, that the enemy had been driven off – that we had been hit twice – and that we rejoined *Champion* and were ordered to base at 1 p.m. on 1 June.

Having shipped a new gun from *Petard*, who was temporarily out of action, and fitted patches over our honourable wounds, we reported that we were ready for sea and, three days later, we were off again on a reconnaissance sweep with a squadron of cruisers.

The Fleet did not subscribe to the alarmist convulsions in the press. There was a current feeling that we had been tried and not found wanting and this gave a boost to general morale. There was, however, an atmosphere of anti-climax. Having witnessed the escapist manoeuvres of a reluctant enemy, the consensus of opinion saw little promise of another fleet action. One of the results of the battle was to be a shift to unrestricted submarine warfare that would strain the Navy's resources to the utmost for a further two years. Now the Grand Fleet took up again the burden of blockade and as the weeks slipped past there was no relaxation. We spent as many days at sea as in harbour and steamed hundreds of miles, screening, patrolling, examining merchant ships and doing odd jobs for the big ships.

The King visited the battle-cruiser force at Rosyth and we marched past in unsteady formation, lacking the polish of peace, but none the less loyal for that.

We carried out gunnery practices at Cromarty, fired torpedoes in Scapa Flow and took advantage of our trip to the north to hold a flotilla regatta which, as many of the sailors were 'hostilities only' whose education had not extended to learning one end of an oar from the other, bore resemblance to Saturday aquatics on the Serpentine.

Discussion in the battle-cruisers revolved round their apparent vulnerability to internal explosion. It was at first assumed that plunging enemy shells had penetrated the armour protection and exploded stocks of cordite in the magazines. Later this theory was discounted on the grounds that in other ships which had been hit and survived there was little evidence that German shells had broken through and exploded beneath the armoured decks. The problem was so vital that high-powered committees were already under way urgently analysing the known facts to establish the cause of the explosions. So far as was known at the time the German ships, though repeatedly hit, had not been rent apart by magazine explosions. Some argued that their apparent immunity derived from the failure of British shells to penetrate through to the magazines, others that the explosions in the British ships could only be accounted for by faults in gun mounting design. After exhaustive enquiry the latter theory prevailed and it was accepted that the fatal explosions had been caused by the 'flash' of ignited cordite passing down through the trunk of the turret into the magazine. There were, of course, some anti-flash devices but it was demonstrated that when the gun-loading cage was in motion it lifted a flash door and thus opened a passage through which flame could conceivably pass.

The loss of the three battle-cruisers was attributed to this shortcoming in design and, once the defect had been discovered, it was a relatively simple matter to guard against disaster by fitting all ships with anti-flash revolving doors between magazines and handing rooms so that passage between these two vulnerable compartments was always proof against flame.

After the war it became known that the German battle-cruiser *Seydlitz* at the Battle of the Dogger Bank had been saved from a similar disaster by quick flooding of a magazine. This narrow escape alerted the enemy to the danger of 'flash' and all German heavy ships had been immediately equipped with adequate anti-flash doors.

Throughout the Fleet there was intense disappointment that the

High Seas Fleet was not intercepted in the vicinity of Horns Reef at dawn on 1 June. It has been widely assumed that had contact been made the power of the British battle line, which was virtually at full strength, would have annihilated a harassed and faint hearted enemy. Given ideal conditions and plenty of sea room the annals of the Navy might well have recorded a second 'Glorious first of June'.

But weather conditions were bad. Scheer, at dawn, was approaching Horns Reef and Jellicoe would have had to bring him to action before he could run into his bolt hole. We knew, from personal experience, that the maximum distance at which ships could be sighted was barely two miles and under such conditions the chance of bringing capital ships into general action would have been highly problematical.

This essential fact seems to have been overlooked by historians with the result that failure to re-engage at dawn has been branded as a tactical blunder.

Two months ebbed past and a clammy low water feeling damped exuberance. It was, therefore, a welcome boost to hear that we were to spend the better part of August at Leith for docking and refit.

Leith, though in reality a drab commercial port, sparkled with promise as we locked into the basin. Wasting no time we dispatched half the ship's company on a week's leave and as the libertymen smugly hurried over the brow, self-consciously fending off ribald advice from well wishers, those remaining on board took consolation in looking towards Edinburgh and its manifold delights only a short tram ride up the hill.

I took the night train to London, a long but consistently convivial journey enlivened by a carriage full of Highlanders on their way back to the trenches. The train was past York before we lapsed into silence and King's Cross on a drizzling morning was peculiarly uninviting. There had been no time to make arrangements for my leave and in any case the war had thrown friends centrifugally to all points of the compass.

Londoners, after two years of war, were feverish. The reality of deadlock on the Western Front, and the seemingly inexhaustible demand for more and more men to dam the dykes against the

German flood, was rammed home daily by the appalling pages of casualties in the newspapers. The carnage was on a scale beyond comprehension and individuals, in the face of stark predicament, sought anodyne in hectic activity, which in most cases was self-sacrificing and praiseworthy. But the West End which I frequented overflowed with a frivolous fringe of synthetic patriots only too ready to encourage returning warriors to drink and be merry and anaesthetise thoughts about the pitifully short expectation of life for those in the front line.

At this time the national resolve was hardening. The optimism of 1914 which boasted peace by Christmas, the processional bands leading flower-showered volunteers to embarkation and the white feathers pinned to those who watched – these and many other early naïveties were swept away by a flood of realization that war was a muddy, bloody business waged in the main by the chap next door. With returning casualties, maimed in body and mind, came tales of inconceivable hardship and courage and this gave rise to growing fears that the deadlock would not be broken until the nation had been bled white. With the public in this state of mind the press reported advances of even a few hundred yards, involving massacre of thousands, as victories presaging breakthrough and the nation, stunned by the sacrifice entailed, bit on the bullet and resolved to see it through.

I returned to Leith in sober mood rather thankfully stepping back into a world of order and discipline. During my leave I had met men from the trenches, many even younger than myself, who, despite their outward cheerfulness and saving sense of humour, transmitted the horror of their existence through sunken eyes and I thanked my stars that it was my destiny to be embraced by the cleanliness of the sea rather than the mud of Flanders. I reflected that though life in a destroyer had its tribulations and perils we had, at least, reasonable comfort and could recoup in a warm bunk each night. The ship's company, too, returned in a contemplative frame of mind, not perhaps relishing the idea of taking up the common task but resigned to the inevitable and indulging in the sailors' prerogative to stave off the prospect of boredom with a good grouse.

We rejoined the Flotilla just in time to screen the battle-cruisers in a sweep to the Dogger Bank and, after a battle with a nor-wester which washed away the dockyard cobwebs, we returned salt-laden to our familiar buoy at South Queensferry. Within the flotilla we formed a sort of Subs' caucus which met, when occasion offered, to discuss affairs of state over a gentle gin in a friendly mess or, in greater seclusion, in the saloon bar of the Hawes Inn, that unfortunately named hotel hard by the pier at South Queensferry, which lodged our Captains' wives.

With the wisdom of adolescence we held advanced views on everything but, in the main, we 'cagged' about which line of specialization would most quickly lead us to appointments offering proper scope for our undoubted talents. The majority of us opted for destroyers and we drank a toast to the immortal memory of seamen coupled with our own salty aspirations. It was, therefore, with a mind full of possible alternatives that I went ashore in Blyth and by one of those chance encounters which curiously shape our lives I altered course to an entirely unsuspected point of the compass.

Meeting Jefferson, who had been our much respected Sub of the Gunroom in *Orion*, I was invited to see over the submarine of which he was First Lieutenant. Intrigued by this novel experience and fascinated by his eulogy on life in this new branch of the Service I recapitulated the arguments about specialization and asked his advice. 'Why don't you volunteer to become a Submariner?' he said, 'It's a damned good life, you have an interesting box of tricks to look after, you get early command and you work with the best men in the Navy.'

I found this entirely convincing and hastened back on board to write an official letter begging to submit that my name might be forwarded as an applicant for a Submarine Course. Mixing this fateful missive within a pile of incoming correspondence I placed the sheaf of papers on my Captain's desk and stood back with the feelings of an *enfant terrible* who had dropped a fire cracker under the table at a Bishop's tea party.

In due course I saw him read my letter and, in silence, lay it aside. Picking up the discarded papers from the out-tray I was beating a retreat when he cleared his throat – 'Hurrumph! So you want to hide yourself under water – eh? I hope you know what you're doing.' I didn't, but stammered an affirmative to which he replied, 'Very good Sub, if this is what you really want I won't block your ambitions.'

In a state of confusion I returned to my cabin doubtful if I had made the right decision. But, for better or worse, the die was cast and I tried to figure out how my life would be affected by my somewhat hasty impulse.

CHAPTER XIV

Fort Blockhouse

FORT BLOCKHOUSE stands on a spit of land forming the western shore of the narrow entrance to Portsmouth Harbour. From the sixteenth century onwards this area has been the site of defensive fortifications. As early as 1522 there is record of a 'myghtie chain of iron' for drawing across the mouth of the harbour. It is said that when Parliamentary troops captured Southsea Castle in the Civil War they were bombarded by loyalists manning the guns of Fort Blockhouse.

The present Fort had its beginnings early in the eighteenth century and the fortifications were strengthened during the Napoleonic era. Blockhouse had been the main depôt of the Submarine service since 1905 in which year it was decided to set up a shore base for a newly formed flotilla of 'submarine boats'. In the following year an accommodation ship, H.M.S. *Dolphin*, arrived in Haslar Creek, a narrow inlet bounding the northern perimeter of the Fort, and in this creek jetties were built to provide berthing for the submarines.

Ten years later, at the end of 1916, I took passage from Portsmouth in an ancient dockyard launch and set foot for the first time in an establishment which was destined to become the centre of my career for many years to come.

That evening the six members of my 'Submarine training class' huddled in a corner of the Wardroom trying to be inconspicuous in a patently esoteric and sophisticated society. Bright and early the next morning we were shepherded into a wooden hut to begin three months' instruction into the mysteries of the 'trade'.*

Training for service in submarines had always been based on practice rather than theory. Our teacher, a senior Lieutenant who had recently returned from command of a submarine in which he had successfully penetrated into the Sea of Marmora, was a quiet, unflappable man with an authoritative air of command.

Our formal lectures were set against an historical background so that we could appreciate the evolution of the submarine.

In 1877 John P. Holland, an inventive Irish-American, began the development of a series of submarine boats. For twenty years he persisted and, despite disheartening frustration and disasters, eventually built his Holland VIII which, in 1899, at long last, convinced the American Navy Department that he had 'produced an engine of warfare of terrible potency which the Government must necessarily adopt for the Naval Service'. Holland had not been alone in his experiments. By the turn of the century France and Italy had submarines in operation. The performance of all these early submarines was affected by fundamental difficulty in maintaining a steady depth when diving, a problem which was eventually solved by fitting horizontal rudders (hydroplanes) at bow and stern. They were also greatly hampered by lack of efficient power units for propulsion on the surface, and when submerged, until the internal combustion engine and the electrical storage battery had been developed to a pitch that could be trusted to give reliable service.

The British authorities took scant notice of these experiments and trials abroad and the Admiralty were resolute in refusing to be submerged in the rising tide of foreign enthusiasm for underwater warfare. It was argued that the submarine was a defensive weapon which might be developed by inferior maritime powers but that there was no requirement for such cranky, ineffective vessels in the British Navy and that under-water attack was brutish and uncivilized. But, in 1900, public opinion expressed in Parliament brought pressure to bear and the Admiralty ordered five Holland type submarines from the Electric Boat Company

* In the early days the big ship Navy looked upon the submarine service with suspicion and scornfully referred to submariners as pirates following a disreputable 'trade'.

in the U.S.A., saving face by stating that the reason for this change in policy was to test the value of the submarine boat as a weapon in the hands of our possible enemies.

Accordingly the Naval Estimates for 1901–1902 included, for the first time, an appropriation of money for submarine construction.

By 1904 the five Hollands had completed their trials and were assembled at Portsmouth. These original submarines were, in truth, unseaworthy, unreliable and dangerous to handle. Furthermore, they were manned by officers and men who, though filled with venturous spirit, had little to guide them in mastering the complexities of their new profession and had, perforce, to gain experience by trial and error.

The Hollands were diminutive vessels, packed with machinery and even when in full surface buoyancy they had very little freeboard. Navigation was difficult and when submerged their periscopes were of such poor optical quality that they were virtually blind. The petrol engine and storage battery exposed the crew of nine to toxic fumes and hydrogen gas, both of which, in concentration, could be dangerously explosive. Despite the difficulties and hazards which they faced those first submariners not only demonstrated that they could operate under water but showed that, given improvements, the submarine had definite potential.

The Hollands led the way to the construction of the A and B classes which, being larger and with slightly greater surface buoyancy, had better sea-keeping qualities. By 1906 the C boats were coming into service. This new class, though bearing evolutionary similarity to their predecessors, were larger ships of 280 tons displacement and, with more than 30 tons of buoyancy on the surface and better machinery, they proved their seaworthiness.

We were instructed in one of this class and, within a few days, embarked in C34 for our first dive. Our knowledge was elementary and we were bemused by the mass of machinery crammed into restricted space and by the plethora of pipe lines spreading everywhere.

On our way out to the diving area in Stokes Bay we toured the compartments trying to hoist in our instructor's complicated explanatory comments on the functions of valves and switches which hemmed us in on all sides. At first sight it all seemed uncomfortably cramped and, in the engine room, distressingly noisy. The whole interior of the submarine was saturated with an overpowering stench of petrol.

When the crew closed up at 'Diving stations' we assembled in the Control Room and sat on the deck out of harm's way. I do not know what my classmates anticipated at that moment but I braced myself for some sort of violent sensation. The engines were still, the crew impassive and we waited in silence. The Captain's legs appeared down the conning tower ladder and stepping to the periscope he casually ordered 'Close lower lid', 'Half ahead', 'Open main vents' and finally, to the Coxswain and Second Coxswain at their hydroplane wheels, 'Take her down to twenty feet.'

There was a snort of venting air, a gurgle of water flooding into the ballast tanks, a faint hum from the main motor driving the propellor and an almost imperceptible inclination down by the bow. The Coxswain, in sepulchral tones, reported 'Twenty feet, Sir.' This was it, and I found difficulty in realizing that we were actually diving until, in my turn, I was invited to take a look and saw water splashing over the top of the periscope. It was all rather an anti-climax; no sensations, no claustrophobia.

For our instructional benefit the submarine's crew were put through a series of simple evolutions. I tried my hand at the fore hydroplanes, gripping the operating wheel fiercely and gazing fixedly at the trembling depth gauge needle, and at the after hydroplanes with my eyes glued to the inclination bubble.

Finally, with a loud hiss of compressed air blowing water from the main ballast tanks, we surfaced from the quiet depth to begin our noisy passage back to Blockhouse. With some relief I climbed up on to the jetty gulping in the fresh sea breeze to drive away the splitting headache induced by breathing petrol-laden air. After an eventful day we foregathered in the Wardroom for a gin before dinner and aired our slender wisdom in a mood of pleasant sophistication.

The next day in the lecture room the instructional diagrams hanging on the walls took on a new and purposeful significance.

The C class, like their predecessors, were of a type known as 'single hull' which meant that the water taken in to cancel out buoyancy was admitted to ballast tanks within the strong, circular section, pressure hull of the submarine. Pretty well the whole of the lower half of the area within the pressure hull was taken up with space for ballast water, fuel and a number of trimming tanks used for adjusting the weight to meet varying circumstances,* so that when the ballast tanks were filled the submarine was in a properly trimmed state of neutral buoyancy and readily susceptible to easy control by angling the hydroplanes even at slow speed.

We were instructed that all the ballast and trimming tanks were connected to a pipe system and all were fitted with 'blows' to drive water from one tank to another or to push it overboard. Alternatively water in the tanks could be sucked out and discharged overboard by an electrically driven pump.

We had two days to crawl round C34 and in a surprisingly short time the multitudinous members of the whole box of tricks became old familiars. We then studied the main engines, auxiliary machinery and electrics which were rather more complicated.

All submarines, with few exceptions, have the same layout of propulsion machinery. On each propellor shaft† a sequence runs from the engine room aft comprising main engine, engine clutch, main motor, tail clutch and, finally, propellor. On the surface with both clutches engaged the main engine is directly connected to the propellor with the main motor turning idly as a sort of fly-wheel. When diving the engine clutch is disengaged and the main motor, drawing electrical energy from the storage battery, drives the propellor. When re-charging the battery in harbour, or at sea, the tail clutch disengages the propellor from the shaft and the main engine revolves the main motor which, as a dynamo, generates electricity to replenish the storage battery with energy.

Our training class quickly grew into close companionship, bonded together by rising enthusiasm and by our need to preserve

* For example, it was necessary to compensate for the dead weight of six officers under training by pumping an equivalent amount of water out of a trimming tank.

† After the C class virtually all submarines were twin screwed.

an identity in a privileged society which, at first, took scant notice of our existence. We had all been afloat for two years and took full advantage of our freedom to catch the seven bell boat and push off to Pompey to look for innocent gaiety for which, as often as not, we hunted as a pack.

Blockhouse, for us, was not exactly the height of luxury. We slept in barrel vaulted caverns burrowed into the base of the ancient fortification wall. These dank dormitories lacked windows and heating and were far removed from what were euphemistically called 'ablutionary amenities'. This did not worry us overmuch as we were usually flat out at night.

In compensation the Wardroom was comfortable and, as submariners were spared the rigours of rationing, food was plentiful. As far as we were concerned it was all a rollicking interlude in the war and, apart from occasional nagging doubts about the passing out examinations, we had not a care in the world.

Fort Blockhouse has a distinctive character. When taken over from the Army in 1905 the old fortification structures were converted into quarters and so, paradoxically, the youngest branch of the Navy lived in surroundings redolent of the past in odd-shaped rooms with domed ceilings.

The Commanding Officer lived in splendid isolation in Ivy Cottage, a tiny two-roomed bungalow overlooking the submarines lying in Haslar Creek. Years later when this miniscule official residence had to make way for the Admiral's office the workmen demolishing Ivy Cottage unearthed a female skeleton but, as far as we knew, she was not deposited in our time.

Half-way through our course we progressed to study of submarines of later construction than the C class in which we had been instructed. The year 1909 had marked a definite step forward when the first of a new D class came into service.

The older, single hull, submarine suffered the disadvantage that its ballast water was carried internally within the pressure hull and this not only took up much space but also subjected the flat tops of the ballast tanks to the full pressure of the sea when diving and this was recognized as a weakness. To overcome these disadvantages D1 was designed to carry ballast water externally in tanks arranged longitudinally outside the pressure hull on either side.

These 'saddle tanks'* were made of comparatively light plating, a revolutionary feature which sprang from the realization that, since ballast tanks are full of water when diving, the pressure within and without the saddle tank plating would be equalised at whatever depth the submarine was operating. D1 proved the practicability of this innovation and, thereafter, with few exceptions all submarines were designed to carry ballast water externally, allowing greater buoyancy in surface trim and a welcome increase of space within the pressure hull. The D class were also the first submarines to be propelled by diesel engines running on a heavier fuel and thus avoiding the use of the volatile and dangerous petrol which caused so many headaches in the earlier days.

The D boats were half as big again as the C class and, with 50 tons of positive buoyancy on the surface, much more seaworthy. D1 herself surpassed even optimistic expectations when, in the 1910 naval manoeuvres, she voyaged alone from Portsmouth to the west coast of Scotland, patrolled off 'enemy' harbours, and attacked two cruisers before returning in triumph to Blockhouse. This and other spectacular proofs of the efficacy of the new submarine weapon, though convincing enough in submarine circles, were unfortunately not generally appreciated by the Navy as a whole which still ignored the threat of submarine attack when war came.

Almost alone in high places the redoubtable 'Jacky' Fisher had foreseen that the submarine was destined to become a major factor in warfare and, as First Sea Lord from 1904 to 1910, he ceaselessly demanded that Britain must build submarines in large numbers. With this powerful support the submarine service entered into a period of expansion and, profiting by experience gained in operating D boats under taxing conditions, plans were laid for the construction of an improved model.

The first of this new class, E1, left her builder's yard for trials in 1912 and in a short time it was apparent that the years of research and development had come to fruition. The E boats with 80 tons of surface buoyancy were a leap forward in sea-keeping

* A name derived from resemblance to the positioning of a pack saddle on a horse.

qualities and reliability. Equipped with five 18″ torpedo tubes and a 4″ gun, a surface speed of fifteen knots and an endurance of 3,000 miles these ships were formidable and far-ranging instruments of war. Progenitors of a long line of ocean-going submarines, the E boats were superior to submarines of any nation.

The submarine service continued to expand at the maximum rate practicable in peace time until, in 1914, the demands of war and the urgent need to replace the older classes by submarines with more power and radius of action set in train a greatly accelerated programme of construction. New types were designed to meet special requirements, shipyards hitherto unaccustomed to submarine work were dragooned into construction and, by the end of 1916, no fewer than 83 submarines were on active service in the North Sea and many more were on the building slips.

Blockhouse was alive with activity as new submarines arrived to work up prior to departure on war service. The Wardroom teemed with birds of passage and veteran visitors whetting our interest with first-hand experience of events in the waters of the Heligoland Bight. Tales of adventure came rolling in to be retailed with pride and the exploits of submarine captains, such as Holbrook (B11), Boyle (E14) and Nasmith (E11)* fired the imagination.

It was barely ten years since the Hollands had made their tentative dives and a number of officers and men who had blazed the trail were still in the submarine service. We revered those early pioneers who created the submarine lore which became a tradition for their followers. Handling primitive machinery had demanded skill, ingenuity and improvisation. Exposed to risk by failure of equipment and by lack of experience in their slender crews, they learned that they were all members one of another and from this grew a strengthening sense of mutual dependence and trust. All, officers and men alike, exercised self-discipline in their determination not to be found wanting in moments of crisis. They developed 'submarine sense', a constant awareness that the sea, ceaselessly striving to breach watertightness, is a real contender that must be thwarted.

To overcome such difficulties thorough practical knowledge

* All three were V.C.s.

of equipment, understanding of the duties of shipmates and an instinctive attitude of careful foresight must be the basic essentials in a submariner. All this was rammed home by our Instructor, who repeatedly emphasized that as First Lieutenants of submarines we would carry responsibility for the training and morale of our crews and for maintaining the equipment which they handled in a state of high efficiency.

'Contrary to bad habits you may have picked up in the big ships,' he told us, 'it is hallowed submarine practice for officers to take off their coats and get down to it with their men in the job of keeping everything in the submarine on the top line and ready for immediate service.'

The qualifying examinations at the end of our course of instruction, some being severely *viva voce* in C34, were an ordeal, but we all managed to scrape through.

The day the results were announced we sensed a subtle change in the Wardroom, when as fledged submariners we joined the charmed circle of First Lieutenants and parked our bottoms on the club fender round the ante-room fire.

We were full of conjecture when we went off on leave pending appointment to a submarine. The chances were that we would fetch up in one or other of the eight flotillas on the east coast, and hoped that we would have the luck to be sent to one of the E boats which were currently active in the more advanced patrol areas.

CHAPTER XV

Submarine Patrol

FROM August 1914 British submarines kept watch off that part of the German coast fronting the North Sea, and throughout the war a constant patrol was maintained in an area enclosed by a quadrant stretching from Horns Reef, 120 miles north of Wilhelmshaven, to the Island of Terschelling off the coast of Holland. The submarines given responsibility for this duty were drawn from the VIIIth Flotilla based on Harwich and Yarmouth. Their function of advanced reconnaissance in waters that would have to be crossed by German ships breaking out into the North Sea was similar to that of the frigates of the eighteenth century which, by keeping a close watch off harbours, were able to give early warning of enemy movement. The submarines could not keep German harbours under visual observation, but by maintaining an offshore diving patrol in the Heligoland Bight there was a good chance of sighting enemy ships and reporting their presence by wireless. Submarines on patrol also kept watch on the German mine sweeping activities which customarily preceded an enemy excursion and gathered constant information about routine clearance of swept channels through the offshore minefields.

British submarines on patrol were generally under orders to abstain from attacking outgoing heavy ships and were expected to keep their heads down until it was safe to surface and make a wireless report. This prohibition was irksome to submarine captains who could see no sense in letting a fat target go waddling past without having a bash at it. Homeward bound ships were free for all, and considering their limited opportunities for attack the VIIIth Flotilla clocked up a number of successful hits.

German surface ships seldom ventured to sea after Jutland, but the development of unrestricted submarine attacks on merchant ships resulted in an ever increasing number of U-boats crossing the Bight on passage to and from the trade routes, and submarine versus submarine encounters were not infrequent. The participants were wary and the one who managed to dive first had a chance of a snap shot before his opponent woke up to his perilous state. If both dived there was little that could be done except to hang about and hope that the U-boat would be foolish enough to surface and continue his passage. The waters in the vicinity of Light Vessels, Terschelling in particular, were fruitful places for such contacts because the submarines of both sides tended to close these sea marks to check their position in the clouded, tidal areas of the southern North Sea.

Mines were a constant menace, but since the majority were set shallow to catch surface ships it was possible to seek immunity by diving deep unless the submarine was unfortunate enough to be snagged up with the mooring wire of a mine. To protect against this all submarines were fitted with 'jumping wires' running from the bow over the periscope supports to the stern, and wire rope guards on the hydroplanes to ward off mines or sweep wires.

On returning to Fort Blockhouse from leave I was appointed as First Lieutenant of submarine V4, one of a group of eleven H and V class submarines of the VIIIth Flotilla based at Yarmouth.

On arrival I found *Alecto*, the depot ship wearing the pendant of Commander (S), berthed at a wharf near the centre of the town. Her submarines lay alongside a fishing jetty a quarter of a mile down river. Though *Alecto* loomed large in the modest River Yare she was in reality a small yacht-like vessel built as a tender for the submarines of earlier years. Her mess deck space was very limited and the submarine crews were housed in a warehouse that had been converted into barracks. The submarine officers lived in two requisitioned houses on the water front, in one of which I shared a small bedroom with two others.

Reporting to Commander (S), a rotund and genial personality bearing resemblance to a 'laughing Buddha', I was told that my

Captain was on leave and that I should make myself at home until his return.

I walked down the road and found V4 berthed outside three sisters. She looked small but very exciting. Having but recently come in from patrol half her ship's company were on leave and I found the remainder busy in chaos. As I went through the boat with the Coxswain, who turned out to be a true friend and staunch support, my feelings were as confused as my surroundings. Loose gear, stores and stripped down machinery littered every compartment and the boat still had that musty, stale oil-laden stench that accumulates in a submarine at sea for any length of time.

As my Captain, Lieutenant A. N. Lee, was not due back for three days I had breathing space to study the ship's drawings and ferret through the boat. V4 was one of a class of four small submarines designed and built by Vickers. Slightly bigger than the C class they embodied some of the characteristics of the larger E boats, including diesel engine propulsion and external ballast tanks. They were lightly armed with two 18″ bow torpedo tubes and manned by a crew of three officers and sixteen men. The internal layout was conventional. Right forrard the 'fore end' housed the bow tubes and two spare torpedoes, and this space was separated by a bulkhead from a 'battery compartment' leading on to the control room amidships. Abaft this there was space for the two diesel engines and their associated main motors.

The seamen messed in the fore end, the stokers right aft and the petty officers and officers were accommodated in a living space over the batteries.

The V's, having a good margin of buoyancy on the surface, were seaworthy craft but lively in foul weather. They had good, but not outstanding, diving qualities and the pressure hull was strong enough to withstand the water pressure in the region of 150 feet, that is the equivalent of their own length. On the surface they had a cruising speed of twelve knots and when diving the battery had capacity to give a speed of nine knots for one hour or two knots for twenty hours.

V4 was comparatively new when I joined her and throughout her nine month's life she had been engaged on war operations in the Heligoland Bight.

My Captain returned and under his guidance I began to prepare the submarine for her next trip to sea. He was a Lieutenant of elfin proportions but what he lacked in inches he amply made up for in alertness of mind.

V4 was his first command and we were, therefore, in our respective spheres somewhat green – a state of affairs which can make for scratchy relationships – but we dovetailed to each other without aches and pains.

I found that actually shouldering responsibilities was vastly more onerous than I had anticipated. Like all 'qualifiers' I had passed out from my training class under the illusion that I was a submariner. I soon realized that in practice I knew little.

All new 2nd Dickies* go through a salutory period during which they rely on the old hands in their crew to keep them out of trouble. I leaned heavily on my stalwarts, who never failed to prompt me until I found my bearings.

Within days we were caught up in one of the periodic flaps which occurred whenever the Admiralty got wind of a possible raid by the enemy on the east coast. Hastily grabbing sacks of meat and bread we bundled on board and slipped down river. Our orders were to patrol an area outside the Scrobie Sands with the object of attacking enemy ships approaching to bombard Yarmouth. We were to keep submerged during daylight hours and to surface at predetermined intervals to listen in for reports of enemy movements.

On reaching our billet the Captain said that he would dive to 'catch a trim'. I had adjusted the amounts of water in the various trimming tanks rather hurriedly on our way out to sea, but, being unfamiliar with V4, I was not sanguine about my calculations.

When I knew the Captain had shut the upper lid at the top of the conning tower I ordered 'Open main vents' with what I hoped was an outward air of assurance, and told the Second Coxswain to 'Take her down.' We dived. The depth gauge needle whizzed round, the Coxswain growled 'She's very heavy, Sir,' and the

* In the early days it was the custom to refer to a submarine Captain's principal assistant as his 'second hand' and to additional officers as 'third and fourth hands'. The 'second hand' (i.e. First Lieutenant) was commonly called the 2nd Dickie by his crew.

Captain said 'Blow main ballast,' adding as we rose to the surface, 'you'd better start again, Number One.' In a state of agitation I pumped out tons of water, most of which had to be taken in again to get the submarine to dive. At long last we submerged and undulated like a love-sick porpoise for a solid half hour before I was able to catch a controllable trim. There is nothing more frustrating and humiliating than trying to cope with a recalcitrant submarine under the deepening frown of a Captain whose patience is obviously wearing very thin. V4 could certainly be a little bitch when she felt obstreperous. It took me weeks to learn to master her trick of compressing herself at 25 feet and, becoming suddenly heavy and expanding at nineteen feet, to rise buoyantly and unashamedly to the surface.

Our patrol was uneventful. Whatever the Germans had in mind they thought better of it and after a day spent circling round at periscope depth we were recalled to harbour.

Prior to the war submarines had been manned by two officers only, the Captain and his 2nd hand. The stress of active service necessitated an increase in complement and in 1914 new ground was broken by the enlistment of RNR officers into the submarine service. These 'Rockies', as they were called, had been trained in practical navigation in the merchant service and, though new to submarines, quickly proved their worth. As Navigators they had to work under difficult conditions with equipment that was inimical to accuracy. Their mainstay was a small portable magnetic compass which, because of electrical fields within the submarine, could be used only on the surface. A gyro compass, impervious to magnetic disturbance, had been recently introduced but this original equipment was in an early stage of development and uncertain in performance. These 'Sperry' gyro compasses were undoubtedly a boon but the maintenance of their delicate and intricate mechanism was a tricky business and, in semi-skilled hands, the gyro compass was prone to break down or, more subtly, to wander from its 'true' line.

As a legacy from the days before gyro compasses were introduced submarines retained a small magnetic compass housed in a brass watertight casing outside the pressure hull in a position above the helmsman in the control room. This 'diving compass' was connected to the interior of the submarine by an optical tube through which an image of a section of the compass card was projected on to a ground glass screen in the control room, but misted lenses or a flooded tube often made this image indecipherable.

Despite the difficulties under which they worked and their uncertain aids the Rockies gained a reputation for uncanny navigational knack and gave yeoman service throughout the war. Our Rocky was an irrepressible optimist, filled with good intentions but somewhat ham-handed in execution, but as a navigator he knew his stuff. He sometimes provoked the Captain into blowing his top but, on these occasions, his contrition was mournful.

Our submarines were exacting in their demands and quick to avenge lax attention. Hardly a day passed without the discovery of some minor fault and we invariably came in from sea with a crop of defects to be taken in hand. Our flotilla worked to a regular cycle of eight days on patrol followed by a fortnight's recuperation in harbour. It was the rule to send half the crew on five days' leave after each patrol and, on their return, we had our work cut out to get shipshape in time for the next excursion. The business of husbanding our individual submarines left little time for relaxation. Yarmouth was an empty and rather forlorn town, offering minimal enticement and, apart from an occasional run ashore for a convivial evening, we saw little of the place or its inhabitants.

Life within the flotilla was self-contained, congenial and exciting enough. The efficiency of the submarines was the sole concern of all and, providing that our captains were satisfied on this count, we were subjected to little interference from above. The discipline within our submarines was beyond reproach. The crews willingly accepted the self-discipline that is essential for efficient teamwork. We had no need to apply harsh disciplinary techniques for our submarine sailors were all volunteers, specially chosen for their integrity and a sense of mutual inter-dependence bound officers and ships' companies into warm relationships, which not only smoothed the path of daily work, but gave strength at moments of crisis.

The Captain of a submarine in action is a lone figure standing in the centre of the control room with his face pressed against the rubber eyepiece of his periscope. Only he knows what is happening up top and in his rapt concentration he gives little evidence of what is in his eye and mind. Nobody can assist him as he makes his estimation of the enemy's range, course and speed or prompt him as he manoeuvres his submarine on to an attacking course. The submarine captains of the First World War had nothing but their periscopes to aid them in attacking. From brief and indistinct glimpses of their target they built up an evanescent picture in their minds and on this slender basis they hastened to swing round into a firing position before fleeting opportunity passed by.

The whole operation was largely a matter of using a sound sense of orientation to keep track of the surface picture when manoeuvring at depth and a quick eye which could instinctively judge the critical angle to fire torpedoes ahead of the target so that they would, some minutes later, converge on the speeding enemy. This gift of 'eye' was an essential faculty. With some it was inborn, with others it had to be cultivated. Opportunities for practice attacks were few and the majority of the younger captains of submarines had to rely on the innate senses they happened to be born with if chance sent an enemy their way.

At the time when I joined V4 a total of 70 submarines were operating in the North Sea, of which our VIIIth Flotilla comprised eighteen E boats based at Harwich and our contingent of eleven smaller submarines at Yarmouth. The maintenance of ceaseless watch off the German coast had its hazards. The patrols took their toll and in the years 1916 and 1917 no less than fourteen submarines failed to return to harbour, a figure representing nearly one-third of the total of 47 British submarines lost during the four years of war.

We were lucky at Yarmouth and, with the exception of H8 who struck a mine but miraculously struggled back to harbour, none of the submarines in our section of the VIIIth Flotilla suffered serious damage in those two fateful years.

*   *   *

Throughout 1917 German submarines became increasingly active and vicious in their attacks on defenceless merchantmen.

British submariners at this stage of the war lacked the opportunities of earlier years when warship targets were more plentiful. The High Seas Fleet showed no inclination to seek further engagement but there was always the possibility that they might do so and the cordon of VIIIth Flotilla submarines was drawn tightly round the Heligoland Bight throughout the year.

Seldom less than half a dozen submarines were on watch in the area and patrol followed patrol with persistent regularity. Though actual contacts with enemy forces were comparatively rare, our eight-day patrols did not lack incident.

Preparing for sea one Friday afternoon I was singling up the mooring wires on the fore casing when someone in the submarine berthed inside us belted something with a heavy hammer making an ominous sound like a tolling bell. 'That's a good start that is,' muttered the 2nd Coxswain, 'an' wot's more it's the thirteenth of the month.'

Dropping down the river on the last of the ebb we cleared the estuary and turned north to make for the entrance to the swept channel leading away towards the Bight. Passing the Haisborough Sand we noticed an armed motor launch made fast astern of the lightship and, grumbling that some people had all the luck, we altered to an easterly course. We had not gone far in the twilight when the Signalman reported gun-flashes astern. 'Hell's teeth,' cursed the Captain, 'that damned motor launch has woken up from his siesta. Clear the bridge I'm going to get out of it.' I hurried down to the control room and the Captain, following me down the conning tower ladder, pressed the button of the klaxon horn diving signal and within a couple of minutes we were comfortably out of sight. When it was fully dark we surfaced and settled down for a night's run towards our patrol billet, a twenty-mile square to the northeast of Terschelling, which we could easily make by daylight. I put on a running charge to boost the battery up to its full capacity. The ship's company, accustomed to the routine, were clearing up after supper and getting their heads down. As I had the middle watch I lost no time in following their example.

At midnight it was dark, wet and miserable on the bridge. The wind was freshening and the submarine cavorted in a rising sea. Apart from the discomfort and that vague sense of 'first-day' depression which nags imagination into seeing things that are not there and pictures mines menacing the forefoot, I had an uneventful watch until, at 3.30 a.m., we lurched in the seaway and the telescopic mast carrying the wireless aerial came down with an alarming clatter. The cause was a broken hoist wire but, unfortunately, the mast in its precipitous descent had buckled itself and was out of action for the remainder of the trip. The telegraphist rigged up a small jury aerial on which he said he could receive signals but could not transmit. However we decided that the jury aerial should suffice for short distance transmission and with its aid we could, in emergency, relay enemy reports through another of the five submarines on patrol in the Bight at that time.

Arriving at our billet shortly before dawn we dived at 60 feet until full daylight when the view through the periscope revealed such foul weather that we were thankful to be well out of it in peaceful seclusion. The visibility remained poor and beyond putting the stick up for a look-round every ten minutes we ambled along with a few hands at 'watch diving stations'* and the remainder coiled down asleep in their favourite dossing places. At seven bells in the afternoon watch I sat with the Captain at our little Wardroom table discussing our patrol orders, the routine for the night and a few minor defects which had been reported. Rocky was on periscope watch in the control room. The Able Seaman who looked after us flourished a plate of hot toast with the panache of a head waiter. He was an engaging character who took pride in ministering to our needs even to the extent of turning out at night on his own initiative to carry a cup of hot cocoa up the vertical conning tower ladder to revive the Officer of the Watch on the bridge. The 'skipper's flunkey', as he was called by the ship's company, was a fair plain cook and he worked wonders on the little electric hot plate which was all he had in the way of appliances. The Wardroom hardly merited such a dignified title being no more than a space about fourteen feet long in the passage between the control room and the fore end. Our mess resembled a tube train carriage with ventilation trunking and pipe lines cluttering the rounded shape of the pressure hull above, so

* An organization which allows for the submarine to be controlled by one-third of the full crew required for 'Diving Stations'.

that there was little headroom. Beneath our feet a carpet of painted canvas shielded the portable battery boards against accidental influx of salt water. It was usually chilly inside the submarine, because the surrounding sea water cooled the pressure hull but, with the aid of a few small electric radiators and the accumulation of human warmth, it was reasonably tolerable in the temperate waters of the North Sea. We lived in a state of dripping humidity because the warm air inside the submarine condensed on the cold pressure hull.

As the light faded we closed up at full diving stations and brought the submarine up to fifteen feet on the depth gauge, so that the Captain with about six feet of periscope above sea level could see over the waves and take a careful sweep round the horizon. Seeing nothing but wind-driven waters, he told me to prepare for surfacing in half-an-hour by which time he estimated it would be fully dark.

Immediately after ordering the main ballast tanks to be blown the Captain mounted the conning tower ladder and, when I reported that we were breaking surface, he opened the upper hatch and climbed out on to the dripping bridge. If all was clear he passed down word to open up the bridge voice pipe and, after judging the way the submarine was riding the sea, he directed me to flood an appropriate proportion of the main ballast tanks to 'trim down' to a state which would materially reduce the time required for crash diving in emergency and yet leave us sufficient buoyancy to lie comfortably in the prevailing sea. This done I told the Chief E.R.A. to start up one engine connected to its propellor to keep the submarine moving ahead with steerage way and to put the other on to charging the battery at maximum rate.

The duty watch then closed up at their surface stations, the helmsman remaining at the control room wheel with his ear to the bridge voice pipe, and the lookout going up on the bridge with the Officer of the Watch. I then went 'rounds' with the Coxswain to ensure that gear was properly secured and to check that the battery ventilation fans were operating correctly.

We passed the word to carry on smoking and the Coxswain gingered up the 'gash party' to gather buckets of refuse and carry them up top to ditch over the side. This was not quite the simple operation it sounds. The main diesel engines when running sucked in quantities of induction air and this drew a considerable flow of air down the conning tower against which one had to fight to climb up to the bridge. It requires knack to carry a brimming bucket up a vertical ladder in the teeth of a breeze of gale proportions and the unfortunate who let his load slop over, or blow out of his bucket was not popular.

All being well I then took over on the bridge. In all submarines at that time the bridge was no more than a small deck at the level of the upper conning tower hatch surrounded by a brass rail to stop one falling overboard. A canvas bridge screen could be spread on the rails, but as one had to be ready for an instant crash dive this was always kept furled when on patrol. This bridge was, therefore, merely a platform on which the Officer of the Watch and the lookout stood bleakly unprotected from the elements and, when trimmed down, only a few feet above sea level. In calm weather this was not so bad but in a gale it was eerie to stand a watch in lonely isolation whipped by the wind and seeing nothing in the pitch darkness except the faint loom of angry wave crests breaking in confusion. Providing that one headed the sea at just sufficient speed to keep steerage way, or ran slowly down to lee-ward the bridge was surprisingly dry even under foul conditions, but there was always the rogue wave which reared up in spite to smother the bridge and send a cascade of water down the conning tower to the fury of anyone who happened to be climbing up at that moment. The diesels' insatiable demand for air made it essential for us to remain on the surface until the battery was fully charged. In summer, after a long day's diving there was barely time to replenish the battery during the short hours of darkness, but in winter we had ample time and usually managed to finish by 10 p.m.

Rocky, on that overcast evening, had had no sight of a star and was not too sure of our position, but he estimated that when we dived we were over a twenty fathom patch. The Captain decided that to save energy we would sit on the bottom so that we would have a more or less full battery at dawn.

A submarine is little affected by wave disturbance below twenty feet but on, or near, the bottom there can be, in heavy weather, quite a ground swell which can cause a rise and fall of several feet. On this occasion I took her to 100 feet and then slowly down until, at 135 feet on the depth gauge, we felt a tremor as she touched bottom. Putting a couple of tons of water in a forward tank as an anchor we left her to settle comfortably, slightly down by the bow. We were unlucky. The ground swell with maddening persistence kept lifting and dropping us on to what must have been hard packed sand with a disconcerting bump. The Captain stuck it for a bit until in prudence he came to the conclusion that it was too much of a strain. We blew out our anchor water and shuffled off. Three times we tried to settle and were growing thoroughly irritated and on edge with the shuddering bumping when, at our fourth attempt, we found a soft bed to lie on and with relief turned in for an undisturbed night's sleep.

The next day was uneventful until, just before noon, the Captain, who was keeping periscope watch, roused us with a call to 'action stations'. On arrival in the control room, in a dead heat with the Coxswain, I found the Captain crouching on the deck looking through the eyepiece of the lowered periscope and cursing the watch diving planesmen for letting the submarine rise above her proper depth. We got her in hand and the Captain in a state of suppressed excitement ordered full speed on the main motors and full starboard helm.

He told me to lower both periscopes into their wells while we turned and during this brief breathing space vouchsafed that he had sighted a U-boat on the surface. On his directions I gave the order to flood both tubes and, a few minutes later, reported that the torpedoes were ready for firing. As we swung round towards our attacking course the Captain ordered dead slow speed and gingerly raised the periscope. Feverishly wiping the misted eyepiece he took a quick sweep round. Halting his circling he said quietly, 'There she is. Stand by to fire.' On tenterhooks I watched him set the periscope at a firing angle and fervently hoped that my precious fish would not disgrace themselves. And then – the father and mother of an anti-climax.

As he was about to fire the Captain was mortified to see spouts of spray as his victim opened her vents and, seconds later, disappear from view. With a snort of frustration he snapped, 'Take over Number One,' and left the control room in disgust.

Monday was a day of calm sea, blue sky and a clear horizon. We surfaced a few minutes before midday to obtain a meridian altitude of the sun to check our latitude.

The Captain, remembering that this was just what our U-boat friend had been doing the day before, told Rocky to slap it about and not to waste time fiddling with his sextant. Within a few minutes we were up and down again with a shot of the sun that put us about eight miles south of our billet, a discrepancy we remedied while charging on the surface during the night.

Tuesday, another day of good visibility, passed uneventfully except for brief excitement when we saw smoke to the south east but too far away for us to determine its origin. This was also the day for our ceremonial mid-trip wash. It seemed hardly worth the effort to strip off layers of sea clothing and our ablutions in a small tip-up basin were more in the nature of gestures to convention than active scouring evolutions. But we always went through the ritual and felt virtuous.

That night Rocky, when on watch during the charging, sighted what appeared to be an approaching black shape against the slightly lighter horizon. He touched off the klaxon and, ostrich like, we buried our heads at 80 feet and listened to the noise of propellers rattling overhead until whatever it was had passed on its way and all was clear for us to surface and carry on with the charge.

Wednesday was a day of internal difficulties. Our battery had been showing signs of senility and prior to surfacing I had been lifting the battery boards to see how several ailing cells were faring and I was badly shaken to find half a dozen dry cells lacking the liquid electrolyte which normally shows to a depth of about an inch above the level of the lead plates. I rightly surmised that the electrolyte had drained away through cracks in the containers and this was cause for concern. I hastily peered down the sighting hole to see if there were traces of acid on the floor of the battery tank and, to my consternation, saw liquid reaching up to a level half way up the surrounding cell containers. This was serious because the sea was obviously penetrating into the battery tank and, if allowed to rise further, the salt water would overflow the tops of the cells and generate highly toxic chlorine gas.

I went into a huddle with the Captain who, as was his wont, took a philosophical view. Though well aware of the gravity of our situation he was reluctant to abandon the patrol and return to harbour unless forced to do so. A tank beneath the battery had been recently open to the sea and therefore subjected to water pressure and we deduced that, at some time in the past, acid had accumulated on the floor of the battery tank and, finding a flaw in the bitumastic coating, had attacked a loose rivet and eaten a small hole through to the trimming tank beneath. Possibly the bumping on the bottom had aggravated this defect with the result that sea water, in some profusion, had forced its way through the small hole up into the battery tank.

We decided to pump out the trimming tank underneath the battery and to bale out water through the sighting hole and, if the floor of the battery tank remained dry, we would carry on with the patrol. These measures were effective and when, on our return to harbour, we lifted the battery we found that our diagnosis had been more or less correct.

Thursday turned out to be a day of fog and as we could see nothing through the periscope we spent an easy day on the bottom.

The engine room was in trouble in the evening. Half way through charging the battery the starboard engine with a resounding bump came to a grinding standstill. I hovered at the forrard end of the engine room until the Chief E.R.A., scowling with irritation, reported that No. 4 piston had broken adrift and crashed through the back of the engine casing narrowly missing a stoker who had been standing nearby. This startled man, a newcomer, seeing a plunging mass of angry metal brush past him, nipped round to the Chief E.R.A. asking querulously, 'Is that likely to 'appen often Chief?' It transpired that a fractured bearing on the crank shaft had caused the accident and the revolving crank, catching the loose connecting rod askew, pushed the piston through the back of the engine breaking the cooling water system and thus contaminating the lubricating oil with salt water making it unserviceable.

Throughout that night and well into the next day the engine room staff laboured unceasingly to 'sling' the damaged piston clear of the crank shaft with such success that by the time we surfaced on the Friday evening the Chief was ready to give the errant engine a gingerly run on light load. Fortunately the contaminated lubricating oil had not damaged the bearings elsewhere and the engine ran sweetly, though on reduced power, until our return to harbour. This professional skill in overcoming breakdown was typical of the magnificent resourcefulness of Submarine Artificers and there were many tales current at the time recounting extraordinary ingenuity in tackling seemingly impossible repairs without the aid of workshop facilities.

Lacking recent sight of sun or stars we were very doubtful about our position and the Captain decided that he would try and get a positive check before setting course for home, which involved running through a narrow swept channel in a known minefield. With this in mind we spent most of Friday diving to the south west in the expectation that we would be in the vicinity of the Terschelling light vessel when we surfaced at dusk and be able to pick up the dim light which was all she displayed during dark hours. I had the afternoon watch and took advantage of a brief glimpse of the sun to take note of the bearing through the periscope. On working this out I found to my astonishment that according to the Sperry compass the sun was on an easterly bearing, whereas I knew on the evidence of my own eye that it was patently in the west. Obviously the gyro compass was in one of its wandering moods. I told the helmsman to steer by the diving compass but, on switching on its light no image appeared and I realized that the optical tube had flooded and that this compass too was out of action.

This was a bit of a poser and as we had no way of steering a course I called the Captain into consultation. Looking through the periscope he noticed that the sky was conveniently clearing and that the rays of the brightly shining sun were passing through the lenses and throwing a brilliant spot of light on to the wall of the control room.

'That's it,' he beamed, 'we can calculate the correct bearing that the sun ought to be on and the spot of light will give the helmsman a basis on which to steer a steady course.' This original compass worked well enough and kept us headed in a south westerly direction until sunset.

We surfaced at dusk and, after cruising round for a bit, thankfully sighted the small light we were seeking. With the bridge compass in its normal position and the gyro compass apparently behaving itself after removal of a speck of dirt from a roller contact, we set off confidently for the eastern end of the swept channel.

Our jubilance was short-lived. Round about 10 p.m. there was sudden commotion when electrical fuses blew out, plunging us in total darkness. To add to the excitement we could see through the murk that the main switchboard was alive with flashing sparks and that insulation on electrical cables was on fire and filling the control room with the choking fumes of burning rubber. We stopped the engines and, coughing and gasping, brought fire extinguishers to bear on the switchboard. The fumes from the extinguishers were more tiresome than the smoke but, in the intervals of going up top to be sick and fill our lungs with fresh air, we quelled the fire and set about clearing the atmosphere inside the boat. None of the ventilation fans was working and, to clear away the smoke we shut the conning tower hatch and started up one engine to suck out the noxious gases.

We then surveyed the damage which, luckily, was not serious and after rigging up temporary circuits to get some light on the scene and to boil up water for cocoa we were soon under way again.

When I took over the morning watch on the bridge the weather was calm and, on looking at the chart, I saw that our estimated position was half way through the swept channel. After a few minutes to accustom my eyes to the darkness I checked the ship's head reading on the gyro compass by which we were steering with the reading against the lubber line on the magnetic compass alongside me on the bridge. They were wildly at variance, which pointed to the fact that the Sperry was up to its wandering tricks again. I brought the helmsman up to the bridge wheel where he could steer by the magnetic compass. It then occurred to me to wonder how long the Sperry had been wandering. This was a matter of importance because we were in a narrow channel with a minefield on either side. I sent down and roused the drowsy Rocky and asked when he had last checked the gyro against the magnetic compass. It was standard practice to do this at frequent intervals and he staggered me by shamefacedly confessing that he had not taken this prudent precaution during his watch. This meant that, for perhaps four hours, we had been wandering about the sea at the whim of the wretched gyro compass. I called the Captain, and hoping that our aimless circling had been short-lived we optimistically went on steering a course that would take us through the swept channel. Soon after full daylight the sun rose clear of a hazy horizon. When it reached an altitude of 15° the Captain, impatient to know where he was before making landfall, thought we might take a sight so as to obtain a better horizon we climbed down on to the fore casing and lying down with sextant and stop watch we both took altitudes of the sun. Our respective position lines when we laid them off on the chart were comically apart but by taking the mean we estimated that we were still some 30 miles off the coast of Norfolk. We knew only too well that our night's navigation had been 'by guess and by God' and, as our ideas about our position were as hazy as the visibility, we trimmed down so that if we inadvertently touched a sandbank we could readily blow out main ballast and back off into deeper water.

We kept an anxious look out ahead and, an hour later, we were rewarded by a faint sight of land which turned out to be the small cliffs of Cromer. By plotting our positions during the night we found that, by sheer luck, I had spotted the variance in the compasses about the time the Sperry went haywire and that we had, in fact, steered slap down the middle of the swept channel but were farther ahead than we thought we were.

As we came up to the river entrance, Yarmouth sparkled with a brightness that matched the feeling of the ship's company, who with cheerful back chat squared up the boat and closed up at stations for entering harbour.

We secured alongside and, stepping ashore, I was buttonholed by a Lieutenant R.N.V.R., who anxiously enquired about our welfare. It turned out that it was his motor launch that had chased us into the darkness eight days earlier and, having confidence in his gunnery prowess, he had promptly reported that he had destroyed an enemy submarine. Commander (S) in *Alecto* had brushed this claim aside and pending news to the contrary assumed that we had gone blithely on our way. The poor skipper of the motor launch had spent a miserable week convinced that he had our innocent blood on his hands and he expressed his relief by profuse offers of liquid entertainment which we gladly accepted that evening.

Being due for a periodical docking we went to Ipswich, where our defects were taken in hand. Two weeks later, refurbished and refreshed, we went to sea for the next trip.

Patrol followed patrol with but slight variation throughout 1917 until, on Christmas Eve, I returned to harbour to find that, after only nine months in V4, I was appointed as First Lieutenant of Submarie K6, one of the mammoth Fleet Submarines in the XIIth Flotilla attached to the Grand Fleet.

CHAPTER XVI

Fleet Submarine

In 1914, when ruling Naval thought was convinced that command of the seas depended upon an ultimate trial of strength between opposing battle lines and that total victory could only be achieved by virtual annihilation of the High Seas Fleet, much thought was given to the development of tactics that would ensure this objective. Admiral Jellicoe had been vexed by the problem that would arise if his opponent in a Fleet action, reluctant to engage in a heavyweight fight to the finish, turned away and, in so doing, imposed a long, and probably inconclusive, stern chase upon the Grand Fleet. The ideal solution would have been to frustrate evasive tactics by detaching squadrons of fast battleships to work round to the disengaged side of the German line. This tactical plan was ruled out because in the early stages of the war the margin of heavy gun superiority over the High Seas Fleet was insufficient to justify departure from the basic principle that force should be concentrated to the maximum possible extent.

The experience of war intensified anxiety about the potency of torpedoes and mines and many of the Commander-in-Chief's 'Battle Instructions' were designed to counter the possible use of these weapons in the course of a Fleet action. It was firmly believed that a turn away by the enemy might indicate a deliberate attempt to draw the ships of the Grand Fleet into waters infested by submarines or over a freshly laid minefield.

Study of this possibility gave rise to the thought that, given suitable torpedo- or mine-carrying ships, similar measures would be advantageous in discouraging the German C.-in-C. from adopting evasive tactics. This led to discussions with the Admiralty on the practicability of designing submarines that could work with the Grand Fleet and be deployed to attack the disengaged side of the German battle line. In January, 1915, Admiral Fisher, who had succeeded Prince Louis of Battenberg as First Sea Lord, endorsed the proposal by saying 'Without any doubt a fast Battle Fleet which can be accompanied always by submarines under all circumstances would possess an overwhelming fighting advantage.' However, there was a fundamental difficulty in fulfilment because the Grand Fleet had an operating speed of twenty knots and accompanying submarines would, of necessity, have to have a margin of speed above that figure.

In 1915 the E class, powered by two 1,700 h.p. diesel engines, had a full speed of sixteen knots which was clearly too low for operating with the Fleet. With great urgency the Admiralty designed and laid down eight J class submarines powered with three diesel engines which, it was hoped, would give them sufficient speed to accompany the Grand Fleet. Unfortunately the J boats fell short of expectations and their best speed on trials did not exceed nineteen knots.

At the same time Vickers, the experts on oil engine propulsion, gave a considered opinion that the existing designs of diesel engines were verging on their limit of power and speed. This setback had the effect of focusing attention on the possibility that greater speed could be achieved in a submarine propelled by steam turbines. As far back as 1913 plans were in hand for the construction of a steam-driven submarine named *Swordfish*, but the difficulties in design and construction were such that two years later this experimental submersible was experiencing teething troubles of such an intractable nature that it had become apparent that she would never be a really viable proposition. Undeterred the Director of Naval Construction, Sir Eustace Tennyson d'Eyncourt, put forward a revolutionary design for a large 24-knot Fleet submarine. This was, to a great extent, a plunge in the dark involving not only construction of a submarine of dimensions considerably greater than anything previously attempted but also one embodying two steam boilers and turbines and all the apparatus necessary for operating this equipment within the limited confines of a submarine hull with a maximum diameter of eighteen feet.

Despite considerable opposition which held the view that submarines and steam were totally incompatible the Admiralty design was accepted and, in June, 1915, Vickers were given a contract to construct submarines K3 and K4 and, at the same time, Portsmouth Dockyard began building K1 and K2. These, the prototypes of the new Fleet submarines, were in commission by the end of 1916 and were the forerunners of thirteen more of the same design all of which were completed and on active service by May, 1918.

The building of seventeen of these phenomenally large submarines, filled with novel and untried equipment, in the short space of three years was a truly remarkable feat. Furthermore, the fact that the K boats gave satisfactory service and were capable of performing the function for which they had been designed constituted one of the most outstanding engineering achievements of the First World War. The opposition to the idea of steam propulsion came mostly from submariners who, rather naturally, inclined to the view that when preparing to dive the fewer holes to be shut the better. In a diesel driven submarine on patrol there were three only and these, being accessible and hand operated, enabled the submarine to be shut off for diving in about 30 seconds. Shutting off a steam-driven submarine was more complicated and time-consuming. It was necessary to operate power machinery to lift and capsize the two funnels clear of the boiler uptakes to leave room for heavy circular doors to swing over and seal the apertures. In addition to this the air supply necessary for boiler combustion had to be shut off and this involved power operation to close four very large mushroom valves tightly down on their rubber seatings. The very existence of these six large holes and the fact that they were power-operated and inaccessible was anathema to submariners in general and, it must be admitted, that the act of shutting off for diving carried great significance to those who served in K boats.

The K boats were specifically designed for high speed on the surface and this prime requirement took precedence over other considerations and, in consequence, certain diving characteristics had to be sacrificed in the interests of seaworthiness. They were long slim ships with considerable structures superimposed above the pressure hull to enable them to maintain speed in foul weather. Their great length of 340 feet made them difficult to control when submerged and rapid diving was out of the question because the drill for shutting off took the best part of five minutes.

It was accepted that the Fleet submarines were in reality surface ships with capacity to submerge rather than submarines designed specifically for 'crash diving' and good underwater performance.

As the K boats came into service they were formed into two flotillas attached to the Grand Fleet and Battle-Cruiser Fleet respectively. The first nine arrivals (K1 to K9) joined the XIIth (Grand Fleet) Flotilla led by Captain (S) in the light cruiser *Fearless*. The remainder (K10 to K17)* were formed into the XIIIth (Battle-Cruiser) Flotilla led by a Commander (S) in the destroyer *Ithuriel*.

In January, 1918, I travelled north once again to take up my appointment at First Lieutenant of K6, attached to the XIIth Flotilla. It was over a year since I had left the Battle-Cruiser force and during that period Admiral Beatty had taken over as Commander-in-Chief and was now wearing his flag in *Queen Elizabeth*. It had been decided that the Battle Fleet should be based further south and as a result the waters of the Firth of Forth were tightly packed with Grand Fleet ships.

I found the Fleet submarines of the XIIth Flotilla berthed on *Royal Arthur*, an ancient cruiser, lying at a mooring on the south side of the Firth almost within the familiar shadow of the great Forth Bridge. The submarines of the XIIIth Flotilla were accommodated in pens in Rosyth Dockyard.

The K boats were designed to be self-contained and their ships' companies lived permanently on board. Conditions were very

* Submarine K13, when carrying out acceptance trials in the Gareloch on 29 January, 1917, dived with the four large boiler room air intake valves accidentally open and sank to the bottom. After a long struggle the submarine's bow was raised to the surface and forty-seven of the crew and builders' employees were rescued. Thirty-one lives were lost. The submarine was subsequently salved, re-named K22, and joined the XIIIth Flotilla at Rosyth in October 1917.

cramped and *Royal Arthur* gave the submarine crews limited, but very welcome, elbow room for relaxation when they were in harbour.

From the deck of *Royal Arthur* I looked down at the submarines secured alongside. I had anticipated that the K boats would be large, but I was taken aback by the sight of submarines of such gigantic proportions. Like great whales they lay sleek and quiescent in the winter sunshine and as my unaccustomed eye scanned their length I felt intimidated by their sheer size. When I later made comparisons with other ships in which I had served I discovered that they were nearly two-thirds the length of *Orion* and nearly twice the displacement and eighty feet longer than *Obdurate*.

I crossed the brow and boarded K6 which on closer acquaintance seemed even more impressive. This was a far cry from the diminutive V4 and as I climbed down the fore hatch I felt I was entering a strange new world. I made my way aft to the Wardroom which, though seemingly large in comparison with smaller submarines, was not exactly spacious, and as my appearance coincided with the arrival of a new Captain and a relief for the Engineer Officer I was immediately embroiled in congested and animated discussion.

K6 was manned by five officers and a ship's company of 52, and her designers had shown great ingenuity in squeezing in living space for so large a complement. The Wardroom over the battery in a space about 30 feet long was relatively free from bulky equipment. The various messes for the ship's company, spreading fore and aft through the compartments of the submarine, were little more than odd spaces unencumbered by encroaching machinery with bare room for portable tables, stools and small lockers for personal belongings. It was a constant wonder to me that the crew managed to live in amity in a state of such congestion and, what is more, that they contrived to maintain a high standard of hygiene and turn themselves out in trim smartness when occasion required even though each man had but a 25th share of a lavatory seat and had to wash himself and his clothes in a bucket.

It is never easy to live cheek by jowl when virtually every act or movement discommodes a messmate. The K boat sailors were outstanding in their cheerful forebearance and unselfishness.

Much of the equipment in K6 bore family resemblance to that to which I had been accustomed, but on a larger scale. We had similar 18″ torpedo tubes, four in the bows and four 'beam torpedo tubes' running athwart the ship in a compartment just abaft the control room. So, with the spares, we had sixteen torpedoes in all, but my cares in this respect were greatly lightened by the fact that I had an expert Gunner (T) and a superb Torpedo Gunner's Mate.

The control room was fitted with equipment which allowed central control of valves for 'blowing' the multitudinous tanks, and a large 'telemotor' panel by means of which we could operate all the main ballast vent valves from a centralized position.

The battery, though considerably larger than that fitted in V4, performed a similar function and gave rise to the same problems. The main propulsion machinery was, however, entirely new to me. This comprised two steam boilers housed within a large 35-foot-long compartment placed amidships in a position where the circular section pressure hull had its maximum diameter of eighteen feet. Immediately abaft this, in the engine room, two sets of turbines drove the twin propellers through reduction gearing. When diving the turbines could be isolated from the propeller shafts by the operation of an 'engine clutch'. As in all submarines the main motors, in addition to their propelling function when submerged, could be utilized as dynamos for charging the battery.

When the K boats were designed it was recognized that it would be undesirable for the submarines to have to raise steam specifically for charging the battery in harbour, and to avoid this necessity all the K. boats were fitted with a single 1,800 h.p. diesel engine directly connected to a dynamo. The diesel unit had an additional and useful function. On surfacing it took time to fire the boilers and, in the interim period until steam was raised, the diesel was used to generate electricity to supply the main motors with sufficient power to achieve a maximum speed of nine knots. The diesel was also useful as a standby means of propulsion if, through misadventure, the boilers became unserviceable. The whole of the engine room department came within the province of the Lieutenant (E) who, in his capacity as Chief Engineer, answered to the Captain for the efficiency of the staff and machinery in his charge.

From an external viewpoint K boats were of distinctive and impressive appearance. Despite a substantial surface buoyancy of 800 tons they lay low in the water and presented a small silhouette in comparison with surface ships of similar size. At sea the Fleet submarines had to operate in company as a flotilla and manoeuvre in much the same way as destroyers; but, unlike destroyers, they had a large turning circle and lacked the power to pull up swiftly in an emergency.

The bridge was loftier than in earlier submarines and a 'wheel house' was superimposed above the upper hatch of the conning tower. In this small free flooding space* the helmsman and the operator of the engine room telegraph were shielded from the worst of the weather, but the view through the surrounding windows was so restricted that the Officer of the Watch and the Signalman had to stand their watch on the roof of the wheel-house.

Watchkeeping in this exposed position was always uncomfortable and a drenching ordeal in dirty weather. On this bare and isolated perch the Officer of the Watch was entirely dependent upon the watchkeepers in the wheelhouse to obey his orders correctly for their actions could not be visually checked. Station keeping was not easy in such conditions and navigational activities were hampered by the need to climb down a vertical ladder to the wheelhouse to look at the chart.

The K boats were originally designed with a long low bow structure formed by building a free flooding casing above the pressure hull to a height of seven feet above the water line. On service it was found that when steaming at speed into a head sea this low bow tended to burrow into the oncoming waves, with the result that heavy water swept aft and damaged the bridge structure. This so restricted operational performance that it was decided to build up the fore casing into a bulbous bow rising to a height of twelve feet above sea level. K6 was the first to be fitted

* A 'free flooding' space is one which is freely open to the sea when diving.

with this curiously shaped 'swan bow' which, though not adding to her beauty was certainly effective in giving her bow a lift when thrusting into a head sea.

At the same time we were fitted with lengthened funnels in an attempt to overcome the K boats unpleasant habit of taking heavy spray over the top of the funnels and thereby temporarily smothering the updraught and subjecting the unfortunate stokers in the boiler room to risk of distressing flashback.

Water entering the big mushroom air intake valves was an endemic defect in K boats. These large valves, and the funnel operating gear, were enclosed in a long free flooding casing running aft from the bridge and in reasonable weather this was effective in protecting the air intakes which were only a few feet above the water line from green seas. In foul weather, particularly with a following sea, the waves tended to mount up and force water through the many free flooding holes cut in the side of the casing and this inevitably found its way through the open valves down into the boiler room to the discomfiture of the oilskin-clad watch-keepers.

The general scheme for operating the Fleet submarines was, in the main, devised by our Captain (S) in *Fearless* who, as one of the original pioneers, was a submariner of great experience. Captain C. J. C. Little, a leader of personal charm, was held in universal respect for his awareness of K boat capabilities and for his sympathetic understanding of the problems faced by those who served in them. We had implicit trust in his ability and we were sanguine that, if humanly possible, he would lead us to an advantageous tactical position.

When cruising with the Fleet at sea a K boat flotilla as a body was stationed in a position mid-way between the phalanx of capital ships and their screen of cruisers twenty miles ahead. On receipt of contact reports from the reconnaissance antennae, it was planned that Captain (S) would increase to full speed and lead his flotilla forward to gain as much ground as he could. As successive reports came in and it became possible to make a rough estimate of the path of the enemy the K boats would be turned on to a converging course to make for a position in advance of the main body of the High Seas Fleet. Captain (S) was given freedom to act on the information at his disposal and when he sensed that his flotilla was somewhere ahead of the enemy battle fleet he dispersed his K boats in pairs to positions which, in his estimation, would cover a reasonably wide area. The pairs of submarines on arrival at their positions opened out to a mile apart and trimmed down ready for instant diving as soon as they made visual contact with hostile forces. Having dived they were relatively immobile and their chances of success depended on worthwhile targets coming their way.

It was all based on theory, albeit carefully worked out, and sceptics abounded. Within the Fleet submarine flotillas we recognized that there was a big element of chance in our operations, but were confident that some of us would have an opportunity to give the British Fleet that 'overwhelming fighting advantage' which Jacky Fisher had prognosticated.

CHAPTER XVII

Black Night

THREE days after my arrival, when I was still in the throes of
taking over my responsibilities as First Lieutenant, we were ordered to sea for a series of exercises with the Grand Fleet. These
included attacks by K boats under simulated battle conditions
and I was pleased at this prospect of seeing Fleet Submarine tactics tried out in practice. Still feeling rather green I had not worked
up much confidence and it was a relief to be given this opportunity
to watch events from the stalls, so to speak, rather than having to
take my place on the stage as one of the cast.

My new Captain had not yet assumed command and, to avoid
overcrowding, it was decided that I should go to sea as a passenger
in another submarine for the period of the exercise. This suited me
well enough and, on the afternoon of 31 January, I rustled up a
hammock from *Royal Arthur* and joined K7 as a supernumerary.
The hands were preparing for sea and as Dick Lindsell, the First
Lieutenant of K7, was busy I settled down in the Wardroom to
browse over the operation orders.

It happened that the Commander-in-Chief and the majority of
the Battle Fleet were at Scapa Flow and the sailing orders directed
ships in the Firth of Forth to leave harbour in company that evening and make for a rendezvous with the rest of the Grand Fleet
in readiness for the exercises that were due to start on the following day. The Vice Admiral in command of our contingent, wearing his flag in the new battle-cruiser *Courageous*, had signalled his
intention to weigh and proceed at dusk and he directed the re-

maining ships under his command to follow him down the Firth of Forth with the leading ships of squadrons and flotillas spaced five miles apart.

The orders indicated that *Courageous* on reaching a position to the north of May Island would increase speed to twenty knots and alter course a point to starboard to make for the rendezvous on an easterly course and following ships, on reaching this position were told to conform.

The order in which we were to leave harbour, which as it turned out had a marked bearing on subsequent events, resulted in a long line strung out over a distance of sixteen miles with each ship steaming in the wake of her next ahead.

The Admiral, at the head of the line, was to be followed by ships in an ordered sequence:

Courageous (Vice Admiral)

Ithuriel (Commander (S) XIII) K11, K17, K14, K12 and K22

*Australia** (Vice Admiral) *New Zealand, Indomitable* and *Inflexible*

Fearless (Captain (S) XII) K4, K3, K6 and K7

*Barham,** *Malaya* and *Valiant*

There was nothing unusual in this; I had been present on many occasions when *Obdurate* had accompanied the battle-cruisers making similar night departures, and I could readily visualize the quiet measured procession to the open sea. Reading the orders I noticed that our contingent, after passing May Island, would traverse a familiar swept channel running eastwards out into the North Sea which was worked over daily by minesweepers as a matter of routine.

At this stage in my studies I heard the word passed for the hands to close up at stations for leaving harbour and, putting on a duffle coat, I climbed up to a vantage point in the wheel house from which I could watch unfolding events. K7, in the outside berth, was first away. Casting off we moved slowly astern and, waiting until the other three submarines had dropped back and formed up, we took station at the rear of the line. It was nicely timed and, within a few minutes we saw *Fearless*, with dimmed

* Both *Australia* (2nd Battle-cruiser Squadron) and *Barham* (5th Battle Squadron) were accompanied by their screening destroyer flotillas.

navigation lights, coming under the Forth Bridge making a lamp signal ordering her flotilla to take station astern. It was a calm night and I watched with interest as we moved slowly ahead gliding in silence through the still water until, behind K6, we swung round to follow *Fearless* and increased speed to sixteen knots. Accustomed to the rumbling chatter of a diesel exhaust our progress seemed effortless and unnaturally quiet. Presently I climbed to the bridge and, joining the Signalman by the after periscope standard, looked round to get my bearings. The night was overcast and the darkness, accentuated by intermittent drifts of low-lying mist, was intense.

There was not much to see. To port we passed a flashing buoy and to starboard I could just make out a dim light marking the northern edge of Inchkeith Island. It was clear enough to see the shaded stern lights of the ships ahead of us in line without difficulty. All was tranquil and as nobody seemed inclined for conversation I soon decided that it was fatuous to suffer unnecessary chilly discomfort and went below to the warmth of the Wardroom.

The Captain joined us for supper, but he had hardly started when he was called to the bridge by a message reporting a slight decrease in visibility.

About 8.30 p.m. I was yarning rather drowsily with Dick and we had just agreed it was about time to turn in when we were shaken by a shuddering bump. It was not particularly violent, but obviously we had hit something and together we ran forrard to investigate. Nothing seemed to be amiss and we returned aft to the control room closing watertight doors behind us.

As we arrived word came down the voice pipe ordering the First Lieutenant and 2nd Coxswain to the bridge. We could tell by the absence of vibration that the ship was stopped and as we climbed the conning tower ladder we wondered what was happening up top. On the bridge the Captain, calm but clearly puzzled, said quietly 'One of the submarines ahead of us has been rammed. Get some hands forrard Number One and stand by to pick up survivors.'

Gathering heaving lines we waited for orders. We had not an inkling as to what had occurred and it was an eerie business standing on the low fore deck of the submarine gazing out over the dark welling waters for signs of life. Half a mile away the searchlight of a ship, which we correctly guessed to be *Fearless*, cut bright swathes in the black night. Closer we could see the navigation lights of two submarines.

K7 moved slowly astern sweeping the near water with the beam of a signal lamp. Catching a glimpse of movement we stopped abreast a small group of swimmers hailing faintly to attract our attention. There had not been time to launch the dinghy which was secured in the after casing but, being only four feet above the water line, it was not too difficult to heave the sodden men to safety. Most had strength to grab the lines we threw to them, but we could see one man about 50 yards out in difficulty. Dick, pulling off his boots and asking me to keep an eye on him, went over the side to tow the distressed man within our reach. We were just securing a line round the inert body when to our discomfiture *Barham*'s destroyer flotilla crashed past at high speed setting up a succession of waves which, when they hit us, swept across the low foredeck throwing our life saving into confusion and washing two of our number overboard. Luckily no harm was done and fishing our wet and angry shipmates out of the ditch we lowered, with some difficulty, the unconscious survivor down below and laid him on the deck in the Wardroom. We tried artificial respiration but soon began to fear that he was beyond any aid which we could give him and were relieved when the Surgeon Commander from *Fearless* arrived in a whaler and took over but, despite his efforts, the patient died. The remainder of the men we had picked up, eight all told, were stripped and warmed externally and internally with blankets and rum. Dick was shifting into dry gear and I went round the survivors to see if any were in urgent need of medical help. Though still cold and shocked they all seemed in fair condition and were able to give me their names and ratings. All were completely bewildered as to what had happened but one, a Lieutenant (E), the only surviving officer, told me that he was in the Wardroom of his submarine when she was hit forrard on the starboard side. He ran aft to the control room and tried to close the watertight door behind him, but the submarine was flooding fast and with others he climbed to the

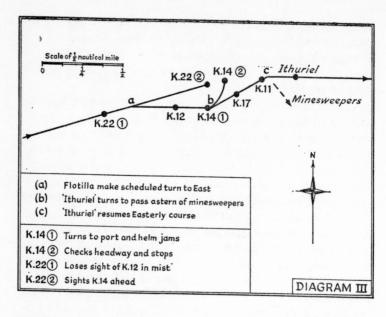

Scale of ½ nautical mile

K.22 ②   K.14 ②   c *Ithuriel*

a   K.11
                    b   K.17   *Minesweepers*
K.22 ①   K.12   K.14 ①

N

(a)	Flotilla make scheduled turn to East
(b)	'Ithuriel' turns to pass astern of minesweepers
(c)	'Ithuriel' resumes Easterly course

K.14 ①	Turns to port and helm jams
K.14 ②	Checks headway and stops
K.22 ①	Loses sight of K.12 in mist
K.22 ②	Sights K.14 ahead

DIAGRAM III

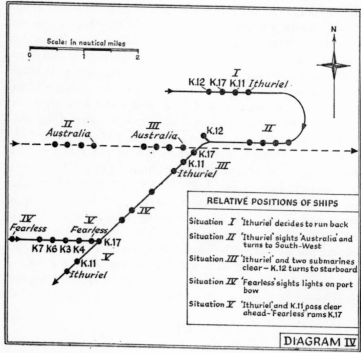

Scale: in nautical miles

N

I
K.12 K.17 K.11 *Ithuriel*

II   III   II
Australia   *Australia*   K.12

K.17
K.11 *III*
Ithuriel

IV

V
Fearless

IV
Fearless   K.17
K7 K6 K3 K4   V
K.11
Ithuriel

RELATIVE POSITIONS OF SHIPS

Situation I   'Ithuriel' decides to run back

Situation II   'Ithuriel' sights 'Australia' and turns to South-West

Situation III 'Ithuriel' and two submarines clear – K.12 turns to starboard

Situation IV   'Fearless' sights lights on port bow

Situation V   'Ithuriel' and K.11 pass clear ahead – 'Fearless' rams K.17

DIAGRAM IV

bridge in obedience to an order to 'Abandon ship'. After that he had little recollection of events until he found himself swimming.

I had assumed that the sunken submarine was one of our own flotilla and was astonished to discover that all the men we had picked up were survivors from K17. I knew from the sailing orders that the XIIIth Flotilla to which K17 belonged had preceded us down the Firth of Forth in a station at least ten miles ahead and the circumstances which had led to a mix up between the two submarine flotillas was deeply perplexing. I hastened to the bridge with this surprising news carrying with me the names of survivors to pass on to Captain (S).

I found that there had been an interchange of signals and the Captain told me that K17 had been rammed by *Fearless* and, to my horror, that K4, the leading submarine in our line, had also been rammed and sunk. It was, in fact, the unfortunate K4 which we had bumped over as the sinking submarine was making her final plunge to the bottom.

Despondent at this double disaster we carefully searched the area, but found no further signs of life.

At the time the situation was utterly confusing. Apart from the information that the K boat flotillas had been involved in a major catastrophe and that K17 and K4 had been sunk we knew nothing of the events that had led to such a tragic result.

Several weeks later official enquiries unravelled the tangled story. When the full tale became known we realized that we had witnessed only a part of a series of misjudgements and accidents that had bedevilled that black night.

It transpired that *Courageous*, on reaching a position to the north of May Island, punctually made her slight alteration of course and increased speed to 21 knots. A German submarine had been seen by a seaplane off the Firth of Forth that afternoon and the five-knot increase in speed was a predetermined measure to ensure that the outgoing line of ships would pass through the danger area at high speed to minimize the risk of night attack by the enemy who might be still lurking in the vicinity. A mile astern *Ithuriel* and her flotilla of five K boats followed in the track of the flagship. A patch of mist temporarily blotted out sight of the stern light of *Courageous*, but Commander (S), knowing he had reached the specified position, made his scheduled alteration of course.*

At this juncture the XIIIth Flotilla – *Ithuriel*, K11, K17, K14, K12 and K22 in that order – encountered two darkened mine-sweeping vessels which, when they realized they were being over-taken, switched on their navigation lights. *Ithuriel* and the submarines in succession made temporary turns to port to pass clear astern.† K14, in her turn, made this slight diversion but, when the order was given to reverse the rudder to follow the course of the flotilla the helmsman reported that the wheel had jammed.

The Captain, who was on the bridge, seeing his submarine turning well out to port, went astern on his starboard engine to check the swing and, because K14 had accidentally sheered out of line, he switched on his navigation lights as a precautionary measure. Within a short time the defect in the steering mechanism rectified itself and K14 went ahead and began to turn to star-board to catch up with the flotilla.

Unknown to anybody K22, at the rear of the line, had previously lost sight of the stern light of K12 in the patchy visibility. Out of touch she had not noticed her flotilla's scheduled change of direc-tion and had continued on her east-north-easterly course. At the critical moment when K14 was struggling with her jammed wheel K22, slightly out to port of her line, was coming up at nineteen knots with the Officer of the Watch and Signalman alert to pick up the stern light of their next ahead. Peering through the misty darkness they were suddenly alarmed by the sight of red and white lights fine on the starboard bow indicating a ship about to cross their bow from starboard to port. The other ship was very close and despite an immediate order to turn to port there was insufficient time for the rudder to bite and swing K22 clear. Col-lision was inevitable and within seconds her stern plunged into the port side of the other vessel. Though the Captain of K22, who was on his way up to the bridge in response to an urgent call, realized almost immediately that he had run into another sub-marine, it was not until some time later that he established her identity. She was, in fact, K14 who at the moment of collision

* See Diagram III. Position a.   † Diagram III. Position b.

226

had just regained the use of her rudder and was turning to starboard with gathering speed.

Providentially K22 had just begun to swing to port with the result that she struck K14 a glancing blow well forrard on the port side. Even so the impact was violent and both submarines were in dire trouble. Surface buoyancy in the K boats, as in all submarines, was limited and even when in full surface trim any major loss of buoyancy was a serious matter.

In K14 the pressure hull was badly holed and sea water rushed through the breach. The men in the forward compartments, appalled by the menace of the flooding water ran aft and managed to reach the control room where the First Lieutenant with quick initiative closed a watertight door against the onrush of the encroaching sea. With the exception of two seamen who had been unable to make the control room in time all the crew were in relative safety. The submarine herself, however, was in mortal danger. Through the flooding of all the forward compartments she had lost nearly one-third of her surface buoyancy, and had taken up an angle down by the bow. Because of the planing effect of this inclination she was unable to make headway without risk of submergence. In this state of distress she asked K22 to stand by and signal for help. K22, though damaged, was in no immediate danger. At the moment of the collision it so happened that her Coxswain, Chief Petty Officer Moth,* was in the control room and realizing the gravity of the situation, he immediately ran forrard. Here he heard from a Leading Seaman that the torpedo tube compartment was open to the sea but that he had been able to close the watertight door at the after end of that compartment just as the water was lapping over the sill. Moth, gathering all available hands, shored up the bulkhead against the pressure of the sea water.

* CPO Moth, the Coxswain of K22 was a veteran submariner and a great character. He was one of the survivors of K13 which foundered on trials in the Gareloch, and when that submarine was salvaged and recommissioned he volunteered to continue as Coxswain. He told me later that on the evening of 31 January he was yarning to a messmate and ruminating that it was the anniversary of his escape from K13. A few minutes later this same submarine, now re-named K22, came into violent collision with K14.

The Captain of K22 in the knowledge that with only one relatively small compartment flooded he had a good margin of buoyancy was contemplating getting under way when he received K14's signal asking him to stand by. It was about 7.15 p.m. when he made a wireless signal to his Commander (S) in *Ithuriel* reporting that he had been in collision with K12 and that both submarines were flooded forward. In the darkness and confusion attending the accident this mistake in identity was understandable. K22 had been following K12 in line and it was natural to draw the conclusion, wrongly as it happened, that she had run into her next ahead.

This mistake, though it confused the issue for a time, was not of urgent importance. A much more vital matter, as the Captain of K22 quickly appreciated, was that both the disabled submarines were in the direct path of the 2nd Battle-Cruiser Squadron. Pointing his stern towards the west he rigged up a cluster of lights and prayed that this illumination would be seen and avoided by the oncoming ships.

At 7.30 p.m. the battle-cruiser *Australia* leading *New Zealand*, *Indomitable* and *Inflexible* had just passed the specified position for altering course and had increased speed to 21 knots when red Very lights, fired by K14, were sighted fine on the port bow and, a few minutes later, a number of low-lying white lights were seen on the same bearing.

A signalman then reported a message reading 'Have been in collision require assistance.' There was no preamble to this signal and nobody on the bridge of *Australia* suspected that it was a call of distress from a submarine.

As the battle-cruisers swept past leaving the stationary lights well clear on their port hand the Rear-Admiral in response to the appeal for help detached a destroyer to investigate.

By chance *Inflexible*, at the rear of the battle-cruiser line, had, like K22 earlier on, temporarily lost sight of *Indomitable*'s stern light in a patch of mist and in catching up was slightly out to port of the line.

The Officer of the Watch saw K14's red Very lights and in the vicinity a white light ahead which he took to be the stern light of *Indomitable* switched on to full brilliancy because of the poor visibility. Seconds later, coming up fast, he appreciated that the white light was stationary, that it was not *Indomitable* and that whatever it was he was in danger of running it down. Putting on starboard wheel he ordered 'Full astern' on the starboard engine and felt the great ship quiver as she began to turn.

The Captain of K22, relieved at having seen the dim outlines of *Australia* and other big ships passing clear, was suddenly transfixed by the sight of a great dark shape bearing down on him. There was no time to take avoiding action and he gripped the bridge rail bracing himself for an inevitable and fatal crash. *Inflexible* rushed past so close that the flare of her bow struck the wireless mast stepped on the starboard side of K22's fore deck. But this, terrifying enough, was not all. *Inflexible* was steaming at high speed and, under full rudder, her stern, swinging to port, swept along the starboard side of the submarine and with a rending crunch tore away several of her starboard external ballast tanks. K22, reeling from this terrific blow, heeled over to an extent that made those on board fear she would roll on to her beam ends and flood through the boiler room intake valves. Miraculously she righted and lay battered but intact with a list to starboard. Fortuitously the pressure hull, apart from the bow torpedo compartment, was unbreached and by pumping out fuel and ballast water she was able to regain an even keel.

By 8 p.m. a destroyer and a trawler were standing by illuminating the submarines in the rays of a searchlight so that the 5th Battle Squadron and their destroyers were able to give them a wide berth. Throughout the night the two submarines limped homeward, K14 under tow stern first and K22 at slow speed under her own power. Next day they were dry docked together at Rosyth.

While all this had been going on *Ithuriel* and the three remaining submarines of her flotilla had continued their easterly course at 21 knots quite unaware that K14 and K22 were no longer in company. The wireless signal from K22 reporting the collision had been delayed through an error in coding and three-quarters of an hour passed before it was known that two of the submarines of the flotilla were in distress.

By this time *Ithuriel* was nearly twenty miles beyond the estimated position of the accident but, despite this, Commander (S) decided that it was his duty to run back to rescue survivors if, by misadventure, one or both of the disabled submarines had foundered.*

Acting on this impulse he turned *Ithuriel* on to an opposite course and ordered his submarines in company to follow in his wake. He made a wide turn to starboard and switched on navigation lights confident that this manoeuvre would take him clear of the line of advance of *Australia* and her battle-cruisers which he knew were five miles behind him in the sequence in which ships had been ordered to proceed during the night. But in taking this action Commander (S) overlooked the possibility that squadrons and flotillas might not be traversing identical tracks.

It was a night of varying visibility and in these circumstances ships, when north of May Island, were a little uncertain of their exact positions and, in consequence, did not all make their ordered turn to the east in precisely the same place. *Ithuriel* herself, possibly because of her encounter with the minesweepers was actually a little to the north of the tracks taken by following ships. She had barely steadied on her westerly course when Commander (S) was shaken by the unexpected sight of *Australia* dead ahead. Realizing that he was in the path of the remainder of the Fleet he made a sharp turn to port with the intention of running farther to the southward to make sure he would be clear of following ships.

Submarines K11 and K17 followed close astern of their leader on to a south-westerly course.† K12, at the end of *Ithuriel's* line of submarines, had been slightly astern of station when her flotilla turned and steadied on a south-westerly course. She saw *Ithuriel*, K11 and K17 jinking to port to avoid the battle-cruisers, but realized that if she waited to follow in their wake she would be in grave danger of being run down by *Australia*. Her Captain took quick action and saved his ship by breaking out of the line and turning to starboard. He told me later that it was a close run thing and that he had barely time to ring down to the engine room for emergency full speed.

When *Australia* crossed his stern his signalman, startled by the

* See Diagram IV. Situation I.   † Diagram IV. Situation III.

sight of a monster ship rushing past with a noise like an express train, clutched his arm and shouted 'Gawd, Sir, that's the narrowest escape we'll ever have.' To which the Captain replied 'Not a bit of it – there are more to come.' In tense silence they watched the huge shapes of *New Zealand*, *Indomitable* and *Inflexible* pass clear astern. Somewhat unnerved by this alarming experience K12's Captain stopped engines while he took stock of his situation.

At 8.15 p.m. *Fearless*, on a track a mile or so to the southward of that taken by the battle-cruisers, was steaming east at 21 knots with K4, K3, K6 and K7 astern. The flotilla was in a position well past May Island, the night was dark but starlit with a smooth sea and a light southerly breeze. The signal from K22 reporting the collision had been intercepted but it was clear that *Fearless* was, by now, beyond the scene of the accident. Captain (S) had no reason to suppose that any ships, except *Australia*'s squadron five miles ahead, were in his immediate path. Everything was perfectly normal and no change in the situation was anticipated until dawn.

Five minutes later, at about 8.20, those on the bridge of *Fearless* were surprised by the sight of the masthead and starboard side lights of two vessels fine on the port bow and crossing from port to starboard.* No ships other than those of the outgoing Fleet had been reported as being in the vicinity and the identity of the crossing vessels was puzzling. It was at first assumed that they might be minesweepers. The lights of a third ship, more than half a mile astern of the other two, were then sighted broader on the port bow. Bearings were taken and it was soon apparent that the first two ships would pass across the bow in safety. The bearing of the third ship, however, remained steady, indicating that if present courses and speeds were maintained there was risk of collision.

Captain (S) immediately gave orders for his navigation lights to be switched on and waited for five minutes with growing anxiety as he watched the unknown vessel grow closer on a constant bearing. The 'Rule of the Road' governing the actions of crossing ships lays down that it is the duty of a vessel having the other on her own starboard hand to give way. It is also obligatory for the other

* Diagram IV. Situation IV.

vessel to maintain course and speed until the moment it is apparent that there is a definite risk of collision. *Fearless*, therefore, was correct in standing on and she was perfectly justified in anticipating that the other vessel would also observe the 'Rule of the Road' and turn to starboard to pass safely down the port side of the XIIth Flotilla.

But the unknown ship held on. At 8.30 Captain (S), by now thoroughly alarmed, appreciating that collision was imminent, took urgent action. Shouting to the Quartermaster to turn the ship to starboard he rang down full astern to the engine room and sounded three blasts on the siren to indicate to the other vessel, and to his submarines following astern, that he was checking his way.

It was too late. Two minutes later *Fearless*, still making considerable headway crashed into the starboard side of the crossing ship.* The shock of the collision was so violent that *Fearless* was brought up all standing. At the moment of impact it was realized with horror that she had struck a submarine and a few seconds later it was established that her victim was K17.

Captain (S), in great distress at this ghastly calamity, guessed correctly that the two vessels which had crossed his bow in safety must have been *Ithuriel* and one of her submarines, but what the XIIIth Flotilla was doing steering south across his path was beyond comprehension. It was not until later that he was handed a signal from *Australia* reporting that she had passed *Ithuriel* and three submarines inward bound.

K17, hit on the starboard bow, slewed round and drifted down the port side of *Fearless*. Her bow was already awash, men could be seen climbing on to the after casing and it was only too obvious that she was mortally damaged. Minutes later she disappeared from view. *Fearless* herself was in trouble with 30 feet of her bow stove in. Fortunately watertight doors had been promptly closed and she was in no danger of sinking, but it was some time before the extent of the damage had been assessed and she was able to get under way.

The sudden stoppage of *Fearless* dead in her track had immediate and disastrous repercussions upon the four submarines

* Diagram IV. Situation V.

following in her wake at 21 knots. The three siren blasts had given them short forewarning of impending danger. The leading submarine, K4, reacted quickly and sheering out to starboard she went full astern and came to a halt with her navigation lights switched on. On the bridge of K3, the next in line, the Officer of the Watch, realizing he was coming up rapidly on his next ahead, stopped engines and veered out to port, narrowly missing the stern of K4 in the process.

The First Lieutenant of K6, the third submarine, who was on watch at the time, had seen the lights of the ships crossing ahead of *Fearless*. Shortly after hearing the siren blasts he saw the stern light of K3, his next ahead, growing out to port and simultaneously caught sight of the masthead and green starboard light of another ship more or less ahead and apparently crossing ahead of him from port to starboard. Making a quick decision to pass under her stern he put on rudder to turn to port and stopped engines. A moment later he recognized with a shock that the other ship was not, in fact, moving ahead and that K6 though under full rudder would not have time to swing clear. She went full astern but before the engines could take effect K6, still making considerable headway, crashed into K4 who was lying stopped in the position in which she had pulled up to avoid hitting *Fearless*. The bow of K6 penetrated deeply and K4 immediately settled by the stern.

The Captain of K7, the last submarine in the line, alerted by the siren signals, but knowing nothing of events ahead, suddenly found that he was rapidly overhauling the stern light of his next ahead. Putting on starboard wheel and going full astern he passed very close up the starboard side of the unaccountably stopped K6. Seconds later he saw a sinking submarine right ahead, and, with headway nearly checked, K7 bumped gently over the foundering bow of the stricken K4.

Though it takes time to relate, this tragic sequence of events was swift in action. Within the space of a few short minutes our flotilla had passed from calm normality to stunned awareness of loss. K4 and K17, who but a bare quarter of an hour since had pulsed with life now lay side by side deep flooded in death.

Apart from the eight men saved by K7 there were no survivors and we heard later that 107 officers and men had lost their lives.

Captain (S), rounding up his flock, enquired about our health. K6 signalled that she had a damaged bow but was otherwise sea-worthy. K3, K7 and K12* reported that all was well.

Two hours later *Fearless*, having made temporary repairs, was able to get under way and, in slow procession, we set off to the westward at three-and-a-half knots and reached harbour the next morning without further incident.

Clustered alongside *Royal Arthur* there was a general feeling of depression and confusion as we tried to fit together the bits and pieces of the disaster into a coherent picture. K6, in particular, was in sombre mood when I took over my duties as First Lieu-tenant for she had been on terms of close relationship with the absent K4.

I heard that at the moment of fatal collision the engines of K6 were turning astern and this, to a minor extent, reduced the force of impact but she was unfortunately making enough headway to thrust her bow deeply into the engine room of K4. The mortally wounded submarine flooded instantly and the embedded bow of K6 was dragged down until she reached an angle when her own buoyancy pulled her clear of her foundering sister ship. Despite the violence of the collision the injury sustained by K6 was sur-prisingly slight as we discovered when we dry-docked at Leith a few days later. The stem was crushed and the outer ends of the torpedo tubes were distorted but, beyond this, there was no serious damage and after a few weeks in dockyard hands we were once again ready for sea.

In the weeks immediately following the catastrophe there was a general airing of opinions on what had caused the accidents but, as nobody knew the full facts, much of this was unenlightened and it was not until details were revealed at a Court Martial that it was possible to see events in true perspective.

On the 22nd March Commander (S) was arraigned on a charge of 'Negligently or by default suffering H.M. Submarine K17 to be lost'. I attended this trial and listening to the first-hand narra-tives of the witnesses I felt ready sympathy with them in their

* K12, after her alarming encounter with *Australia*'s squadron followed *Ithuriel* to the southward and in so doing had unwittingly joined company with *Fearless* and her flotilla.

various dilemmas and found it difficult to criticise the actions that had been taken in moments of crisis.

Divergent views were expressed on *Ithuriel*'s action in turning to go to the assistance of K14 and K22. There were those who argued that Commander (S) was too far from the scene of the accident to give effective aid and that he took a definite risk in leading his flotilla back towards the oncoming ships of the fleet. Others took the view that since his flotilla ran back with their navigation lights switched on at full brilliancy his action was justified.

The members of the Court evidently accepted the latter view and, after long deliberation, they found the charge against Commander (S) not proven and acquitted him from blame.

There was much argument about this verdict. It seemed inconceivable that no one was held to be accountable for events leading to a major disaster.

The evidence before the Court made it clear that *Ithuriel* and her submarines were acting normally in altering course to avoid the minesweepers; that K14 took quick action to counter her swing out of line when her steering failed; and that K22 was behaving rationally in speeding up to regain her station. Taken in isolation none of these incidents called for more than heightened vigilance and seamanlike action. By sheer coincidence they were fused together in a patch of poor visibility.

Similarly it was coincidental that, at a later stage, *Ithuriel* in making her way to the southward ran foul of the other submarine flotilla. A few minutes either way would have avoided this meeting but, by a chance in a million, the XIII Flotilla happened to be on a collision course with *Fearless* and this set in train a disastrous sequence of events.

In retrospect one can draw the conclusion that the impulse that prompted Commander (S) to turn back was an error of judgement which indirectly led to the loss of K17 and K4. One can also see that K17 was at fault in not adhering to the 'Rule of the Road' governing the actions to be taken by crossing ships.

There remains the question as to whether the K boats with their somewhat limited facilities for accurate station-keeping, their unwieldy size and relatively small surface buoyancy, should have been operated in close order as if they were highly manoeuvrable destroyers. At the time it was generally agreed that, despite some shortcomings in manoeuvrability, the Fleet Submarines had to operate in conjunction as a flotilla in order to perform the function for which they were designed and that, under the active service conditions then obtaining, it was necessary to accept the possibility of accident as a justifiable risk of war.

CHAPTER XVIII

Armistice

On our way back to rejoin the Flotilla we dived to test for water-tightness. This, for me, was a somewhat nerve-racking experience. K6 was never easy to control when submerged and, though I soon became reasonably sensitive in anticipating her singular habits, on this initial occasion I felt insecure.

In a small submarine the First Lieutenant had a comfortable feeling that he was in personal touch with the ship's company, who seemed to be within the compass of his personal control. In K6 I lacked this sense of personal contact and felt cut off from events. In time one learned to trust the system of communication which was in fact quite adequate, but until accustomed to exercising remote control from a central position the mind was beset by doubts about what was happening at the extremities.

A sense of heightened tension was a common experience in all K boats immediately prior to diving. The lesson of K13 was fresh in mind and we were cautious. In K6 the Engineer Officer, whose responsibility it was to check that the drill for shutting off the boiler room had been meticulously completed, was required to come forrard to the control room to make a personal report that, as far as his department was concerned, we were ready to dive. This was fine when we had plenty of time but, when the Captain was in a hurry and breathing down my neck, impatience prevailed and, on these occasions, I always felt slight hesitation in giving the order to 'Open main vents' on the sole assurance of a muffled telephone message from the Engine Room.

Discounting the time taken for shutting off, K6 submerged quite smartly. Though there were no less than ten external ballast tanks on each side these were amply vented and filled quickly. The hydroplanes, forrard and aft, were disproportionately small for our length and bulk and, in consequence, they had a diminished effect in controlling the angle and depth of the submarine.

We had a large number of relatively small internal trimming and compensating tanks and catching a trim was usually a laborious process. As control by the hydroplanes was not very effective at slow speed it was necessary to adjust the weight and balance of the submerged submarine with precision, and the finicky business of adjusting the trim by shifting small quantities of water with clumsy blowing and pumping arrangements was equivalent to knitting in boxing gloves.

The K boats, because of their length, had a large vertical turning circle under water and if they took up a steep angle down by the bow they required depth to turn to an upward inclination. In the shallow waters of the North Sea this process could quite possibly result in hitting the bottom with a resounding bump or, in deeper waters, there was a risk that, unless quick action was taken, the submarine might dive to a depth that subjected her to dangerous water pressure. As both these alternatives were undesirable I used to watch the inclinometer bubble like a hawk and, if we angled to more than 8° down by the bow, I blew the forrard main ballast tanks instantly and hoped that, when the plunge was checked and I reopened the main vents, I would be able to regain control before the submarine broke surface. The Captain did not like this much but he appreciated my point of view and was very forbearing on those occasions when I was not quite quick enough and we bobbed up to the surface.

My new Captain, Commander W. R. D. Crowther, was a 'brass hat' of some seniority and the Senior Submarine Officer in the flotilla and as such he was not a figure to be trifled with. I quickly found that he was not one of the piratical fraternity and that he saw no reason why a submarine should be less strictly disciplined than other ships. Having come straight from the chatty and happy atmosphere at Yarmouth this brought me up with a round turn. I was back in the Fleet with a vengeance.

The K boats were intricate craft and their crews had to be trained to a high pitch of all-round efficiency. My Captain was well aware of this. He chased me and I chased the ship's company and for some weeks all hands were vexed by harassment. I did not enjoy this and resented the prick of the Captain's carping thrusts but, as time passed and we reaped the benefit of his stringent criticism, I came to respect his disciplinary wisdom in whipping us at the outset rather than letting us muddle through by trial and error. As we improved the Captain relaxed and our personal relations blossomed into a warm friendship which lasted many years.

Living on board was an acquired taste. At first one felt constrained to the extent that even the daily routines of life such as dressing or washing were tiresome in execution. One seemed to be perpetually brushing past or climbing over and inextricably entwined with the irritating habits of one's messmates. In time we became accustomed and the limited space in which we lived expanded in proportion to the forbearance we exercised in adjusting to our little commonwealth. The starboard side of our mess was taken up by our five bunks arranged in two pairs and, at the after end, a single bunk with drawers under for the Captain. These three seven-foot spaces were divided by wooden partitions and screened by curtains. There was insufficient headroom for the paired bunks to be vertically separated and, as a result, the lower bunk was, in effect, a large drawer which could be pulled out to give the occupant breathing space. The Captain, behind the privacy of his curtain, had just sufficient room for a little desk and a small armchair. Immediately forrard of our sleeping quarters we had the use of a minute bathroom sandwiched between the officers' heads and a pantry. Apart from the fact that one had to be a contortionist to get into the Lilliputian bath and that if one stood up one's shoulders made painful contact with a scalding hot water tank, this was an unprecedented luxury of which we were smugly proud. The port side of the mess was taken up by a table and chairs and, at the foremost end of the compartment, beyond a large air compressor, we had space for chests of drawers in which to stow our personal gear.

The Gunner (T) was a truly professional submariner with innately sound judgement and a personality that charmed us all. Rocky, a dour Scot of quiet temperament, was an astute listener whose rare, but pungent, comments were lit by pawky humour. He had matured in E boats on patrol in the Bight and had the true navigator's knack of always knowing where he was. My confrere, the Lieutenant (E), was a plump figure topped by a round pink plastic face. He had a keen mind with an over-developed sense of the ridiculous that unerringly picked on the comical in even commonplace happenings. He conducted his engineering affairs with pernickety professionalism and was acutely jealous of real, or imagined, intrusions into his domain. In a K boat environment overlapping responsibilities tended to make relationships between the 'Chief' and the 2nd Dicky a bit tricky but, apart from times when I trod upon the sensitive toes of my opposite number, we were blood brothers.

In harbour we were fully occupied in maintenance and making good defects which, in our cramped working conditions, was a laborious process. We were frequently at sea with the Fleet on operations or exercises and from time to time we were sent out individually or in pairs to patrol the approaches to the Skaggerak. This seagoing varied the monotony of waiting for the still-hoped-for chance of having a crack at the High Seas Fleet and we experienced enough foul weather to keep us seamanlike. Living permanently on board as we did, seagoing made little difference to our mode of life except that, in heavy weather, conditions became irritatingly uncomfortable, particularly for the engine room staff.

Life in the boiler room was, at the best of times, unenviable. Cramped in a narrow passage between the hot boilers the watchkeepers sweated in the heat which, inevitably, accumulated in such a confined space. Tending the boilers was arduous enough under normal conditions but in bad weather the stress was barely endurable. As Officer of the Watch on the bridge one might well be stung into cursing the elements, but one was ever conscious of the squad below anxiously keyed up for instant action to cope with fluctuations in boiler performance as spray swept over the funnels; soaked by water pouring down the air intakes and sliding uncontrollably on the wet and oily floor plates.

One dirty night we had a tussle with a rough equinoctial gale on an occasion when four of the flotilla were at sea with Captain (S) on passage to Scapa for gunnery exercises.

Taking over the middle watch I climbed up from the wheel house to the bridge and meeting the full strength of the gale realized that there was vice in the weather and resigned myself to a dreary vigil. The vengeful wind, broad on the port quarter, swore at us in ugly blasts and showed no signs of abatement. It had been blowing fresh for some time and in its present fury the wind was fretting the sea to angry tumult. Steep-sided waves surged out of the darkness and imperious crests bared white teeth as they broke in savagery.

The submarine wallowed in the seaway and the helmsman had difficulty in controlling the yaw from side to side of the course. Ahead I could see the stern light of *Fearless* weaving a gyratory pattern against the black pall of night, and I could just make out the dim shape of K7 following steadfastly in our wake. There was no urgency in our passage and we were steaming at twelve knots, which happened to be an awkward speed for the length of the prevailing sea, and looking aft I could see that as the stern dropped into the trough of each passing wave its successor tended to poop us with swirling water building up, and sometimes surmounting, the long after-casing of the submarine. The wind and sea being abaft the beam it was comparatively dry up top apart from an occasional flurry of spray whipped by the wind over the bridge and funnels. All was reasonably normal and bracing myself against the corkscrew roll as the ship staggered in the sea I curbed nostalgic thoughts of my warm bunk down below and endured the lagging minutes. Things always look brighter after four bells and a cup of cocoa, and I was yarning with the Signalman when an unusually heavy lurch threw us off our balance. As I watched the spent white water streaming off the top of the casing I wondered how they were faring down below and passed a message to the engine room enquiring about their welfare to which the E.R.A. on watch replied that everything was in hand, but that a lot of water had accumulated in the boiler room bilges and that they were having a spot of bother in clearing away a fid of cotton waste which was choking the pump suction pipe. I waited a quarter of an hour and was then told that the water level in the bilges was rising, but that efforts to clear the suction pipe promised success. It transpired later that these efforts meant that volunteers had plunged down into inky surging water in their endeavours to tear away the obstructing waste. As time went on I became increasingly concerned as successive messages reported that more water was coming down through the air intakes and that the level of water had risen above the floor-plates. I called the Captain, told the engine room to start up the diesel and shut off steam, hauled out of the line and signalled to *Fearless* that our maximum speed was nine knots. Captain (S), who always had a sympathetic ear cocked for a *cri de coeur*, reduced the flotilla to seven knots and we went on through the night in comparative comfort.

With the approach of autumn the tempo of the war at sea slackened though the great armies on the Western Front were still locked in deadly clinch. Few, if any of us, could foresee an early end to the holocaust to which the nation had become wearily resigned and, apart from the remote possibility that the High Seas Fleet would challenge our formidable superiority, there seemed no prospect of action and we saw no alternative to yet another winter of watching and waiting.

We were not aware of the creeping deterioration in the morale of civilians in Germany and when, early in November, the enemy collapsed and the Allied armies broke through the hitherto impregnable line we were taken by surprise. It seemed inconceivable that the mighty and menacing force with which we had been so bloodily embattled for so long should disintegrate. We were still half doubting the credibility of the staggering reports of victorious advance when we received the Admiralty's general signal to cease hostilities. On that memorable day our first reaction was one of astonishment. It was impossible to grasp the realization that after what had felt to be a lifetime of war we were in a state of peace.

It did not take long for the glorious reality to sink in and by that evening every ship in the Fleet effervesced in disorderly exultation. Ships, so long darkened, blossomed in light and their companies, enspirited by tots of rum, miraculously appearing from who knows where, cheered themselves hoarse in vain competition against a cacophony of sirens. The submarines added to the carnival spirit by letting off recognition grenades. Those devices fired from a rifle barrel, burst in the heavens to release a bright string of coloured flares to parachute gently, and most decoratively, into the sea.

It was strange to lie in harbour with nothing much to do except keep ourselves clean and ships' companies relishing their relative idleness took quite kindly to the rebirth of spit and polish but this passive occupation soon palled. Waning enthusiasms were fanned into temporary flame when the Commander-in-Chief issued his orders for the ceremonial reception of the surrendering High Seas Fleet.

Early in the morning of 21 November the Battle Fleet with its attendant cruisers and destroyers assembled off May Island and in mighty strength steamed slowly eastwards towards the specified rendezvous. The K boat flotillas were not included in the reception party but the big ships, sensing that we might feel rather out of it, were generous in sending invitations to join them on this momentous occasion. I embarked in *Ajax* and as the significant hour approached I climbed, full of breakfast, to the fore top which seemed as good a place as any to have a grandstand view.

On this dull winter day with little wind the patchy visibility was barely eight miles. By signalled orders from Admiral Beatty in *Queen Elizabeth* the capital ships and cruisers formed up in two long columns six miles apart. It was some time since I had been to sea in a battleship and, having become accustomed to the relatively slender frailty of small ships, I felt awe at the sheer solid power of the battle line as the great grey ships manoeuvred purposefully into their appointed positions. All ships were closed up at 'action stations' and, after the flurry of orders as the guns were cleared away, *Ajax* was wrapped in watchful quiet broken only by the distant sound of air being sucked down to the boiler rooms, and the faint swash of the bow wave breaking on the face of the placid sea. Despite the outward calm the ship was charged with tense excitement. I gazed with eager eyes through my binoculars to catch my first sight of the enemy since that hectic moment at 'windy corner' two-and-a-half years back.

Being mid-way down the column our first intimation of contact came from a hoist of signal flags at *Queen Elizabeth*'s yard arm ordering leaders of squadrons to turn to a reciprocal course and for remaining ships to follow in their wake. A minute or so later we sighted the light cruiser *Cardiff*, which had been sent on ahead, leading a single line of enemy ships into captivity.

At the executive moment the string of coloured flags came down at the rush and with spectacular precision the leaders of squadrons swung round together and took up close station abreast the long line of German ships. In obedience to this sole signal the whole Grand Fleet, in grave and dignified silence, turned for home flanking the defeated enemy on either side.

From our position about two miles out from the German line it was possible to make out a fair amount of detail. Our opposite number, the *Kaiserin*, dirty, unkempt and well astern of her station, steamed dejectedly under a pall of black coal smoke. Groups of sailors on her fo'c'sle seemed, even at a distance, to be sullen and mutinous. To a sailor a ship is a living entity with its own dignity, pulsing energy and strength and it is always distressing to see one down and out and beyond redemption. The sight of these once proud but now humiliated men of war under stern escort was tantamount to witnessing a string of bedraggled miscreants shuffling prisonwards and I was not alone in having my exultation quenched by their obvious degradation.

The day which had dawned with exciting promise came to a sombre end when, that evening, Admiral Beatty slammed the gaol gate with a curt signal. 'The German flag will be hauled down at sunset today, Thursday, and will not be hoisted again without permission.'

We were very conscious of the immediate significance of this spectacular climax to four years of bitter warfare. Later, when we came to review the panorama of the past twenty years, we recognized that we had witnessed the fulfilment of Admiral Fisher's great reforms. Tracing the measured progress of his deliberate policies we paid tribute to the uncanny perception of that astonishing prophet who not only saw the imperative need for a strong battle-line but who also had the foresight to predict that the submarine would become a major weapon of warfare.

Had it not been for the providential presence of a seaman of truly exceptional vision backed by resolute politicians ready to accept and implement his professional advice there would have been no Grand Fleet at Scapa Flow in August 1914 and, lacking this great instrument of sea power, our maritime nation might well have been forced to succumb to the pressures of continental militarism.

At the time we tended to look upon the 'surrender' as the final phase in the drama of Jutland but we gradually came to recognize that, in the longer perspective, it was the pressure of sea power rather than pitched battle that had defeated the High Seas Fleet.

*　　*　　*

Pending the signing of a 'peace treaty' it was considered necessary to keep an adequate naval force intact and ready for unforeseen emergency and, throughout the twilight period of Armistice, the main body of the Grand Fleet languished at their war station swinging idly round their moorings.

This tiresome time of anti-climax was gradually ameliorated as ships were withdrawn for repair and recommissioning. Our turn came when, in the spring of 1919, K6 was ordered to proceed to Barrow for a major refit at Vicker's great shipyard. We made out an impressive defect list, packed up our gear and sailed north-about round the coast of Scotland.

This ultimate voyage was memorable because we were, for the first time, making a passage free from war's seagoing anxieties. I felt extraordinarily carefree steaming through the dark waters of the Pentland Firth, secure in the comfort of brightly burning navigation lights and warmed by the sight of the sweeping beams of lighthouses cheering us on our way.

Index